The Social Roots of Discrimination

The Social Roots of Discrimination

Peretz F. Bernstein

With a new introduction by Bernard M.S. van Praag
Translated by David Saraph

Transaction Publishers
New Brunswick (U.S.A.) and London (U.K.)

Library of Congress Catalog Number: 2008035347
ISBN: 978-1-4128-0866-8
Printed in the United States of America

Library of Congress Cataloging-in-Publication

Bernstein, Perez, 1890-1971.
    The social roots of discrimination : the case of the Jews / Peretz F.
    Bernstein ; with a new introduction by Bernard M.S. van Praag.
        p. cm.
    Includes index.
    ISBN 978-1-4128-0866-8
    1. Antisemitism. 2. Bernstein, Perez, 1890-1971. Antisemitismus als
    Gruppenerscheinung. I. Title.

DS145.B44 2008
305.892'4--dc22

                                                    2008035347

The author wishes to acknowledge his indebtedness to Messrs. Leo Auerbach and Jacques Torczyner for their cooperation in preparing the American edition of the book.

TABLE OF CONTENTS

Introduction to the Transaction Edition

Bernard M.S. van Praag

The classical serendipity dream is that you find unexpectedly along the road a gold treasure. For scientific researchers, the analogue is that you find a totally forgotten and overlooked publication that is of the highest quality. *The Social Roots of Discrimination* is just such a work. Written by the late Peretz Bernstein, it was first published as *Der Antisemitismus als eine Gruppenerscheinung* (1926) by Fritz Bernstein. The first English translation was titled *Jew-Hate as a Sociological Problem* (1951).

I will start with a few biographical facts. Then I will consider the experiences of the book from 1926 up to now. In the second section I will describe the contents of the book and in the third section I will try to place it in the world of today.

The Author

Fritz Bernstein was born in 1890 in the provincial German town of Meiningen. His family was a conservative but non-orthodox Jewish family. Although his parents planned for Bernstein to go to university like their older children, due to financial difficulties, Bernstein received only intermediate education in trade and commerce. Before his military service, he went to Rotterdam for an apprenticeship. After his military service, he returned to Holland in 1909 and got a job at a coffee trade firm in Rotterdam and, soon after, he became the son-in-law of the Jewish owner. Some years later he started a firm of his own in Rotterdam and became a friendly competitor of his father-in-law. Apparently, the market was sufficiently profitable for both of them to make a comfortable living. Bernstein then became quite active in the Dutch Zionist movement and was president of the Dutch Zionist Federation (DZF) for the period 1930-34. He was especially active in providing Zionist schooling to the youth and he was chief editor of the DZF's weekly. The DZF at that time had a membership of about 3000 members all over Holland. By 1936 Bernstein had become a wealthy man and could stop working. He went on *alyah* (emigration to Palestine). Soon he became chief editor of the Jewish daily *Ha-Boker* in Tel-Aviv and he became politically active in the non-socialist non-religious General Zionist party. In 1948 he was one of the 36 signatories to the Israeli Declaration of Independence and became a member of the first Israeli Parliament, the Knesset. He was minister of economic affairs in two cabinets and member of Parliament from 1949 until 1965. He died in Jerusalem in 1971 at the age of 81.

Fritz Bernstein must have been a remarkable person. Apart from his organizational activities, he wrote a large number of articles, the book we have before us, and several other tracts, partly in Dutch and in Hebrew, about aspects of the "Jewish problem."

His most important book was certainly *Der Antisemitismus als eine Gruppenerscheinung,* with the sub-title *Versuch einer Soziologie des Judenhasses*. The English translation (1951) of the title read: *Antisemitism as a Group Phenomenon, Attempt of a Sociology of Jew-Hate.*

The book was completed in 1923, but Bernstein found it very difficult to find a publisher. He submitted the manuscript to the Jüdischer Verlag in Berlin, which was at that time the prominent publisher for modern Zionist authors like Buber, Bialik, Gordon, Chaim Weizmann, and numerous other celebrities. After much delay, Bernstein's book was accepted and published in 1926. The book got about twenty reviews in Jewish and non-Jewish dailies and weeklies in Germany and Holland, which were generally favorable. However, the problem was that the book was not reviewed in scientific journals to my knowledge, and that it consequently received no attention at all in academic circles. The only exception was Prof. Dr. Theodor Lessing, a famous German/Jewish philosopher and Nazi-fighter, who was killed by the Nazis in 1933 in Marienbad, Czechoslovakia. The reasons why the book received hardly any attention in German academic circles are not hard to guess. First, the author had no university education and consequently he had no academic title. He had lived outside Germany for about 16 years and consequently had no German academic network whatsoever. The discipline of sociology was young and scarcely represented at German universities. The title suggested that the main subject was anti-Semitism and since most German university professors at that time were not very Jew-friendly, to put it mildly, they were not interested in what a non-doctored Jewish businessman from Holland, publishing at an outspoken Jewish publishing house, could have to say about a subject that could only be interesting to those in Jewish/Zionist circles. Finally, the book itself was not written in the usual German academic style of the day. It did not contain the typically German half-page long sentences, it did not quote other authors, it did not contain the usual irrelevant footnotes and finally there were no references at all. In short, in our eyes it was an ideally readable and transparent book, both for academics and intellectuals at large, but in the 1920s it was far ahead of its time stylistically. The most important reason for the meager interest was perhaps the title of the book, which suggested a book on anti-Semitism. The main subject of the book is definitely not anti-Semitism, but a new theory on social groups, a great deal of which was developed by Bernstein himself. This newly developed theory is applied in the last chapter on the explanation of anti-Semitism as a special instance of the theory developed. From a marketing point of view the choice of the title was definitely a misnomer. Therefore, the present edition has been given a new and more appropriate title—*The Social Roots of Discrimination: The Case of the Jews.*

With hindsight and knowledge of the events to come in Germany (Hitler wrote his *Mein Kampf* at about the same time), it does not come as a surprise that the book was a complete failure in terms of sales. Of the 2000 copies printed, at most 500 were sold in the usual way. The only place where the book was read, known, and admired was in Dutch Zionist circles. In 1934 Bernstein bought the remaining copies and shipped them to Amsterdam, where a local bookseller kept them in stock. Even after World War II, the Jewish bookseller in Amsterdam was selling out a fair number of copies of the book. According to some autobiographical notes, Bernstein realized in about 1930 that his ambition for a sociological academic career had to be abandoned.

After World War II, Bernstein had become a very prominent member of the Zionist world movement and he became close[1] with Rabbi Abba Hillel Silver, one of the American Zionist leaders in the 1940s and 1950s. Silver convinced Bernstein that his book deserved an American translation. The book was excellently translated by David Saraph, a son of Bernstein, and accepted by the Philosophical Library Inc. at New York in 1951. The original 1926 text was translated unchanged and a short prologue by Bernstein was added to the book. The prologue commemorated the events between 1926 and 1951, but did not add anything substantially new. Bernstein, who was a prominent Israeli politician at that time, apologized that he had had no time for revising the book. This text is now reprinted unabridged.

The Philosophical Library Inc., nowadays virtually un-known, was in the fifties a rather small and highly distin-guished publishing house, which vanished somewhere in the seventies. The main editor was Dagobert D. Runes, a prolific and influential author on philosophy himself. Other authors, who were published in that time by The Philosophical Library, were, e.g., Karl Jaspers, Maeterlinck, Jacques Maritain, Sartre (probably the first American edition of *Existentialism*), Karl Barth, Albert Einstein, and Max Planck. We may say that most of the authors belonged to the *fine fleur* of European philosophy and literature, but whatever their prestige, were not real bestsellers in America in the fifties.

The book was sent for reviewing to various scientific jour-nals, but it was not reviewed to my knowledge, except in 1956, after five years of delay, in an anonymous eight-line review in *The Western Political Quarterly*. The review said: "Although the psychology is schematic and incomplete, this is the most

---

1. This and other information I received from Mr. Moshe Imbar, Jerusalem, who is one of the sons of Peretz Bernstein.

useful work in group theory for political scientists; it is an enormously significant book."[2]

We may conclude that again the book failed. Although it was published by a very prestigious publisher, its marketing was not targeted at the relevant readership, consisting of social scientists and Jewish and non-Jewish intellectuals in general. Bernstein might have found a bit of consolation in a letter in German that Runes received from a colleague. The letter (dated 28/1/1951) read in part: "[A]ccording to my conviction the book must be considered as a classical masterwork.... I can only congratulate you that you have acknowledged the value of this book...." Runes' colleague was Bernstein's fellow author at The Philosophical Library: Albert Einstein!

Still, the tale does not end here. After Bernstein's death in 1971, the book was translated into Hebrew in 1980. It was again reprinted in German in 1980 by the post-war successor of Jüdischer Verlag. This new printing contained a new short epilogue by the British scholar Henri Tajfel, who was one of the most prominent European social psychologists of the time. According to his epilogue, Tajfel was generally very fond of the book. He failed to notice, however, that the ideas of Bernstein were certainly relevant for his research and that of his contemporaries. From private correspondence, in which the German editor invites Tajfel to write an epilogue, it emerges that the initiative for the reprint came from the editor, but that Tajfel did know the original German book before and immediately accepted the invitation. Although the book is certainly relevant for modern social psychological research, it is striking that neither Tajfel nor anybody else from his school ever refers to Bernstein's book before or after 1980.

---

2. The Western Political Quarterly, Vol. 9, p. 1014.

At the risk of becoming monotonous, I note that the book's reception in 1980 was again poor—I cannot find any reviews. Even a notable contemporary connoisseur of literature on anti-Semitism during the Weimar period confessed to me that he had never heard of the book.

The reader will agree that this story is highly unusual and that it can only imply that this must be a book that raises a reader's curiosity. Could it be a hidden pearl that should be brought into the open, or would it be best to leave it in the dark as one of the many scientific mediocrities? In the following pages I will try to summarize the book (of about 300 pages). I must warn the reader that this actually implies a mutilation, as the book is so full of content that it cannot be summarized without dropping much of its richness.

I will end by giving an evaluation of the book related to the time of its conception. Moreover, I will have to ask the question whether, if the book had become known, it would have had any impact on the development of social sciences. Finally, the question arises whether the book still has value in the twenty-first century.

An Introduction to the Content

Bernstein's stated objective was to explain the phenomenon of anti-Semitism. He therefore starts out looking for "objective" *reasons*, why anti-Semitism could flourish in Germany and other European countries in the 1920s, the time of the writing of his book. Although one cannot deny that anti-Semitism still exists in many parts of the world, there is a marked difference in dealing with anti-Semitism in continental Europe in 1920 and the anti-Semitism in, for instance, the United States in 2000. In the twenties there was no moral ban in Germany on being anti-Semitic and to speaking in such a manner. Many people today would consider it as uncivilized, but the existence of *superior* and *inferior* human races was accepted as a fact of life and as a scientific truth long before the Nazis came to power.

For German Jews, although legally emancipated since about 1860, many civil offices remained inaccessible in the 1920s. This held, for instance, for academia, for becoming a judge, and for getting jobs in private industry. There was no legal obstacle, but it was the result of a silent understanding between "true" Germans: Jews had to be excluded, just because they were Jews. Actually, Bernstein himself fell victim to this habit in about 1909, when he was refused an appointment as a *Feldwebel* (a very low officer rank) in the reserve army, after that he completed his military service. The officer said that he could only get the higher rank if he converted to the Christian faith. This was the immediate cause for his immigration to the Netherlands at the age of twenty. The result of this de facto exclusion from the German workforce was, as we know, that Jews overwhelmingly earned their incomes as independents, e.g., as lawyers, doctors, musicians, shopkeepers, by setting up their own firms or by working in firms owned by other Jews. In addition to that, the Jewish proletariat was massive. This does not deny that there have been exceptions to this rule. Since Moses Mendelssohn, Heinrich Heine, and much earlier the "Court Jew" Jud Süss, there were rare Jews who succeeded in finding a place in German Gentile society. These Jews, however, almost always paid the price by assimilation, personal isolation, and mostly conversion—at least of their offspring.[3]

---

3. See, e.g., W. Michael Blumenthal (1998), *The Invisible Wall between Germans and Jews: A Personal Exploration.* New York: Counterpoint.

Apart from this widespread but informal anti-Semitism, there was a religious and a "scientific" anti-Semitism. The scientific branch tried to argue why Jews as a group were inferior, or at least that a good Gentile society should not have a Jewish minority in its midst. It was this current that made anti-Semitism respectable and paved the way for Nazi anti-Jewish philosophies. In other European countries anti-Semitism existed as well, but with gradual differences.

In chapter 2 Bernstein begins to look for the reasons behind the phenomenon of anti-Semitism. The first reason, which was the main driving force until the emancipation, was the *religious* one. Jews had killed Christ. However, as no Jew living almost 2000 years later could have had anything to do with that, and the fact that many Jews were non-believers or even baptized, the force of this argument was already weak in the time of Bernstein. For many devoted Catholics and Protestant farmers in Bavaria and elsewhere, however, it was still a popular notion. The second reason is "cultural parasitism." Jews would not be creative but only imitate and reproduce Gentile culture. That reason is also untenable, unless (in Bernstein's words)

> one helps oneself by the fiction that not the Jewish but the Dutch flowerbed has produced Spinoza; Mahler becomes an Austrian composer, Heine a German poet, Bergson a French philosopher, Disraeli an English statesman, and so on, and so forth (p. 54).

As Bernstein states, the majority "of the non-Jewish population cares nothing for sophisticated distinctions between creative and derivative cultural capacities; they are incapable of perceiving the difference and therefore unable to react to it. The man in the street, who hears about Jewish inferiority, takes it to mean that Jews are 'bad'..." (p. 56).

Another type of anti-Semitism is "economic anti-Semitism." However, enmity against capitalists and capitalism cannot give a real clue either, because there are many more Jewish proletarians and paupers than Jewish capitalists. Moreover, among Gentile capitalists one may find the most active representatives of anti-Semitism (e.g., Henry Ford). After having looked for the main reasons, which are proposed for the existence of anti-Semitism, Bernstein discovers that there are always individual Jews, who are guilty of some of the allegations, which are to justify anti-Semitism, but that they are no reason to hate the group of Jews as a whole. This implies a gross and unwarranted generalization. Moreover, he argues: "Anyone who looks with open eyes at his fellow-Jews and fellow-Gentiles, will find himself face to face with a never expected reality: numberless Gentiles behave in the way expected from Jews, and numberless Jews act as if they were anything but that" (p. 62).

This recognition brings Bernstein to the conclusion that there may be motives for hating some individuals, who happen to be Jewish, but that there is no convincing motive to hate every individual who is Jewish, that is, to hate the whole group—the great majority of which the individual does not know and will never meet. If Bernstein's analysis ended here, it would have been an eloquent and rather objective (as far as possible) analysis of the anti-Semitic phenomenon. In its time (1920), when the habit of assigning general characteristics to races and discrimination on the basis of race was completely normal, this analysis was a courageous and convincing treatise. Unfortunately, however, it was only convincing for those individuals who were not anti-Semites and thus did not need to be convinced. As Bernstein recognized, real anti-Semites cannot be convinced by reasonable observations, evidence, and reasoning. Anti-Semitism is a "gut feeling" and has nothing to do with reason.

Mostly, people assume that such a hate must have reasonable causes that justify the feelings of hate. Here Bernstein presents his first rather revolutionary insight: he inverts the direction of causation. He suggests that hate against the Jews, as a group, is the primary phenomenon. As hate has to be justified, the anti-Semite looks for justifications for that hate. These are the so-called causes for anti-Semitism. Bernstein states it is "not the bad qualities [that] arouse hatred, but it is hate which causes the qualities of those who are hated to be regarded as bad" (p. 63). He concludes his chapter 2 by saying: "it is immaterial how the Jews really are; and that it is not even important how we really act; in the first place there exists an aversion to us, and that this in its turn has created the belief in our inferiority" (p. 71).

However, having excluded all reasons for hatred of Jews as a collective group, the problem remains that such a hate exists. Hence, Bernstein makes an attempt to explain the hatred by the working of a more general mechanism. General in the sense, that it has nothing to do neither with specific characteristics of Jews as a collective nor as individuals. In doing so, Bernstein is probably the first who attempts to sketch a general theory of social groups and conflicts between groups.

At this point in his book, Bernstein makes an unexpected and rather revolutionary turnabout. He embeds the problem in a more general theoretical setting. Just as in algebra the fact that $(5+3)^2 = 5^2+3^2 +2 \times 3 \times 5 = 64$ leads to the general theorem that $(a+b)^2 = a^2+b^2 +2(ab)$ for all values of a and b, Bernstein surmises that there are general mechanisms in society that explain why human beings cluster into groups A and

B and why such groups are bound to have mutual conflicts; groups are hating each other, where "hating" may vary from very intense feelings of hate to a slumbering situation of slight uneasiness towards another group. He sees then anti-Semitism as a specific example of a group conflict in terms of a sociological group theory, which he elaborates later on. He replaces Jews and Gentiles, so to say, with the anonymous groups A and B. Firstly, by this generalization to a more abstract level it is possible to find evidence from everywhere for a theory of groups and group conflicts that is applicable to all groups, say, American whites and African Americans, workers and capitalists, Christians and Muslims, Northerners and Southerners, French and Germans, or members of two rival football clubs A and B. By embedding the problem of anti-Semitism in this general context, it becomes possible to construct a general theory based on general evidence. Secondly anti-Semitism loses its unique particularity and becomes one instance of many other group conflicts. Finally, one may nurture the hope that by unraveling the underlying mechanisms, it may be possible to solve conflicts between groups or even to prevent them from becoming manifest.

For a good evaluation of this endeavor it should be noted that at present there is a well-established body of research, known as social psychology and group sociology, but that at the time of Bernstein's writing social psychology did not exist at all. The only influential ideas were those by Freud, mainly dealing with individuals.

The Origin of Enmity

Although Jews sometimes have the impression that they are the only ones who are hated as a collective, this is by no means true. We have as examples the hate between nations (e.g., between Americans and Russians not so long ago), the hate between ethnic groups (like the Hutus and the Tutsis in Africa), and the hate between religions (like Roman Catholics and Protestants). We even have as an example the hate between fans of different European football clubs. All these examples have in common that individual members of two collective groups hate each other to some degree, although the individuals do not know each other personally. These feelings are based on prejudices in their purest form.

If we think rationally about it, hostility between individuals without a cause looks rather irrational and consequently should be rare. However, in the real world such feelings of hostility appear to be a mass phenomenon.

In order to explain this observation, Bernstein starts to ask himself why individuals would hate individuals they do not know. Bernstein formulates an answer by postulating a psychological theory that resembles the ideas of his contemporary, Freud, whom he also mentions as a source of inspiration. Bernstein's theory, however, may be seen as an independent extension of the Freudian way of thinking.

Bernstein starts by observing that each individual, say A, has to accept some suffering in life. This may be caused by another individual, B, one happens to know, and in that case it may be that the other individual B caused the suffering on purpose and is in some sense guilty. In that case there is aggression, which may elicit a reaction by the suffering individual A, who defends himself. However, in many cases the other individual B had no intention to inflict damage to A, but he was just making use of his rights. Apart from specific individuals who cause individual suffering, there are numerous other sources that cause suffering. We may think of the hardships in the labor market, restrictions put in one's way by law, recognized deficiencies in one's own character, innate handicaps, and other hardships caused by nature. Hence, the individual accumulates a stock of sufferings, part of which can be linked to a human cause, but most of the sufferings have to be assigned to anonymous causes or to no cause at all. Some of those sufferings evaporate over time. Some sufferings, which are caused by specific individuals by purpose, can be revenged, but most sufferings cannot be revenged in any way. Either because the initiator of the suffering is unknown or because its guilt cannot be proven, or because the suffering individual is afraid to perform acts of revenge, as the other person is too strong and would credibly threaten to inflict more suffering as a reaction to the act of revenge. Bernstein gives the example of the family, where one person is held in a kind of blackmail situation by his/her partner, as he or she feels unable to react in the natural way towards the partner who causes his/her suffering, lest more suffering might be provoked.

Now Bernstein postulates that individuals cannot infinitely accumulate sufferings without any reaction. One may occasionally batter his table or the wall of the house to force an outlet for the accumulated damage of the psyche, but in general such "hostile feelings are continually directed and discharged against persons who cannot possibly be responsible for their formation" (p. 83). Bernstein illustrates it with an example where a businessman has private difficulties with his wife, but discharges the psychological burden on his person-

4. Allport, G.W., *The Nature of Prejudice*. Cambridge, Massachusetts: Addison-Wesley Publishing Co., Inc., 1954.

nel. Mostly, such actions need some justification, but if there is no justification, pretexts are fast found. The same holds if the businessman has lost an order because a competitor took it away by a better offer. Bernstein continues by assuming

> that every instance of suffering, every feeling of displeasure, by whomsoever and in whatsoever way it may have been caused, whether it arises from the guilt or from the lawful activity of another person, or through the sufferer's own fault, or without any fault, or even without any human influence, tends to transform itself into a feeling of enmity, to direct itself against fellow-humans and if possible to express itself against them… (p. 86). Enmity is suffering projected upon other men.

Referring to common parlance, according to Bernstein, a man is said to have had to "swallow" more than he can "stomach," so that he is "fed up" and must "air" his anger, hate or rage: a simple description of the process that must actually be presumed to occur. "Within the human mind there always exists a reserve of accumulated hostile feeling…" (p. 88). Actually, the so-called "steam-boiler theory," much later formulated by G.W. Allport[4] (1954), is just the same idea.

Obviously, this theory should be and has been qualified by Bernstein himself. The way in which the transmutation takes place depends on the original amount of suffering, or rather the intensity and the frequency of sufferings received, and on the character of the individual involved. Hence, the theoretical model, which Bernstein had in mind, is less mechanical than described in the few words we spend on it here. However, most of us will recognize that we ourselves are also subject to this mechanism. It is also clear, that if somebody inflicts suffering on somebody else without sufficient reason, it will invite reactions of the same type, leading to a propagation and repetition of the process.

If enmity towards other has mostly no real cause, how is it that causes come in? Bernstein's answer is that most individuals feel the need to justify their acts for their neighbors, for the law, and last but not least, for themselves. If there is no valid reason, a reason is just invented. Hence, frequently the observed enmity is not caused by any guilt of the victim. However, the need for justification in the form of assigning a legitimate guilt "is so irresistible, that every expression, and even every feeling of enmity, is accompanied by the compulsive demand for justification by some recognized, assumed, invented, or at least feared guilt on the part of its object" (p. 100).

It is explicitly said that this whole mechanism also holds for "normal" hate reactions where the object of hate has really inflicted suffering on the individual. However, in the case of "group enmity" where one feels enmity towards all (or nearly all) the members of a specific group, of which only a few are personally known, the "normal" hate reaction is irrelevant.

If we accept the idea that individuals have to get an outlet for their feelings of hate, the basic question is: Who can be the target of our feelings of hate? Two precepts seem to be wise. First, do not vent your hate on your family and friends and people upon whom you are dependent. In general, according to Bernstein, "then it becomes imperative to keep the reserve of hate remote from contact with this circle and its intimacy, even to the extent in which it arises from relations within the circle" (p. 107). This again increases, of course, the sum total of hate that cannot be expressed.

Concerning the second precept, Bernstein writes: "Failing a possibility of expression it finds at least its direction where there is some imagined chance of expressing it without punishment, and therefore without danger: it must be diverted from the closer circle and directed outwards" (p. 107). Bernstein continues:

In this way we automatically arrive at the conception of a circle of human beings, which has an inside and an outside: the group as an immediate consequence of the desire to enjoy the advantages of human society—love, sympathy, friendship, consolation, protection, assistance, succour—and at the same time the possibility of directing (and where possible expressing) accumulated and ever present feeling of hate outwards.

We do not consider the groups as a collection of human beings with similar characteristics, established for scientific or other purposes, but as a functional unit within human society, charged with the distribution of feelings of affection and disaffection according to certain principles (p. 107).

Bernstein then observes:

The group appears to be a curious form of extension of the individual. It seems as if under the influence of the necessities of human communal life, human beings who need love and produce hate combine into new collective and collectively selfish individualities of a higher order; directing their love inwards, their hate outward, their social instincts towards the insider, their anti-social tendencies towards the outsider. The group becomes apparent as a functional unit and as the organization, which cannot be foregone, if the enjoyment of all advantages which human society can provide is to be combined with the possibility of expressing the hostile feelings, which always clamour for discharge (pp. 109-110).

Bernstein continues:

[T]he described distribution of functions, namely the outward direction of hostile and the inward expression of friendly feelings, is an exhaustive definition of the cause and purpose of group formation (p. 113).

By this analysis Bernstein describes and explains the reasons for the mechanism of how social groups are formed and maintained. Indeed, from his many examples of groups, ranging from states to local neighborhoods, football clubs, student unions, etc., it is seen that mostly the differences between competing groups are small or even fictitious, but that they serve the job of directing and distributing friendly and hostile feelings excellently.

Obviously there are many ways in which groups may be formed. The main tendency is that members should have similarity according to some characteristics, which have to be easily recognized. Frequently, however, the driving force behind group formation is that individuals have a common enemy or fear. For existing groups, it may quite well be that such an enemy does not exist anymore, but that the group sticks together for historical and traditional reasons. In that case, the group will vanish over time, unless it finds new objectives and new enemies.

Bernstein (p. 129) outlines the main categories according to which group formation takes place are:

a)   Biological categories: Family, clan, tribe, nation, race; occasion-
     ally also sex and age-group.
b)   Local categories: House, street, suburb, village or town, district,
     country, continent.
c)   Cultural categories: Language, religion, philosophy of life,
     similarity of conception and aim in science or art
d)   Social-economic categories: Social circle (clique), club, trade or
     profession, class, also party.
e)   Purposive groups: All groups where an expressly stated material
     purpose or aim appears as the reason for group formation....

Two conclusions may be drawn immediately. First, one individual is simultaneously a member of various groups according to the different group characteristics. This may lead to group-loyalty problems. However, Bernstein solves this problem, somewhat superficially, by defining invariant and variable group characteristics. The invariant group characteristics are individual characteristics that cannot be changed at will by the individual like his skin color, his race, or less so, his language or social class. On the contrary, the hallmarks of the football club, again, are not only variable, but artificial (p. 131). At this point I fall for the temptation to include a quotation, which is perhaps not functional to summarize Bernstein's group theory, but which is very illustrative for the vivid and at times witty style of Bernstein:

> Artificial characteristics have a great attraction for groups, particularly for those whose natural marks cannot readily be recognized at sight, but whose members wish to display their group solidarity in a way that strikes the eye. For the group characteristic is the distinguishing element: it is the banner and uniform of the group struggle: and where the individual has not received any visible mark from his group, a distinctive badge must be found instead. Intended as marks of recognition in battle, the artificial group characteristics become objects of ostentatious adoration; ... the group takes pride in its emblem and its flag. The symbol becomes the embodiment of the principal means of intimidation, the group's authority: the flag is the incarnation of group honour. An insult of the flag is therefore no mere incident, but wounds the whole of collective group sensitivity in the most sensitive spot... (p. 132).

A better description of Germany in his time, but also of the significance of group symbols everywhere, is hard to find. Of course, the whole Nazi-symbolism offers a supreme example.

The second point that emerges is the simplicity by which a group enemy may be defined. Enemies are those who do not conform to the own-group definition. Because they are different with respect to the own-group characteristics, they are easily recognized as members of the enemy. "[E]ven as the own characteristics are objects of pride, so do those of the foreign group evoke contempt; they are regarded not only as symbols but as actual evidence of the foreign group's inferiority" (p. 135).

It is not only symbols that are important for the group's cohesion. The group has to have an ideology, a mission, which is based on something, which has to be improved or maintained. It yields "an idea of justification which supplies the group with the psychological prerequisites for the expression of enmity to any desired extent.... The importance of a well-developed group ideology is so great that no movement of any considerable extent can deploy itself without it, and that even biological groups must frequently be inoculated from outside with a vigorous group ideology."

Hence, Bernstein also sees the ideology not as the cause for the existence of the group, but rather the other way round, the ideology as a necessary means for the continuation and extension of the group. The ideology describes a purpose "which must naturally derive from the category; the social group will find a social purpose, the religious group a religious purpose, and so on. A group always fights another group of the same category" (p. 142).

Following the order of the book, we now return to the question of group loyalties. Bernstein gives an example, which brings the problem to light (pp. 168-169).

> Let us consider the comparatively simple case of an American worker of Anglo-Saxon descent. As a worker he is anti-capitalist (social category); as Anglo-Saxon he is in opposition to ... "Latins" ... the descendants of Mediterranean nations (ethnical category), who ... usually are American ... workers also like himself.... [A]s a white man he detests Negroes (racial category) and as an American he hates the Japanese (national-political category). ... In addition, our American worker probably belongs to some Christian religious community; and even if his loyalties in this respect are not of the strongest, they are sufficient to cause some dislike against other religions....

Bernstein continues:

> In a dispersed people, like the Jews, the interrelation of group allegiances is still far more complicated; we are an ethnical-historical group, but belong individually to the most diverse state, language, social-economic, cultural and philosophical groups; officially, we are regarded as a religious community, while the specifically Jewish religious ideology does not, to say the least, dominate the larger part of the ethnical group. In this case, at any rate, the conflict of claims between the various groups to which the individual belongs has reached such a degree that it cannot but express itself always and everywhere as an

internal conflict of the mind; daily and almost hourly the individual is pressed into different ranks and forced to regard the same person now as friend and then again as enemy in an alternation too rapid for sanity....

[W]e should consider that all the groups to which the individual belongs compete for the dominations of his soul: for the group, being organized for struggle, must make sure that it can always rely on its members, lest, for instance, the worker whom his state has called to the wars lower his arms when he faces his fellow-worker on the other side; even as, on the other hand, the proletariat does not want its solidarity to collapse before the barricades between nation and nation (pp. 171-172).

Bernstein argues (p. 172) that the category that becomes predominant with split loyalties is "that group category which through its ideology most completely saturates the individual mind." Therefore the leaders of the group ... "continuously strive to convince the individual of the outstanding importance of the ideology concerned."

This is the reason for the continuous internal propaganda in groups, be it states, parties, churches, student unions, or football clubs. However, the most important point is whether the group feels threatened or not. Groups living in intensified antagonism will present the predominant category of allegiance. And it is also therefore that the leadership of the group tries to convince group members that the group is in danger and even frequently tries (with brinkmanship) to maneuver the group into a situation of antagonism. This is because, thanks to that situation, the specific group is clearly an operational and efficient instrument to defend its members. We see this phenomenon in the behavior of many different types of actors, e.g., Nazi Germany, Bush administration vs. Iraq, Iran, trade unions, Hamas, and, for instance, in the refusal of Orthodox Jews to endorse the State of Israel in its secular form.

Having come at this point Bernstein has explained the genesis of groups. They are formed to vent off feelings of enmity and to foster solidarity between the group members. In order to get the group-feeling some generalizations are needed. First, the conception of the existence of collective characteristics is necessary for group struggle (p. 186). The group may in reality consist of a large variation of characters. However, the group is assumed to be homogeneous: each member has the same collective properties. This holds as well for the own group as for the other "foreign" groups. But the own group is also considered as superior to the other groups.

> The belief in the collective inferiority of the foreign group finds its complement in the positive part of the [own] group ideology, the missionary idea. The inferiority, then, does not merely appear as an accumulation of faults of all kinds, but its manifestation is particularly seen in the resistance offered by the foreign group to the group mission and the acceptance of its contents (pp. 186-187).
>
> The conception of the existence of collective qualities, therefore, provides the possibility for a general diffusion of feelings of love and hate.
>
> Within the own group, every member becomes, as a bearer of the valuable group characteristics, indiscriminately the subject of friendly feelings; every member of the foreign group, as the carrier of the collective inferiority, becomes as indiscriminately the subject of the enmity feelings directed against his group. Individual activities and inactivities remain in either case without influence upon the group feeling bestowed (pp. 187-188).

We notice that both or multiple groups behave similarly and that the conception of what is right or wrong depends heavily on the standpoint of the group. This holds also for official law, which represents the interests of the ruling classes. As both groups feel the same, mutatis mutandis, it follows that the ground is prepared for tensions and frictions.

> This mode of equalization of all members of the foreign group is well-known. We discern only the typical group characteristics, e.g. with Chinese or Negroes, and we are nearly unable (without training) to distinguish between individuals. The foreign group appears as an agglomeration of similar beings, the foreign individual as an accumulation of average group characteristics. Therefore the stranger appears representative (for his group). His group is judged by his

appearance and behavior. And the group, accordingly demands exemplary behavior from its members abroad, for there they are regarded as representative for the group. As the group is disliked, evil behavior of an individual is seen as typical for the group and confirms the expectations, while good behavior is seen as just an exception on the rule. Hence, any member of the foreign group is made responsible for the behavior of its collectivity. For evil members of your own group there holds a different rule. He is just an exception to the rule of high quality in his group.

Apart from open struggle between groups mostly there will be some tension, which may be high or low. Tension will be promoted by contacts or the possibility of contacts. So tension is border tension. If groups do not live near each other, it is easy to have no tension. It follows that tension will increase with increasing contacts. This is also, for instance, the reasoning of Samuel P. Huntington[5] in his famous book, *The Clash of Civilizations*, where he locates many tensions between Islam and other groups at the borderline of the two civilizations. This clarifies why the tensions in a country are so high when two ethnic populations live among each other. In that case the border area is so large that it may even cover the whole country.

In the previous pages we have mostly tacitly assumed that struggling groups have about the same power. However, the case of a minority group shows that this is not true in many cases. Numbers are not always decisive. A ruling class is by definition a minority group. However, in the Jewish case, the minority group is frequently not the most powerful. If it is also fragmented geographically and socially, the whole group becomes a group border, "an army exclusively consisting of vanguards, and therefore lives over its whole extent in a continuous state of highly increased tension" (p. 220).

5. S.P. Huntington (1996), *The Clash of Civilizations and the Remaking of World Order.* New York: Simon and Schuster.

Finally, Bernstein looks for the possibility of absorption (assimilation) of the minority group into the majority group. He concludes that this is only possible for individuals in small numbers. Formally, they may be absorbed as are, for example, the baptized Jews in Spain and Portugal, but then they will not be seen as "belonging to us," but will constitute their own sub-group.

Bernstein returns at the end of his book to the subject proper: anti-Semitism, which may appear under the headings of "religious," "economic," "political" (by governments using scapegoats or directed against political activity by Jews), "social," "cultural," and "racial" anti-Semitism. On top of that, he distinguishes Jewish anti-Semitism, where Jews hate their fellow-Jews (jüdischer Selbsthass).

Indeed, Bernstein shows that the phenomenon of anti-Semitism is nothing special, but fits neatly into his general theory on group conflicts. He shows that there are no real solutions to the problem of anti-Semitism. But it has also no special and unique significance. Anti-Semitism must be regarded as a special case of a general phenomenon. The only way in which group conflicts can be mitigated is by reducing the contact frequency between the two groups. That means, by trying to shorten their common borders. Therefore he recommends for the Jewish problem the Zionist solution, i.e., a Jewish homeland.

Appreciation and Place in the Literature

The book by Bernstein is one of the most remarkable books I ever read. Although there is no doubt that Bernstein was familiar with the main current thoughts of the day, he was not "academically inhibited," like most of us are in some way. As he stood outside any academic network, he did not feel urged to cast his book in such a way that it would be accepted by the academic (German pedantic) world of his time. He felt completely free to develop his own line of thought. We may see him as an ambitious dilettante. This is not intended to detract the value of his work. Actually, the pioneers in the social sciences, like Freud, all have been dilettantes in some sense. They did not tread on trodden paths, but discovered their own path and developed their own theories, almost always without much empirical evidence except in the form of anecdotal observations and introspection. The problem that Bernstein tried to master is extremely complex, as it needs components from individual psychology, the psychology of groups, and sociology. Moreover, it deals with philosophy and political sciences.

We should not forget that in Bernstein's time, psychology was Freudian psychology. Freudian theory deals with the individual and with the relationship between specific individuals, but hardly addresses the relationship between the individual and the group or between groups. Actually, Freud acknowledged in his *Massenpsychologie und Ich-analyse* (1921) that the individual-group relationship should be considered as a part of psychology, but that book does not offer much of a theory and leans heavily on the famous book by Lebon[6] (1896), which does not attempt an explanatory theory either. The basic question why individuals try to belong to groups and to form groups and as a group are hostile to other groups is not really touched in psychology in the twenties and much later. Hence, Bernstein felt a logical need to formulate a

6. A. Lebon, *La psychologie des foules* (1895; English translation *The Crowd: A Study of the Popular Mind*, 1896).

theory himself. It is the theory of the accumulated frustration, which is neutralized by enmity towards well recognizable or constructed outside groups.

This theory was not part of the established body of psychological literature as far as I know. We have to see it as an invention of Bernstein himself. Is it therefore of less quality or less credible than, e.g., the theory of Freud with respect to the individual? In order to answer this question, we have to ask what a theory in the behavioral sciences is. Actually, a theory is a hypothesis or a set of hypotheses formulated in terms of a metaphor. The theory of Freud turns around the metaphorical concepts of the ego, the superego and the id. Nobody has ever seen those concepts in reality, but the concepts are handy in describing a possible theory on (aspects of) human behavior. When the theory explains and even predicts real-life behavior the theory is accepted as a useful theory, otherwise, it is rejected, refined, or replaced by a better one. In this light, Bernstein's theory is on a par with Freud's basic hypothesis. Obviously, Freud has elaborated his basic theme in many works, especially by providing indirect empirical evidence in the form of patient cases. By this prolonged life-long research and by the work of his followers, an impressive body of evidence has been accumulated for the usefulness of Freud's original paradigm, but it is still a metaphor of which the general validity cannot be proven in a way that would satisfy the modern empirical researcher. This does not reduce the value of Freud's theory by a bit. Rather we should realize that theories do not derive their value of the fact that they can be proven or not. They have to be seen as primary concepts, which may be useful according to whether they explain and predict reality or fail to do so.

In this sense, Bernstein's theory may be seen as a necessary complement to Freud's theory as it describes a model to
describe the formation of groups in society. The way in which
the individual is described as a reservoir of frustrations has to
be seen as a metaphor. The idea that hostility may be directed,
as a rule, at anonymous individuals that are not related to
the original frustrations is certainly not new. It is the biblical
scapegoat. The idea to stipulate it as a large-scale regularity
and to explain the formation of in-groups and out-groups by
the natural need of all individuals to vent their frustrations is
brilliant. As Bernstein himself is well aware of, this idea runs
counter to the concept of humans as rational beings that do not
commit hostile acts or foster hostile feelings without reason.
On the other hand, we have to admit that society is full of ir-
rationality and that finding a fully rational human being is an
especially rare event. Bernstein's giving room to and explicit
recognition of this irrational behavior must be seen as a major
breakthrough in the formation of social theory. Secondly, he
postulates that the individual attempts to justify one's own
behavior by inventing reasons for his behavior, by construct-
ing guilt in the other party. However, the justification and the
invention of arguments why the feelings of enmity are caused
is a secondary activity. Also this sounds irrational, but again,
the phenomenon is generally so well known, that we cannot
deny its factual accuracy.

Starting from a concrete problem, anti-Semitism in Central
Europe, Bernstein tried to put anti-Semitism in a general sociological theoretical framework. The concrete problem was
replaced by an abstract, more general problem of wider bear-
ing. Why are groups formed in any human society? What are
the rules for group formation and why are there always latent

or open conflicts between groups, which are based on the same social categorization principle? Hence, he aims at devising a theory that is as applicable to the ethnically differentiated population of the United States as to the league of football clubs in Germany in 1920 as to Jews vis-à-vis the Gentile population. He is also looking for a theory that is neither time- nor culture-bound. This idea to see anti-Semitism not as a problem as such, but as an instance of a generally spread mechanism, was completely novel, as far as my knowledge goes. Far from limiting himself to fruitless elaborations on the common perceived unpleasant characteristics of Jews, he recognizes that the group is heterogeneous and that the usual arguments to justify anti-Semitism do not have any general validity. They may, however, hold for some specific individuals of the hated group, like individual members of any group may be less pleasant. The same holds, mutatis mutandis, for the collective hate by any group towards another group. It is replaced by the insight that group formation and hostility between groups is an elementary ingredient of society, stemming from individual psychological needs. In its time and probably up to the present moment this insight may be seen as novel.

The core of the book is the development of a new socio-psychological theory. A theory in social science is always a rather precarious endeavor. Is society not a too diverse field to single out regularities, which can be assigned the status of "empirical laws"? Indeed, if we consider social theories, then they will never have the exactitude of laws in mathematics or physics. It will always be possible to find counterevidence. Reality is pluriform. A theory in social science may be seen as a structure, which explains average development and average behavior. A valid theory should also deliver predictions that can be tested on their validity. It is in this sense that we have to view the sociological group theory, developed by Bernstein. We observe that in 1923 sociology was in its infancy and mostly of a descriptive nature. The idea of a general theory describing social groups and their interactions was not known at that time. The theory, as are nearly all theories, is developed by introspection and by observation of the social environment. As such, it lacks any direct empirical validation. The empirical validation Bernstein finds is by looking at societies in the world of 1920 and drawing rather abstract and general inferences out of his observations. This way of setting up a theory was rather usual in sociology until recently. Actually, the approach of, for example, Sigmund Freud to individual psychology was not different. That theory is much more based on critical observation of a rather limited number of cases and anecdotes, which could not be considered as a statistically analyzable dataset.

On one hand the theory that Bernstein offers us on group sociology and inter-group conflicts is a rather consistent theory on a high level of abstraction, but on the other hand it may be translated into and applied on real world situations.

This theory lays also the link between the individual and the group. Here we come to the second part of the theory. Unlike most modern literature in the field of social psychology, which started as a separate discipline after World War II, Bernstein does not take the existence of groups for granted, but inquires why groups are formed and exist. Modern literature is heavily anchored in empirics, however, the behavior and composition of large groups, like those that Bernstein had in mind, was very hard or even impossible to observe. This is especially true in terms of the rigid measurement and observation standards that had come to prevail in the latter half of the twentieth century.

However, this does not imply that Bernstein's subject choice, theory, and methodological procedures are not scientific in the sense of present social sciences. They are logical, testable by comparison to real situations, and highly plausible with respect to conclusions, predictions, and outcomes. The only point is that he was not in the situation and consequently has not set up and performed tests of empirical validation. Actually, we are tempted to say that the problems that Bernstein considered are much more essential and basic for the science of social psychology than the present-day highly fashionable laboratory studies.

The Lasting Significance of Bernstein's Book Today

Finally, we may ask ourselves what is the significance of Bernstein's book today? First, we believe that this unique figure in the history of social science should be recognized as such and be done justice. He made a rather significant contribution to the understanding of our society.

Second, his theoretical insights seem to be now still as valid as at the time of writing. His psychological views give a clue to the genesis of group tensions. Quite surprisingly, tensions could be reduced not only by eliminating the apparent causes, but by alleviating frustrations in general. It would follow that, for instance, the reduction of poverty, or of feelings of being treated unjustly in any domain of life, would possibly reduce group tensions.

It would be possible to compare Bernstein's work more in detail with other literature. Undoubtedly, we would find some important elements also in later work by others, e.g., by Allport and Adorno.[7] I cannot verify that these sociological giants did know of Bernstein's book. However, what is a plain fact is that Bernstein's work was decades ahead on the post-war developments in the social sciences and much of his thoughts are also found in the works of Allport and Adorno. And, but this is a question of personal taste, worded in a much more concise and transparent style. Hence, we see a duplication in independent streams of similar thoughts. It is then clearly as such that we should assign to Bernstein the priority and his due posthumous recognition as an important social scientist.

As already intimated, Bernstein's book was and is still extremely well readable. As the present situation in modern societies and the world as a whole has, deplorably, in essence not much changed since 1920, the book is still as relevant as at the time of writing, more than eighty years ago. This concise text provides an important message both for social scientists and for all intellectuals who are worrying about the many conflicts between nations, races, and social groups, which, if anything, tend to increase all over the world. I can only express the hope that this time Bernstein's book will get the recognition it deserves.

I am grateful to Professor Abram de Swaan and Professor Jaap Rabbie for very valuable discussions.

---

7. Th.A. Adorno et al. (1950), *The Authoritarian Personality*. New York: Harper.

Prologue

(by way of introduction)

This book was published in German in 1926. It had been written in 1923.

I mention these dates in order to explain the painstaking suppression of the emotional moment observed throughout the book. The necessity is obvious: research of this kind cannot be profitably undertaken unless the writer eliminates, as far as is humanly possible, his own feelings regarding a struggle in which he is a party. At that time, the elimination was still possible. Later years brought anti-Jewish persecution and mass slaughter to an unprecedented degree of fierceness; and the most strenuous effort at scientific detachment would have been in vain. I certainly do not regret that in those far-away days I was able to write on the subject with some degree of equanimity. But I want the reader to keep the period of writing in mind, lest he fail to understand how a Jew could permit himself so dispassionate observation of so impassionating a subject.

As the dates show, it took me some time to find a publisher, and not only owing to the usual technical difficulties. In fact, I am now astonished that I ever found one at all. At the time I did not realize how general the aversion to studying the subject was. And it was an aversion: not mere general lack of interest. The question was topical enough; and Jews, at least, discussed it even then not infrequently—but only amongst themselves and, so to say,

1

with muted voices. They did not want to draw attention to their preoccupation. Still less did they want to know what antisemitism really meant. They cheated themselves by a pretended indifference—and at its root lay unmitigated fear.

Nazism, at least as an organized movement, was still in its infancy. Many people shrugged it off as a bad joke; Jews did so almost universally, at least where they spoke more or less in public. As far as they dared mention the subject openly, they seemed to put their trust in the killing power of ridicule. Most people tend to exaggerate dangers which menace them. The Jews, on the contrary, attempt to avoid seeing potential or approaching dangers; less unnatural a behaviour than would seem: for man notices and even exaggerates those dangers which he feels able to avert or to fight, but from the mental pressure of dangers he cannot avert or fight successfully, he tries to free himself by ignoring them as far as possible. The popular belief that the ostrich puts his head into the sand may, zoologically speaking, be no more than a legend. The frequency with which it is mentioned and alluded to is due to the fact that whatever ostriches may do, men use this stratagem by preference when faced by dangers they have no power to counter.

In the case of Jews and antisemitism the problem assumed a more complicated form. Antisemitism was by preference regarded as a prejudice which was expected to vanish, suddenly or at least gradually, before the light of reason; as prejudices are invariably expected to do— at least by their victims. In the Jewish case this was certainly the most convenient sand to put one's head into. Some Jews, however, did not entirely rely upon an automatic increase of the light of reason. Infected by the notion that antisemitism was caused by the supposedly innate evil Jewish character, they tried to prove that, on the contrary, Jews were rather decent people who could boast of quite respectable cultural achievements and had produced something like a galaxy of geniuses or at least celebrities. They certainly declined communal responsibility for offenses committed by individual Jews somewhere or at some time in history. Paradoxically enough there was, at the same time, much internal criticism of Jewish conduct in many fields, and much good advice was given on how to avoid antisemitic reactions by exemplary behaviour. But as a publicistic endeavour an apologetic literature sprang up. I believe that Jews in England and America are spending money on this kind of activity until this very day. But even the apologetic campaign was, in those prehistoric times of contemporary history, conducted only by comparatively few; and nobody, the writers excluded, paid much attention to it. Most Jews feared to take notice of facts revealing antisemitic feelings, for they feared to admit a problem which endangered what to them seemed the most effective safeguard against any threat to their existence: their positions as citizens of their respective countries. The concern was the deeper since those positions were newly won and at the same time subject of intensive feelings. To their consciousness citizenship was not a matter of mere material advantages and legal security. The emancipation gave Jews what they had lacked for nearly 1,800 years: participation in statehood. The participation was largely an illusion, and intrinsically a tragedy; for many of them a major tragedy: the patriotic feelings of Jews were bestowed on the states and countries of nations who tacitly, and afterwards not so tacitly, first in the innermost recesses of their souls, and later quite openly, rejected those Jews as foreign Orientals whose full patriotic solidarity seemed somehow not fully reliable.

So the dread that the position of the Jews as equal citizens might come to be regarded or—far worse—discussed as subject to doubts, assumed such proportions that anything indicative of hostile feelings towards the Jews had to be eliminated from their minds by the process of ignoring or minimising disagreeable facts. Fear that the protecting wall might be breached withheld them from looking at the numberless rifts which were there already, and at the gathering enemy forces.

Who, therefore, would at such a time be interested in some newfangled theory about the probable causes of antisemitism—and not too palatable a theory at that?

But that is only half of the story.

*   *   *   *

If we admit the validity of the apologetics which refute the accusations usually levelled against the Jews—and in a general way the refutation seems to me rather convincing — we will have to find an answer to the question why Jews are nevertheless so universally disliked. The answer which first offers itself is: prejudice. But what *is* prejudice? And then, there is so much prejudice in the world, and not only with regard to Jews either. There are prejudices against Negroes, or coloured races in general; and against aliens, or foreign nations in general; prejudices against religious communities and social classes, against Easterners and Westerners; and, of course, against political parties and so forth. In short: prejudices are not so much directed against individuals as such, but against individuals as members of certain human entities, or, more exactly, against those entities and all their individual members, irrespective of their individual character and behaviour.

Thus I came to focus my attention on these entities. Human beings who belong together in any given way are called groups. They may be associated on the strength of a host of different elements or characteristics. A man — or woman — usually belongs to a number of groups, large and small. Obviously some groiips are highly important, others are relatively unimportant, and in between there are numerous degrees of importance. But all groups seemed to have something in common: some functional element, closely or remotely connected with prejudice. I came to see the group in its various denominations as something instrumental in that sphere of human activities where prejudice flourishes: warfare, contest, dispute, quarrel, strife, struggle. On closer observation it also appeared that a complementary function of the group, that of cultivating friendly feelings and social instincts and activities within the group, could not be disregarded. I had therefore to formulate at least a rough outline of what seemed to be the main functional task of group formation and group life, namely a certain distribution of love and hate, or social and antisocial behaviour, in the life of human masses. In order to substantiate a seemingly very abstract and rigid theory, I tried to describe the distribution of essential functions over the different categories of groups. This, in turn, appeared to be impossible without defining the specific role of the group characteristics which make the individual a member of any given group. For it is obvious that a black or white skin binds a man to a race-group to quite another degree than a membership card commits him to a racing club. It is equally obvious that the importance of any group is determined by the degree of its hold on its members, though this hold need not be of a biological nature.

Once the role of the group as an instrument in mass-or collective struggle was established, it became, strangely enough, necessary to attempt some description of the mental mechanism of strife and struggle. To the best of my knowledge it has never been clearly realised to what extent every struggle is accompanied by and even dependent on the moral disparagement of the opponent, or what this disparagement is meant to achieve. But if one wants to derive the right to fight a certain opponent from his alleged inferiority, moral or otherwise, then a corresponding conviction of one's own superiority becomes a necessary complement. Where group relations are concerned, this appeared to be the so-called group ideology, which consists of a feeling of collective superiority and the notion of some universal mission imposed from on high on the chosen people, nation, community, church, party or whatever the particular entity may be: or a mission simply derived from that feeling of superiority which values the own mental properties — real or imaginary — achievements, customs or institutions, far above those of any other peoples, nations, races, or human entities whatsoever.

Once I had gone so far, it seemed interesting to define the relationship between the individual and the different groups to which he belongs: for he belongs to quite a number of groups of various categories: to a racial, national, religious, social, professional, political group, not to speak of societies, clubs, sports organisations, and the like.

And finally I was tempted to make some tentative guesses about the most obscure of group phenomena: the probable causes of the manifold changes observed in group life, rise and decline, staying power, absorption, amalgamations, splits, disappearance of old groups and appearance of new ones, in the various categories.

So, almost incidentally, out of a research into the probable causes of antisemitism, there grew a general group theory to which antisemitism was related only as a very small, though specific, aspect of a general phenomenon.

As a result of this, in sociological research somewhat unusual, genetic process, the book contains two parts, not less distinct for not being visibly separated.

* * * *

I do not believe that these two parts, the specific and the general, could have been dealt with separately, the general being necessary to explain the specific. But the combination proved to be rather awkward: the few people interested in antisemitism at that time did not care for sociological explanations, and the still far less numerous persons engaged in sociological research were utterly disinclined to pay attention to antisemitism; partly out of general contempt for the subject, and partly because of the prevalent notion that sociology was exclusively the science of class formation and the ensuing processes, which were considered essentially economic in nature.

The combination of the specific and the general, and more particularly the fact that the specific question was the point of departure, had, apart from the external circumstances which caused lack of interest, another undesirable result with regard to the book itself. The specific question, being the first and main subject of research, is treated somewhat too fully in proportion to the general part. This latter, though perhaps not too incomplete in essentials, has been written in a kind of telegraphic style, leaving it to the reader to fill in the well known relevant facts of past and present history; which the writer should himself have inserted in order to relieve the tension of what, expressed only in abstract conclusions, necessarily requires too much exertion on the part of the reader.

But all these shortcomings and difficulties are of secondary importance compared with those arising from the very nature of this kind of sociological research.

If we are studying, say, chemical processes, even on living tissues, we observe and register reactions, draw conclusions, and so may come to learn what is happening. Nobody would dream of complaining about the way those chemical substances react upon each other, or about their specific properties. Nobody would demand that the reactions or properties should be different and more in accordance with what the scientists, for reasons best known to themselves, would deem desirable.

But if we come to study problems connected with human relations the purely scientific approach of registering observed facts becomes immensely difficult. For instead of observing, registering and drawing conclusions we find ourselves praising or blaming, we admonish, exhort; we demand that relations and attitudes be different, we qualify them as good or bad, we classify them as laudable, permissible or forbidden. In short, we treat them, most understandably, as a matter of morals.

But however understandable, such an approach makes correct and dispassionate observation almost impossible:

the description becomes coloured by the moral viewpoint of the describer, and worse of all: the moral postulate cannot afford to understand and explain the forces determining an exceptionable attitude or action since the explanation would become an excuse, and thus blunt or even obliterate the moral verdict.

I realize quite well that I am touching upon one of the least solved and most persistent mysteries of human nature. An overwhelmingly strong conviction of the existence of a free will (librum arbitrium) is immanent in our consciousness; nevertheless we cannot escape the opposite conviction that human action is dependent on forces not subjected to our free will, and that those forces even dictate the decisions of our will. This problem, in some periods of history hotly discussed in the theological and philosophical world alike, has almost vanished from contemporary thought. Perhaps it has been abandoned (probably only for some time) as too tough to tackle. Perhaps it must be forever evaded; for all our notions of right or wrong, and what seem to vis to be the elements regulating (though most imperfectly) human relations, would become problematic without that responsibility which can only be exacted if freedom of will is considered an established fact.

However that may be: as long as group enmity in general and antisemitism in particular are either condemned as reprehensible, or explained as the justified response to the reprehensible activities of some opposite party, we come no nearer to an understanding of what is really happening. We cannot even take the first step of describing, soberly and as far as possible unemotionally, what is really happening.

I have tried to approach a sociological process somewhat along the lines practised in scientific research of physical and chemical processes. After 25 years I know better than then, how little that method appeals to the reader.

But the book had found, nevertheless, a number of friends and perhaps believers, and some of them thought it important that my views should become more widely known, since antisemitism has in the meantime acquired an actuality so ferocious as even I had thought entirely impossible. I was prevailed upon to have the book translated into English.

It has been translated. It should have been rewritten.

Re-reading the book after 25 years of experience—far too much and too painful experience—-I cannot regard the line of thought developed in this attempt at formulating a comprehensive group theory as essentially a failure. I believe to this day that the main points are correct. But a number of shortcomings could have been avoided; some findings could have been formulated more concisely; and I could have inserted a host of facts illustrating what appear only as abstract conclusions.

In any case, external circumstances do not allow me to undertake the rewriting, and so I have to content myself with a few observations.

*   *   *   *

If I had to rewrite the book today, the chapter about "The Origin of Hate" might turn out slightly different. It certainly could not have been omitted. The title of this chapter, with its purposely general and abstract formulation, is intended to convey that the source of hate, as it finds its expression in mass antagonies, must be essentially different from what is usually given as an explanation of such antagonies. The analysis which leads to that conclusion will be found in the book. To me it seems convincing. Therefore an attempt had to be made to penetrate the darkness surrounding what is called "the origin of hate" in the broadest and most general sense.

Notions of right and wrong dominate our mind to such an extent that we are virtually unable to conceive of hatred as a feeling *not* evoked by some antagonist whom we accuse of some wrong or reprehensive action or quality which gives rise to that feeling. The accusation is nearly almost refuted and answered by counter-accusations. Discussions or disputes, more or less heated as the case may be, turn on the justification of the inimical feelings and still more of the actions which betray their existence. The supreme ethical commandment enjoins upon man that he respond to wrongdoing by love and not by hatred: and as is the way of ethical commandments, its performance is rarely if ever achieved. But at least it certainly seems to go against our most deeply rooted convictions to admit that feeling of hate may be due to anything but the wrongdoings of those against w ᵣhom those feelings are directed.

As will be established at some length, it is one of the most striking characteristics of mass antagonies that feelings of the fiercest hatred are directed and discharged against millions of people personally unknown to those who hate them, millions who, if only for lack of opportunity, cannot possibly have done them any harm, who cannot have evoked those feelings by any act which might be resented as reprehensible. In the course of this investigation I have described the psychological mechanisms by which the guilt of these millions nevertheless becomes an acceptable and accepted notion. But it is no more than a notion; and the real source of the hate must be found elsewhere.

This, in my opinion, is the crucial point of the problem.

We come to discover that the urge to direct and discharge unfriendly feelings against someone appears to be *primary.* Again *whom* the feelings are directed and discharged, depends on the conditions described in this book. But if this is so, the, let us say, impersonal source of the primary urge remains to be disclosed.

At first sight there appears to be a close connection between suffering, even if caused by such impersonal agencies as disease, earthquake, or thunderstorms, and the urge to direct and discharge hostile feelings. I have tried to describe the psychological mechanism which converts suffering into the need for directing and discharging feelings of hate. Such a conversion takes place continuously. There are phases of accumulation, and there is an urge to discharge accumulated hate in any practicable direction. I believe, in addition, that the conditions which determine the direction of the discharge and its objects are, in general, described correctly.

But the process must, obviously, also be influenced by differences in individual, and perhaps even collective, disposition. There are people of markedly friendly nature, though their amount of suffering available for conversion into enmity may be no less, or even more, than that of an exceedingly choleric person. The existence of such differences is evidenced by the traditional types of temperaments. Whether this applies to collectives I am not so sure. The so-called peace-loving nations are usually peace-loving while they are weak; and peoples with a reputation of gentle-mindedness become not infrequently as ferocious as any. But at any rate we have to allow for factors which influence the process of conversion and modify what otherwise would seem to be a function capable of quantitative mathematical expression. It is also almost certain that the subconscious, where most of the conversion process takes place, is affected by factors which are residues of former generations probably going far back in history or even prehistory. The contributory experience causing the conversion of suffering into hostile dispositions may therefore be not only that of the living individual, but also that of past generations.

In group relations the conversion of suffering into hate seems, at first sight, much more obvious and pronounced than in the individual case. Nevertheless there are blurred spots in the general picture. If we attempt to verify the general principle by an observation of group processes in past and contemporary history, we cannot always establish an adequate relation between the measure of suffering arid the intensity and scope of the outbreak of hate. But then the contents of the pool in which accumulation takes place are in the collective case still more obscured than in the individual; it is still more difficult to assess the respective shares of individual experience and of the heritage from former generations in the "stock" of accumulated hate and enmity. And it should always be remembered that a suitable opportunity for discharging inimical feelings may reveal an appalling amount of ferocity, hidden in the deeper layers of the soul as long as such an opportunity does not exist, and probably unknown to the owners of such dispositions themselves. On the other hand, lack of opportunity may be so evident that despair smothers the rebellious pressure of feelings of hate accumulated under actual suffering; and it is not even certain whether the manifest inability of discharging those feelings does not result in some process of partial resorption. Such a possibility suggests itself when one witnesses the submissiveness, the patience and the apparent indifference of enslaved peoples or groups to what to us would seem permanent and heavy suffering. One might argue that a state of protracted slavery (I am not alluding to a legal status) blunts the sensitiveness, and that a treatment which to us may seem outrageous and unbearable does not hurt the feelings of those who have become accustomed to it or have never known anything else. But occasional risings of enslaved groups or peoples—as a rule most eruptive and sanguinary affairs—make us doubt whether this assumption is correct.

Though these uncertainties do not, in my opinion, affect the fundamental arguments of this book, they would, if I had rewritten it, most probably have induced me not to go as far as to establish a direct relation between the excess of sorrow and suffering over joy (in German the differentiation used to be expressed by the terms *Lust*—and *Unlustefuehle)* and the excess of hate over love. The relation may well exist. But I would now have avoided this quasi-mathematical construction of an equation in which the terms "joy" and "sorrow", though apparently clear and opposed in their nature, are in reality questionable abstractions which cover a wide range of feelings, sometimes intertwined to such an extent as to obliterate the contrast which is the base of the equation.

Even with these restrictions I am not quite sure now whether the conversion of suffering into hate, though undoubtedly an established fact, provides us with the final and exhaustive explanation.

Somewhere in this book there occurs an almost casual remark, inserted at the time without the full realisation of all its possible implications. After the exposition of the conversion theory alluded to above, I asked tentatively whether in every human being there does not exist some preestablished disposition to joy and sorrow, to love and hate; a disposition which would, of course, be individually different, and which in its expression would obviously, though not to a very great extent, be influenced by external occurrences. Some people are known to preserve a serenity of mind and friendly attitude towards their fellow-creatures under the most adverse circumstances and even under the severest blows of fate, while others are always morose, growling, storming or dejected, though their experience in life would seem to warrant any degree of happiness and a corresponding friendliness in their dealings with the world. It is evident that external happenings in everyday life influence our moods and feelings. But it seems doubtful whether this influence is of decisive importance. I admit that this is a very difficult question, far-reaching in its consequences, and I do not presume to answer it finally.

Even so it remains a fact that an excess of unfriendly feelings creates an urge to be directed and discharged against fellow-beings; but perhaps I should have contented myself with stating this fact without trying to explain it. However, the attempt has been made; and I leave the result as material for thought and discussion.

*   *   *   *

If, therefore, rewriting the book might have meant the shortening of some parts, a number of complementary remarks would on the other hand have had to be inserted about an aspect of the question which has been entirely neglected.

Since we are dealing with matters pertaining to human beings, it is only natural that we inquire into the processes of that organ where the source of human actions and human attitudes seems to be located. The aspect of the inquiry is therefore preponderantly psychological. But it might be asserted that feelings in general are only, like thoughts, the human superstructure of biological processes which also occur in the animal world. Struggle and oppi'ession are not confined to human society. Warlike clashes between organised groups of animals of the same species, it is true, seem to have been reliably observed only with regard to certain ants, but in a general way animal life is also full of strife, struggle and mutual destruction. And in higher animals we observe as incidental to such clashes something akin to what would seem the expression of hostile feelings. On the other hand the animal world is not devoid of social structures, and some are even rather elaborate, so that we must conclude that social instincts exist amongst animals too. So it may be argued that also in human affairs the psychological processes are not the cause of strife and struggle and clashes, but only the mental concomitants of a biological process. One or two of the critics who at the time wrote reviews of the book, condemned the purely psychological approach to the problem as a major weakness, though without going as far as to deny the psychological processes any decisive role.

I admit a very great reluctance to consider this question of the "biological" extension. There are two main reasons for this reluctance.

It is true that some major impelling forces, obviously

biological, like the need of getting food and the mating impulse, to a large degree govern our mental activities, direct our feelings and colour our thoughts; and not only at moments when these needs urgently demand gratification.

It is also admitted that thought and feeling are influenced by and dependent on chemical processes occurring in the body which in turn seem to be determined biologically. But beyond that we do not know very much; and these rough generalities are not very helpful in finding out why mankind tends to group formation and why it uses its groups for the more important forms of its mutual warring.

It might be possible, of course, to base oneself on the established fact that on this planet all living creatures exist by eating one another, and one might suppose that at the root of all enmity there operates some compelling fear to be eaten or the equally compelling urge to eat someone else who does not want to be eaten. But it would be a rather hazardous enterprise to trace the development from such primeval instincts to the actual complications of human struggle. Men, for one thing, can exist by eating plants, who are living beings too, but are not known to resent being eaten, or at any rate cannot struggle against being eaten. Secondly, men, with the exception of relatively very few ones, have ceased to eat one another, while mutual hatred and the ferocity of its outbursts seem to have been greatly on the increase since cannibalism has been abandoned as a generally accepted custom. So why should just mankind, not bent on eating one another, and assured of plentiful food if they stop warfare, have developed a highly complicated group system on the ground of that deep biological urge of getting food in order to exist? Or are we to assume that canni-balistic instincts remain operative in hatred and warfare while its general aim has become, even in the more extreme forms of armed clashes, destruction of the opponent without any indication of even readiness to eat his flesh? It seems a far-fetched assumption and not very apt to provide us with the required elucidations.

The mating urge, enlarged by Freud and his school to the general principle of libido, is thought to represent the comple-mentary tendency of love and social behaviour, though it has been thought to contain also, in its elements of highest excitement, the death-urge, described as a tendency to self-destruction and destruction of others. But even if we accept those very tenta-tive thoughts, it would be a most difficult undertaking to find something of a connecting line between those hidden urges and a highly developed organisation for the partition of social and anti-social behaviour.

Now there is a second consideration causing reluctance to extend this essentially sociological research into the realm of biology.

There is a wide gap between the relatively extensive and also relatively accurate knowledge we have of our own mental structure and the more than scanty knowledge we have of the biological roots which may feed the highly complicated work-ings of our mental apparatus; we know next to nothing about what the so-called higher animals are feeling—or thinking if they do anything like that—when they live their lives of instincts (which word only means that no intellectual activ-ity comparable with our is operative) and we know nothing at all about the question whether the armies of ants engaged in warfare are possessed of anything like emotions, feelings, or thoughts. Even what we try to conclude from the study of the most primitive human tribes about the early mental dispositions of our own remote forebears is scarcely more than guessing.

Therefore I thought it reasonable to transgress as little as possible outside the relatively accessible sphere in which human actions seem to be directed. I myself am convinced that the intellectual activity of thought and reasoning has no decisive part in guiding human actions. The forces of human intellect have achieved marvelous results in the field of acquiring knowledge and in using this knowledge for the satisfaction of human needs and the gratification of human desire. But these forces seem to be subjected to those of the emotions, feelings, desires, urges, passions which either slily use the intellect for their own purposes, or eventually overrule its unwelcome interference.

If we state the undeniable fact that huge amounts of hate and enmity are always ready to seek a chance of discharge, we have a sufficient basis for the development of the general idea which has been worked out in this book.

I wish to conclude by an additional remark about anti-semitism.

* * * *

It has proved to be far more murderous and far more infectious than I thought possible. But then an abyss has been opened which even pessimists had thought closed for ever. The book was written after the first world war, when, despite mutual destruction on a grand scale, human passion seemed to respect limitations to ferocity which in the light of recent experience must be considered severe. Apparently brakes were functioning then which have become ineffective in the meantime. I believe that it follows from what I tried to explain 25 years ago that the Jews necessarily had to become the first and chief victims of this earthquake of hate, and it is a mere chance of war that no more than a third of all living Jews were slaughtered. With some slight delay in stopping the German armies it could easily have been many more. For the Jews were everywhere weak and defenseless minorities and the most tempting object for an outburst of passionate hate which prefers, understandably enough, dis- charge without risk of retaliation or defense. In such an event the mental apparatus, long before saturated with feelings of dislike and aversion with regard to the Jews, easily provides the notion of their being so dangerous and obnoxious that they must be destroyed.

But I cannot say why the brakes which still functioned during the former war have become ineffective, and why its aftermath has let loose such a fury of the most ruthless and ferocious hate. It was not only directed against the Jews. There were other victims too, but they were persecuted for their politi- cal conviction and would perhaps have been no more lenient towards their adversaries, had those happened to be the losers in the game. The Jews had no choice. They were murdered for being Jews.

One must assume that the thwarted ambitions of Ger- many—and thwarted ambitions of men with great vitality cause a profound and soul-devouring suffering—have generated or freed an amount of hate and an intensity of hate almost unparalleled in known history. It seems also probable that the example set by the Germans has loosened repressions that existed elsewhere. For it is notable that neither the persecution of the Jews before, nor their destruction during the war were interfered with.

The chapter is, I am afraid, far from closed. It is generally admitted that, the Jews have no future in Europe; which means, of course, that they are too much hated to hope for even elementary security. Though their number has been so drastically reduced, they are apparently not insignificant enough to escape becoming the victims of the smouldering passions engendered in that war-torn continent. In England, victorious in war but deposed from her rank of first-rate power by the rise of her ally, the U.S.A., and beset by severe financial and economic difficulties, antisemi-tism, formerly almost non-existent, is already on the increase, and shortly after the war produced one of the most significant features of active antisemitism: excesses against manifestly and admittedly innocent English Jews in retaliation for acts perpetrated by Jewish terrorists in Palestine. Here we have the imposing of collective responsibility, which is so characteristic for antisemitism in its purest form. Public opinion in England regarded it as a natural and excusable reaction. This ought to be astonishing. Terror, riots, rebellious actions are not a novel feature in the history of the British Empire. In the course of the same post-war years British soldiers have been ambushed and killed in a number of countries, and the British press scarcely mentioned the incidents. Certainly there have never been attempts at popular retaliation, such as occurred in the case of the Jews. But in their case the objects were ready at hand; and the ground had been prepared, since anti-Jewish feelings had become strong enough in England to make an occasional outburst possible. The people of Britain have not only been suffering hardships, but their

pride is deeply wounded by their having become the poor relation of the Americans. I am not among those who have already
written off Britain, and her recovery may surpass expectations,
but she is no longer the world-dominating power she was, and
the feeling of decline weighs down heavily on every Englishman.
Such a state of mind is an ideal condition for the conversion of
suffering into enmity; and who should be the victims closest at
hand, but the English Jews?

In various degrees of virulence antisemitism exists in the
U.S.A., in Latin America, in South Africa, in fact everywhere.
Whether it will assume threatening proportions depends on developments on which the Jews themselves have no influence. If
and where things are quieting down, and the economic situation
is more or less satisfactory, there are prospects of Jews being
able to live comparatively unmolested. If, on the contrary, new
upheavals are ahead, the prognostics must necessarily be bad
for the Jews.

As for Zionism, it was meant to solve the Jewish problem by
removing Jews from the dangers threatening them as dispersed
minority groups and from the actual evils besetting them in that
position. Territorial concentration of the scattered groups should
provide strength, independence from the good or bad intentions
of majority nations and their governments, security based on
self-defence and the unhampered developments of an own way of
life. Antisemitism, though one of the main motive forces behind
Zionism, could not be overcome by this movement as such. It
should ultimately have vanished for lack of actual or prospective
victims. But from the outset two major questions presented
themselves; whether the greater part of world Jewry would be in-

clined to leave the countries of dispersal, and what territory would be available for the settlement of the scattered groups. As to the first question, comparatively few Jews came to Palestine only on the grounds of Zionist conviction and in theoretical anticipation of possible future calamities. Most of them were driven by actual disasters. This attitude may change after the establishment of the State of Israel, which proves to have a great attraction for Jews all over the world whose actual economic conditions are quite satisfactory and who enjoy at present the measure of freedom customary in their respective countries. The territorial question, on the other hand, causes serious concern. The territory envisaged for Jewish concentration in 1917 was considered sufficiently large for that purpose, and in the light of colonisatory experience in Palestine this assumption seems to be borne out as justified. But two thirds of this territory, namely Transjordan, were cut off in 1922 to satisfy requirements, then considered weighty, of British colonial policy; and recent events which culminated in the establishment of the State of Israel further narrowed down the area destined to absorb Jewish immigration, so that only part of Western Palestine was left. Whether this territory will be sufficient for anything like the solution of the Jewish world problem by the territorial absorption of at least the larger part of World Jewry, remains to be seen. It depends on economic developments the scope of which cannot be forecast; but it seems rather improbable.

The establishment of the Jewish State is certainly a great historical event, and many Jews believe that its existence, even in its actual shape, will favourably influence the position and standing of the Jews throughout the world, and even the general attitude towards them. The future will teach whether these expectations are justified. As far as the solution of the Jewish world problem according to Zkmist convictions is concerned, only further developments can establish whether the new state can play the decisive part originally attributed to its proposed creation.

Tel Aviv, May 1949.

Chapter I

Terminological Confusion

Definitions have a way of being far more difficult than one would be inclined to assume; for they should convey an explanation, while the word itself which requires definition often has the function of concealing the very absence of an explanation. Most of us fondly believe that they know exactly what life and death, love and hate mean. But how many philosophers in the world have even arrived at an independent theory about the essence of life and death, love and hate? So it is hardly astonishing that scholars and laymen keep engaging in endless disputes about the true essence of antisemitism. A factual situation, on the other hand, is, as a rule, established easily enough; the more surprising that, though, in a general way, everyone is convinced of its existence, there are as endless disputes on the question whether such a thing as antisemitism exists at all.

The man in the street, who would be dumbfounded by a question about the real meaning of life and death, is perfectly able to distinguish clearly between, say, a live cat and a dead one. But it is impossible to establish with anything like the same degree of certainty, whether an incident commonly regarded as antisemitic really deserves that designation or not. On the contrary, it may be claimed that whenever an occurrence is characterised as antisemitic, someone can be found to deny it that character. And these denials do not always originate with antisemitic parties, who often feel blamed by such a designation and therefore repudiate it; Jews, and especially the Jews concerned, often disclaim, persistently and indignantly, that what to the bystander seems a clear case of antisemitism has anything to do with it at all.

How is this possible and why does it happen? The two thousand years' migration of the Jews has been accompanied by antisemitism throughout; it has been imported in nearly all parts of the world; it has obtruded itself to the notice of Jews and non-Jews. Why has this phenomenon not yet been sufficiently investigated to enable its diagnosis in concrete cases? Why has not even its theory arrived at the demarcation of clearcut differences of opinion? Why does it seem as if, as soon as this subject arises, all possibility of intelligent communication ceases, and senseless talking at cross purposes takes the place of the exchange of opinions?

Mere theoretical difficulties of definition are hardly a sufficient answer. But the subject is heavily charged with emotional connotations, which always are a stumbling stone in the way of dispassionate consideration. As a result of the wide dispersal of the Jews, hardly anyone remains totally free from all relations with these carriers of problems which are, to say the least, touchy. Even if the relations bear no character of dependence, in judging the problems one cannot dissociate oneself from considerations of their possible influence on Jews with whom one is personally acquainted; and the vivid feeling caused by direct contacts bias observation and warp, or even dictate, conclusions. Nor are the Jews themselves in a situation favourable to the unemotional observation and dispassionate judging of a problem which always goes close to the skin—and often enough gets under it. Only the Zionist may be regarded as something of an exception. His attitude towards antisemitism can be a comparatively objective one; for he considers it as a result of the Diaspora and therefore as a phenomenon which will disappear with the liquidation of the Diaspora: for which, he believes, he knows the recipe. So he, rather than anyone else, is able to remain cool while investigating what he considers transitory. Non-Zionist Jews, on the other hand, cannot but incline towards fighting antisemitism where it makes itself felt, that is, combating the antisemites. For these Jews consider the Diaspora and their connection with it as unchangeable, or even as desirable: their observations and conclusions are unavoidably conditioned by motivation, whether or not on purpose; instead of observing and arriving at conclusions, they will always be tempted to polemise, to repudiate accusations against the Jews and to denounce the iniquity of antisemitism as such. And such an attitude cannot result in anything but war literature.

Nor is motivation the only way in which the will to fight antisemitism falsifies the result of the investigation. The effect is further favoured by the character of enmity relations in general, of which antisemitism is an instance. At the present stage this aspect can only be hinted at; but it will be found that there are fundamental conflicts between men which cannot be explained by elements of guilt, and which find their expression in the most varied incidents. Incidents are appropriate to this purpose, because they provide a justification for the expression of enmity; a justification which consists in an accusation of the other party. The fighting of antisemitism must therefore aim at disproving accusations which, out of their very nature, always derive from incidents of secondary importance. Consequently, the investigation is led away from the nucleus of the problem to the external and misleading surface effects.

It may be difficult to follow this statement without an example. Let us assume that a Jew in a leading economic position excites enmity, either through the very fact of that position, or because he abuses its advantages and establishes a usurious monopoly, or simply by unfair business methods. His opponents will normally stress the fact that he is a Jew. This is called economic antisemitism. In combating it, it will be attempted to establish: either that the man himself is being falsely accused; or that there are thousands of non-Jews who do exactly the same thing; or that Jewry in general cannot be held responsible for an isolated case. But does all this lead to any real understanding of antisemitism? Should we not rather investigate those elements of the accusation which differ from other cases of enmity? Should one not ask why in this case, contrary to the normal, commercial jealousy or even just indignation against objectionable activities finds an incentive in the fact that the object of the enmity belongs to a certain group? Why, again contrary to the normal, the case is felt as typical by public opinion, even if it can be proved not to be so? Why the enmity is extended to persons who possibly suffer no less from the objectionable activities in question than the accusers — frequently more so: for the economic proximity between accusers and accused is often astonishingly close? But these questions lead us to the very centre of the problems of mass-antagonism and their peculiar modifications in the case of minority relations. And on the way we have lost track of the element of guilt, the only one suitable for combating.

That is why the will to fight antisemitism in its incidental effects is such a definite obstacle on the way towards understanding its essence.

The non-Jew who occupies himself with our problem is usually a self-confessed antisemite. He therefore attempts in the first place to find a justification for his emotional attitude, that is to say, he looks for grounds for accusing the Jews. Moreover his judgment is seriously prejudiced by the sentiments which rule him. Usually they are so strong as to make it impossible for him even to notice facts which might interfere with his aims. From him we can certainly expect nothing but war literature.

In Western Europe the non-Jew concerned with antisemitism may belong to circles whose liberality expresses itself in a social convention of tolerance. All so-called prejudices of race, religion and usually also of class are regarded as lack of education; or at any rate it is thought bad manners to vent them publicly. It becomes least desirable to incur the stigma of holding antisemitic opinions where there is a chance of its being objectively justified. In these circles any discussion of antisemitism will in the first place aim at proving how free one is oneself from this "indecent" attitude; a tendency which can not but distort the results of investigation, especially as it is impossible to approach the subject without a certain unmannerly and sometimes even offensive lack of consideration. Moreover, the liberal will not be overly inclined to make a close investigation of enmity relations, as he is *a priori* convinced that they ought to fade away before his ethical postulates.

We have by no means exhausted the conditions to

which the evaluation of antisemitic incidents and antisemitism as such is subject in various human categories; and it is of some importance to arrive at a certain degree of completeness in this respect. But this judgment is influenced to such an extent by a probably unparalleled terminological confusion, that it becomes necessary to discuss first of all the origin of the *word* antisemitism, which more than anything else, is to be blamed for the confusion.

The history of this word carries us amongst a curious agglomeration of things improbable, not proven and not subject to proof. Their final condensation to the concept "antisemitism" is a process which cannot be understood unless it is assumed that behind the creation of the word "antisemitism" there lies a burning desire to accept this result, the pressure exercised by powerful emotions: nothing else could have been persuasive enough to press such a veritable congeries of ideas into the service of a probably not even intentional falsification.

For many centuries enmity against the Jews had been justified to the satisfaction of popular feeling by motives of a religious nature. In the second half of the 18th century, however, the emancipation invalidated, particularly in educated circles, this religious motivation of hate; as the hate itself, however, continued to exist unabated, other reasons had to be found. It is, of course, not to be understood that Gentile society, after reading Lessing's Nathan, suddenly threw away the cross in the name of which it used to kill the Jews, in order to start on a malicious search for a new symbol which could serve the same purpose for modern minds. On the one hand there had never been any lack of non-religious charges against the Jews; whenever excesses became serious, the religious causes for hate had always been accompanied by actual accusations of a criminal character. On the other hand we are forced to assume that the replacement of hate motivation occurs spontaneously and unconsciously; in an atmosphere of inimical emotions the most improbable accusations seem credible even to otherwise clearheaded people: in fact, it is a primary condition for the psychological adequacy of a pretext for hate, that the hater should be convinced of its validity. If, therefore, we speak hereafter of a construction, we mean that under the pressure of the need for justification a conglomerate of in part highly improbable assumptions has been accepted as credible and even established fact. The particular construction found at the time of the emancipation which had to provide new justification for hating the Jews, may be described somewhat as follows:—

1. There are human races. That is to say: beyond the ethnical units of tribe and nation, there may be distinguished larger ethnical entities: the so-called races. Members of the same race are possessed of common racial characteristics which, consequently, form part of the ethnical heritage.

2. Similarities of languages, interpreted as relationship, are the only definite distinctions between races.

3. Because the difference between the Teutonic and the Semitic group of languages is regarded as decisive, all other characteristics, particularly those based on anthropology, are disregarded and it is concluded

      a) that those groups which speak — or at one time spoke — a Semitic language, belong to the Semitic race, which, incidentally, also has clearcut anthropological characteristics; and

b) that those nations whose languages belong to the Indo-Germanic (Aryan) group, though they may have nothing in common from an anthropological point of view (and in this respect even seem in part rather more closely related to the Semites), have nevertheless in times immemorial issued from a— postulated — Indo-Germanic race, to which they consequently still belong.

4. The nations which regard themselves as descen dants or members of the Aryan race are possessed of a number of highly valued qualities, particularly the ability to produce what in Europe are called cultural values. Not only do the Semitic race lack these capacities, but they are also infested with numerous undesirable col lective characteristics. It goes without saying that the former are declared to be absolutely superior, the latter — equally absolutely — inferior . . .

5. Wherefore the superior Aryan race (or at any rate its European branches) is entitled to despise the Semitic race (at least its Jewish representatives) and, as inferior qualities are a danger for superior surroundings, to com bat their carriers, the Semites (i.e. the Jews) ; which in its turn means to render them harmless — in the sense of a preventive war.

The point at issue is not that this construction should be read backwards if one wants to understand how it developed psychologically; nor are we concerned with the scientific value of the theories embodied in it — most of them have meanwhile been given up as a result of farreaching modifications. But it is this construction which has given issue to the term "antisemitism", and no later changes of the theory, which incidentally is still commonly adhered to among the public at large, have been able to dislocate this word. Antisemitism had therefore of necessity to mean something like an inimical attitude toward the inferior Semitic race element, or rather against its bearers, the Jews. All the doubtful elements of this definition will be considered at a later stage. "Inimical attitude" and "inferior race element" sorely need further elaboration. But it may already be stated that the object is not directed against the Semites in general, but only against the Jews. The non-Jewish Semites are a matter of indifference to the antisemite; quite often they are sincerely liked by otherwise confirmed antisemites. This fact, which has never been contradicted as such, but which used to be somewhat difficult to demonstrate on account of the inaccessibility of non-Jewish Semites, has been exemplified in the course of the British occupation of Palestine. In its first stage the tone was set by pronouncedly anti-semitic army officers. Nevertheless they did not only support the (Semitic) Arabs in every possible way—that might have been mere political calculation—but, as has been stated time and again, felt personally attracted by the Arab landowners, in whom they particularly appreciated those qualities of the true gentleman which are reputedly so sorely lacking in the Semitic race and the absence of which is supposed to render it so unbearable, dangerous and objectionable. So "antisemitism" has a meaning different from that implied in the name. This inner untruthfulness has the graver consequences as it has become common usance to qualify every and any unfriendly attitude towards Jews as antisemitic. This goes so far that the persecutions to which the Jews in Yemen are exposed are called antisemitic, while the persecutors are Arabs and therefore equally Semites, and it would seem improbable that what they object to in the Jews is the inferiority of their own racial element.

The surprising result of this idiomatic usage is that by calling all expressions of enmity towards the Jews antisemitic, one ascribes to them a common cause, the will to fight the inferiority of the Semitic race element, while one often does not wish to recognise the applicability of this common cause and, on the basis of the word's real meaning, is often in a position to deny it. In each individual case it thus becomes possible to disclaim the antisemitic character of the incident concerned. It has already been stated that this is often considered desirable; which statement can now be backed up by a demonstration of the trick.

The antisemite needs his theory of inferiority for a collective condemnation of the Jews. Without its aid he would be compelled to keep himself to single cases of Jewish offenses and to lay them at the feet of the community. Without the support of a theory of inferiority which deprives the case of its one-time character and establishes it as a confirmation of a general inferiority, nothing remains but collective responsibility in its crudest form, which hardly agrees with current conceptions of right and wrong. Nevertheless even the theory of inferiority does not protect the antisemite against the necessity of assuming an inimical attitude towards Jews who have never been known to harm anyone and whom he can only attack on the assumption that they might all the same harm someone at some future time. This is preventive war in its crudest form; and unless the tension of hate has reached extremes it is not admitted by that feeling of right which is so necessary to him who hates as justification in his own eyes. Even the anti-semite who is a convinced adherent of the theory of inferiority likes therefore to justify himself in concrete cases of anti-Jewish behaviour by an equally concrete, though if need be invented or exaggerated, case of Jewish misconduct. At the decisive moment he often lacks the courage of his antisemitic convictions. In that case he wishes to establish that his behaviour is not antisemitic in the technical sense of the word, but a normal hate reaction to an offence to which he would react in the same way in the case of a non-Jew. It daily happens that obviously anti-Jewish statements or speeches are introduced by the assertion that the speaker is by no means an anti-semite.

Jews are occasionally tempted to characterise objectively justified cases of enmity against them as antisemitic, in order to establish their personal innocence and to explain the enmity as a result of unjustified prejudice. But far oftener do they desire to disclaim the antisemitic character of occurrences which obviously bear that aspect, or at any rate to deny them a common cause. For outside the Zionist ranks, Jewish minds are obsessed by the wish to overlook the all-Jewish problem which manifests itself in the fact that anti-semitic occurrences have a common cause, and properly speaking in any incident which is definitely established as of antisemitic nature. One fears this problem, fears every new confirmation of its existence and would deny it wherever possible. The demand for an explicit denial arises therefore from considerations of internal Jewish policy. From the personal point of view many Jews would minimise, if not totally deny, antisemitic behaviour to which they are exposed. For they consider themselves as of so outstanding virtue that the accusations on which antisemitism is generally founded cannot possibly apply to them —at least in their own opinion. In this case the desire to deny arises from the belief in personal excellency, which its "owner" likes to consider exceptional. Astonishingly enough, one may hear from practically every Jew in Germany—which is really sufficiently infested by antisemitism—that, though matters are bad enough indeed, the speaker himself has never had to suffer personally from antisemitism; indeed he has a number of very good Christian friends . . . Finally, Jews in Western Europe will as long as possible—and not rarely with tears of gratitude—assert that their country is free, or as good as free, from antisemitism. Their patriotism fathers the wish to attribute something praiseworthy to their non-Jewish fellow-citizens.

Nothing is impossible in this confusion of terminology. One may rely on idiom in order to qualify every unfriendly act against Jews as antisemitic, even if, by way of exception, it is a case of a simple conflict between man and man, without any collective background. One may, on the other hand, invoke the original meaning of the word in order to object to the qualification of each and any incident as antisemitic. For it is always possible to establish beyond doubt that the insulting of Mr. Levi, the murder of the Proskurow Jews, the forgery of the "Protocols of the Elders of Zion" and the spreading of the ritual murder legend do not originate in disgust at the inferiority of Arab culture. And since, moreover, the expression "antisemitism" postulates a common cause for all phenomena called antisemitic, it is sufficient to claim a separate cause for the incident—easy enough a procedure for the superficial mind—in order to dispel any suspicion of its antisemitic character. For the Gentile it is easiest to avail himself of the first, method, for it is logically unassailable. He need but categorically deny the inferiority of Semitic culture, assert his admiration of the Bible, of Arab literature, and in the last resort even his respect for a world-famous Jew or two, and he has already effectively dispelled all suspicions of enmity against Semitic race inferiority. There only remain the faults, vices and misdeeds of "a certain kind of Jews"; and who is to blame the man who condemns them? Usually he need not even trouble to trot out the whole argument. There are Jews who will relieve him of that. For by admitting Jewish guilt—real or assumed—they see a chance of distancing themselves in the eyes of the Gentile from the incriminated case; they find nourishment for their vain hope of reserving something like extraterritorial status in respect of the hatred against Jews; and they can fondle the even vainer illusion that their own excellency is what distinguishes them from the despised Jews and therefore renders them immune to the attacks of antisemitism.

Not always is the Jew quite so blind to actual conditions. But even then he may at least attempt to qualify the incident as a special case by ascribing it to particular, but not of necessity antisemitic, tension. Antisemitism, thus he will argue, is hate of Semitic racial inferiority, while in the case in question we have "only" to do with personal or economic jealousy, political conflict, snobbishness, etc. This is a rather less convincing argument, as antisemitic incidents actually are characterised by unmistakable deviations from the normal development of this kind of conflict. But such subtleties will hardly be appreciated in superficial everyday conversation, the more so as no one really cares to appreciate them.

Take the case of a rich but respectable Jew who is blackballed for a club, while a number of his Gentile colleagues, of the same educational and financial standing, are members. To me this will appear as a clear instance of social antisemitism. My Gentile friend will swear that that is out of all question, for antisemitism is directed against the inferiority of the Semitic race; and as most of the members are good Presbyterians, many of them even with Biblical names, they are obviously fervent admirers of the most outstanding product of Semitic culture. Moreover, Jewish industry and ability are fully appreciated; but, says my Gentile friend, one can have too much of a good thing, and the Israelite gentleman in question had made enemies by too sharp practices. Another friend of mine, a Jew, happens to know that sharp practices are not exactly a rarity amongst the members of this particular club; but he thinks that the grounds for disclaiming antisemitism are perfectly valid; he would rather ascribe the blackballing to a certain social exclusivity, which, after all, recently caused a rich Gentile shopkeeper to be declined as well. Now one might object that a shopkeeper is not admitted as of the same standing because he keeps a shop, while the blackballed Jew is a manufacturer like the other members; so that his inequality can only consist in his being a Jew; but who would forward so devious an argument?

Another Gentile, no friend of mine, also says that in the present case there can be no question of antisemitism; but though he has a number of good Jewish acquaintances and is by no means an antisemite, he must admit that Jews often have a way of being obtrusive; as proved by the present instance. He can understand that one should want to give them a wide berth. Again we might object that a similar application for admission from a non-Jew would not have been felt as obtrusive and that the assumption of obtrusiveness only arose because the man in question was a Jew. But who would argue with an antisemite who has been kind enough to claim that he isn't one and who would only be confirmed in his belief that I belong to that kind of over-intellectual, talmudic-sophistic Jews whose soulless dialectic acrobatics undermine the deep-feeling, spiritual Aryan mind?

Finally, we should not forget that few Jews and less Gentiles have a sufficient grasp of the subject to allow a comparison of widely varying manifestations of antisemitism. Consequently, judging each case on its own merits must become the rule. Not only is there a tendency to accept the circumstances of the particular case as the underlying cause, but quite generally antisemitism as such is substituted by one of the forms in which it appears. Thus an American politician stated that there was no antisemitism in the States; for religious hate was unknown, and racial hate was only directed against yellow and black folk. What was considered as antisemitism, was actually nothing but social snobbishness or economic conflict. Similarly it was said by a British minister that antisemitism was unknown in England; there was only opposition against cheap immigrant labour and dislike of profiteers. It often appears to be profitable to identify antisemitism with one of its manifestations which happens not to occur in the country of which one is speaking. It then becomes easy enough to dismiss the other

forms as not antisemitic. The process is often applied in all innocence.

After these explanations it may be somewhat less astonishing
that all discussions of antisemitism and antisemitic occurrences
are cursed with the impossibility of reaching an understanding;
and that many serious investigations have run foul of terminological difficulties. It has been attempted to replace the insincere
term "antisemitism" by a more sincere and possibly more precise
expression, in order to gain a freedom of movement not permanently handicapped by the need for laborious circumlocution. But
while the word "anti-Jewish" makes a fair adjective, its noun,
which would be anti-Judaism, is, whatever it may mean, bad
English. "Jew-hate" is clumsy; there is also the valid objection
that the use of "hate" is restricted to the more violent and positive
forms of dislike; and the dislike which we quite frequently
meet is, though pregnant with the promise of development, often
of little actual weight, fairly harmless and hardly realised by its
carriers. It is definitely a manifestation of antisemitism, but cannot
be described as hate without farreaching qualification.

Above all, the search for a better terminology conceals the
danger of introducing, together with the new expression, the
assumption, without sufficient proof, of an explanation of
antisemitic occurrences. We therefore have refrained from using a substitute word and shall in general continue to speak of
"antisemitism" and "antisemitic". It is however expressly stipu-
lated that this use shall be strictly in accordance with everyday
usage; and that the term "antisemitism" shall only indicate
the actual object of the relation: the Jews, not the Semites in
general. The original meaning of the word (dislike of and

defence against the dangerous inferiority of the Semitic race element) shall not be considered; and the conclusion of a common underlying cause of all these phenomena, though apparently unavoidable if the adjective "antisemitic" is generally used, shall not be drawn. It will, on the contrary, be the task of the following investigation to establish the existence of a common cause, if any, and of its nature.

Chapter II

Inferiority

The whole complex of admitted and denied manifestations of antisemitism appears most confusing to the observer; but notwithstanding all controversies, all definitions and all terminological balderdash, it is easy enough to determine the element which makes us regard an occurrence as antisemitic. It is not sufficient that a Jew be exposed to unfriendly acts; we only speak of antisemitism where we assume that the Jewishness of the victim influences the enmity. Whether this is so or not, may from case to case be subject to doubt; but where we speak of an incident as antisemitic, we mean that a Gentile would, all other things being equal, have been treated better.

In its outward appearance every enmity seems to be a reaction to some grievance which the person who acts inimically holds against the object of his dislike. Now it can often be established beyond doubt that a given action (whether legitimate or not) gives rise to stronger enmity if committed by a Jew than if done by a Gentile. It is as established a fact that the same acts which are tolerated from Gentiles, are objected to if committed by Jews; not only because it cannot always be helped, but far oftener without any voiced or even silent protest. Moreover, Jews are held responsible for acts not committed by them but by other, totally unrelated Jews, often thousands of miles away or hundreds of years ago. And finally Jews are hated on account of things done neither by them nor by any other Jews, or even by any other human beings. All these manifestations can be supported by a wealth of proof.

It therefore appears that there is something which, in relation to Jews, evokes unfriendly feelings and actions arising from other sources than what might be called normal reactions to misconduct. In fact the qualification of a relationship by the prefix "anti-" merely indicates a certain disposition of unfriendliness towards certain persons, which exists without regard to their individual acts of commission or omission and which arises from that excess of concrete expression of enmity which cannot be explained by "normal" enmity reactions and to which the objects of the "anti-" attitude are exposed. These objects do not, of course, consist of a chance conglomeration of individuals, but of a series of people who, for some reason or other, belong together, and the link between whom may consequently be recognised by definite characteristics.

A series so determined is called a group. The "anti-" attitude occurs in relation to groups of all descriptions; it is directed against national as well as political, social as well as religious groups, or against any other configuration of men with common views on any subject. One may be anti-French, anti-German or anti-English; one is anti-conservative or anti-liberal; there are anti-Catholics, anti-Protestants, anti-classicists and anti-futurists. So whenever we consider ourselves entitled to speak of an antisemitic occurrence, we presume the existence of an enmity directed towards the whole group of Jews and expressing itself in actual clashes in a way and to an extent not sufficiently justified by normal motives.

Where the antisemitic character of an occurrence is denied, the enmity is either regarded as caused in the normal way by purely personal relations, or it is classified under the heading of some other group enmity, in the assumption that it is directed against the economic, social, political, etc., group to which the Jew in question belongs. At a later stage we shall find occasion to investigate whether and when this assumption is justified; at any rate, in its admitted cases antisemitism presents itself as a group enmity, and for the present it will have to be investigated as such.

Remarkably enough, group enmity seems to leave one of the prerequisites of any enmity relation, that of justification, unsatisfied. Is it not unreasonable, unjust and immoral to be the enemy of a person who may be a most respectable member of the community and to whom certainly no individual offence can be imputed save that of belonging to a disliked group? In theory such an attitude is often condemned as immoral or at least as a prejudice, but since in reality group enmities remain active even under the most peaceful conditions, the necessity for a justification of such feelings will seek and find ways and means to establish that justification. Reason, it is admitted, plays a subordinate part in this process; still it would be strong enough to prevent that individual members of the group in question are simply accused of imaginary opprobrious actions. Such a thing only happens when hate reaches extreme levels and reason is completely silenced. Even in normal times reason will, however, be prepared to admit that the enemy group is invested with undesirable *qualities,* for qualities may be believed in without having become manifest. And as it is supposed—though tacitly, as a rule—that bad qualities contain potentially bad (which means noxious and therefore dangerous) activities, any enmity towards such a group may safely be inflated into a kind of preventive defence. For popular ethics do not only permit to hate evil, but also *the* evil *one,* and particularly the evil *ones.*

And thus it becomes sufficient to assume an evil disposition, even if it has not become manifest. This is the foundation of the conscious or half conscious antisemitic attitude of the educated circles as well as of the masses. Out of the whole body of antisemitic would-be science they only realise what, after all, always was intended to be realised as it's principal contents. The Jews are what the educated call "inferior" and the masses simply "a bad lot".

In general it is realised well enough, particularly by conscious antisemites, that enmity towards the Jews is not a matter of chance individual clashes. In concrete cases of conflict with Jews it will of course be attempted to establish their individual concrete guilt as well, but nevertheless the necessity for motivating that *a priori* aversion to Jews which is usually realised, continues to be felt. So it is stated—and, of course, believed—that the Jews are inferior; and this inferiority is considered a sufficient and satisfactory explanation for the manifestations of enmity to which the Jews have been exposed, always and everywhere, and which are now commonly called anti-semitism.

All of which seems the more reasonable, as the assumption of haphazard and independent singular instances is in itself unsatisfactory. For as soon as one begins to compare and correlate those instances and their occurrence throughout time and space, the theory of independent individual causes becomes untenable. Antisemitic manifestations began with the inception of the Diaspora and continue, without interruption, to the present day. The immediate occasions are manifold; the alleged motives change without cease. But as soon as one motivation fails, another takes its place. The fundamentally monotonous effect remains the same. One cannot help suspecting that what for a time seemed to be the cause, is no more than an occasion, actuated by an underlying cause which itself does not change its nature. To the antisemite this underlying cause is Jewish inferiority. Which would provide us with an explanation of really monumental simplicity for all antisemitic manifestations.

There remains a certain difficulty: as a strictly scientific theory this conception has only a limited number of supporters. For the belief in Jewish inferiority is perfectly acceptable within the realm of vague feelings, but cannot be maintained in the more rarefied atmosphere of reasoned discussion; while it is, of course, a theory totally unacceptable to Jews. But in everyday life Jewish inferiority is—without much discussion—emphatically alleged and readily believed in; even, though unadmittedly, by many Jews—who naturally strive to prove themselves the favourable exception to a regrettable rule. But that is another chapter.

At any rate the conception cannot be passed over in silence; if only because there is, if all antisemitic manifestations should have a common cause, only one alternative: either they are due to constant collective Jewish qualities, or they must be ascribed to a constellation which has dominated the life of the Jewish groups since the first occurrence of these manifestations. We shall therefore in the first place have to establish the exact nature of this so-called Jewish inferiority which seems to evoke so universal an enmity.

It is impossible to conceive of inferiority otherwise than as the sum total of collective qualities. Our belief in the existence of such qualities is unshakeable; so is the certainty with which we are wont to describe them. But we usually overlook the fact that it is impossible to establish them objectively. In order to define even a few physical—that is to say, measurable and ponderable—characteristics of a population of very modest dimensions, there would be need for research of an extent and exactitude which are hardly within the limits of technical possibilities. The proposition becomes hopeless if we are to establish psychological qualities, which by their very nature are not measurable or ponderable but can only be approached by way of tentative abstraction from observed actions. Even the psychological structure of a single individual is only revealed by numberless reactions to occurrences of the most varied nature. And even there the most significant happenings, which give us the key to the true aspects of the character, occur only rarely. In order to establish collective characteristics, it would be necessary to observe millions. Reliable methods of investigation are no more available than reliable standards of evaluation. The individual investigator is forced to rely on the approximation of his opinions, which usually cannot even be correlated to fixed subjective standards, and therefore are not even internally consistent. Where collective characteristics are described, it is therefore usually possible to state at the first glance which sentimental bias has been at work. So it is hardly astonishing that the exact definition of what is to be understood by "Jewish inferiority" meets with the greatest of difficulties.

What the man in the street means, is obvious: moral inferiority, or what he calls "badness". Occasionally he may regard the subjectively undesirable as objectively bad, but that is of lesser importance. For the main point about his interpretation is that it is only tenable as long as it is not put to the test. The most elementary of interrogations punctures his conception of "Jewish badness". He will of course mention a number of Jews to whom he takes all kind of exceptions, but as soon as his unjustified generalisations fail to be accepted, our man will, to his and our astonishment, discover that there are, amongst the Jews as well as amongst the Gentiles, "good" and "bad", "decent" and "rotten" people; and that it seems impossible to find abnormally many of the latter kind amongst the Jews.

There is reason to believe that the distribution ratio of the degrees of ethical excellence does not differ to any significant extent with the various races and nations. In the case of the so-called savages, Europeans are again and again surprised to discover this fact. Naturally, the norms of what is regarded as admissible vary widely; but as far as the fundamental principles of ethics go—and, deriving from the same universal social necessities, they are to a certain degree universally valid—the cross-section of any population presents much the same aspect.

It is naturally impossible to present the ethical structure of the Jewish groups in a way subject to proof, for no reliable crime statistics are in existence either in respect of all of them or for any considerable part of Jewish history: they would, moreover, prove little or nothing, for even utter moral depravity need not lead to conflicts with the law, while on the other hand punishment inflicted by the courts does not necessarily allow of conclusions regarding the moral condition of the convicted person. But we may be permitted to remind the reader how difficult Jew-baiters find it to produce any worthwhile number of morally deficient Jews, notwithstanding their doubtless burning desire to do so. Thus proof is regularly supplanted by suspicion or, at best, generalisation of unfavourable isolated cases on the principle of collective responsibility; of which more later.

In Central and Western Europe, incidentally, which would be the natural field of observation for most readers of this book, the Jews keep rather strictly to the moral standards of the social class to which they belong. At the most, their peculiar position may be said to make them particularly careful; which probably explains why Jewish criminal statistics are in general slightly more favourable than those of the peoples among which the relative Jewish groups are found. At any rate, the fact is hardly proof of moral superiority; the incidence of all moral variants (from the lowest to the highest, if one must introduce valuation) amongst Jews does not differ in any demonstrable degree from that in the Gentile world.

Enemy war literature—the antisemitic publications—is naturally full of collective condemnation. "The" Jews are imposters, have no sense of honour, are parasites, usurers, vampires, corrupters of morals. And the oral echo is of course not lacking.

The war (*) and the post-war years have given rise to a whole literature in which all things German are denounced: all imaginable vices, all criminal tendencies

(*) of 1914-1919, of course; though the phenomenon, on both sides, was and is even more evident in connection with the recent effort.

that could possibly be invented, are ascribed indiscriminately to all Germans—and not in the last instance those crimes and vices which take the place of honour in the antisemite vocabulary. Nor were the Germans backward in the bitter collective condemnation of their enemies, with only the one fascinating difference that the worst qualities were in turn attributed to the party which at the particular time seemed the most dangerous. The opponents of Germany had less choice in that respect. These examples are only quoted because their memory is still green and they can be proved daily. The manifestation as such can be demonstrated in the case of any, even the most modest, group enmity.

Now most people are well aware that there are countless Germans, Englishmen, Frenchmen, Italians, etc., of exemplary probity; and the adduced examples of the summary and unsupported investigation of whole nations with the most horrible immoral qualities prove even to the superficial observer that such judgments are the *result* of a hatred already *in existence,* and that any resemblance to actual conditions is purely accidental. But the war against the Jews—lest we forget—goes on.

For the time being, however, we will not yet go into the psychology of hate. Since we have established that our inferiority cannot be translated as moral deficiency, we shall look for an answer at the address where it was first given that name: we shall inquire with the so-called "scientific" antisemitism. We need not take fright at the racial theories invented by the more or less fertile phantasies of its prophets. If one wishes to attribute to a delimited human group a set of qualities of so definite and unexceptionally valid a nature as is done by "scientific" antisemitism, one must, according to prevalent scientific opinion, regard them as based on common hereditary elements (*). Such a "closed historical community with common descent" may be called a race and in this connection, at any rate, it is immaterial how far back one dates its origin and whether, like H.St. Chamberlain, one speaks of a Jewish race, or, like his antisemitic predecessors, one prefers to consider a Semitic race which includes, *inter alia,* the present Arabs.

For us it is important to know what these gentry have to say about Jewish inferiority. For while they were possibly in the first place interested in finding *justification* for their antisemitic attitude, their theories do, no doubt, also contain an attempt at *explaining* antisemitism.

Whatever the professional antisemite may mean by Jewish inferiority, it is not moral deficiency. In this sense the expression is only used by the authors of the cruder lampoons; the leading figures must at least preserve a semblance of the scientific attitude, and so primitive a conception of inferiority would not even agree with appearances. True, even the "scientists" like occasionally to quote from the scriptures to show that what today would be regarded as opprobrious actions are ordained or at any rate not deprecated. The deception of Esau and the extermination of the Canaanites are favourite charges. But these quotations are mere tactics. For if they were considered as characteristic for Jewish psychology, the same would have to apply to the overwhelming mass of commandments and actions which give evidence of the highest ethics; a course carefully avoided. The favoured con-

_____

(*) It is general practice to speak of common "blood". As biology stands at present, it does not seem that the blood has any particular function as carrier of hereditary qualities. But blood still is a word of power; it retains its numinous aspects; and for convenience's sake we shall, without prejudice, make occasional use of the expression.

elusion, on the contrary, is that all Jews who exist and who have at any time existed are treacherous and cruel; for this transference of individual accusations to a whole population—living three thousand years later—is by no means unusual, and reliable in its results; but while it is good tactics to arouse suspicion in this way, the construction is rather too crude for an explicit scientific defence of principles.

So those who are halfway serious among the "scientists" of antisemitism do not explicitly claim that the overwhelming majority of Jews are morally deficient. The real meaning of "Jewish inferiority" can only be discovered after dissection of the general application of the term and elimination of all the particular accusations which are included by way of speculation on the tendency to generalise. What remains is the reproach of a fundamental and really general tendency, which is said to express itself in two widely different actual forms.

What is claimed is, that the Jews are fundamentally parasites. (Even this finding smacks of tactics; for the word leaves an unpleasant taste. But antisemitism is never free of the militant tendencies demanded by its aim.) These parasitic tendencies are said to find their expression in the first place on the cultural level: Jews have no cultural productive genius; what they have, is only the talent and tendency to exploit the cultural achievements of other nations; where possible to their own advantage. In the field of music, for instance, it is denied that the Jews have any productive composers; the Jews only reproduce. In literature they do not create any masterworks: they only excel in superficial journalism. In the plastic arts they do not produce anything at all: they only criticise. As far as science is concerned, it is difficult to allege a lack of

Jewish creative talent in a way acceptable even to anti-semites; but even this is attempted.

It is not easy to deal with these curious products of the human mind on the assumption that they are based on some sort of reality. It seems unlikely that an observer who would be able to free himself from the mental atmosphere of the Jewish problem and the resulting sentiments, could regard such theories as originating anywhere outside a madhouse. Even at the first glance one discerns the hatred which has begotten the conception of Jewish cultural parasitism. But for clarity's sake we shall not continuously refer to later investigations into the nature of enmity; we shall, for a while, yet attempt to behave as if there could possibly be some reality behind the anti-semites' claims.

The term "parasite" originally meant a poor idler who lived at the expense of a rich idler. Later it was applied to biology and used to express human annoyance at the fact that certain living beings devour each other in a way which seems undesirable from the viewpoint of human advantage. But let us keep to the common conception that a man who lives with and at the expense of another, on the proceeds of the other's labour and to his damage, is a parasite worthy of hate. It is not easy to apply this definition at the cultural level, but the attempt must be made.

But first we shall have to find out how exactly the cultural value of a nation is established. The usual way is to measure this value by the number of famous men which the nation in question has produced in the field of statesmanship, legislation, science, literature and art. The nation appears as a flowerbed of a fertility commensurate with the number and dimension of the reputations which it has brought forth. Their fame, again, is of course heavily underscored by propaganda in favour of the flowerbed concerned. The usual upshot of the system is a spate of national bragging intended to prove the right of existence or expansion (defensive or aggressive position) of the nation concerned. But let us apply the system to the Jews. The conditions of struggle in which the Jews live turns the depreciation of Jewish prestations by the surrounding world into a necessity. But notwithstanding frantic efforts it remains impossible to deny the importance of a quite disproportionate number of outstanding Jews. Wherefore necessity has fathered a really ingenious corrective: these Jews are simply adopted by the surrounding nations. One helps oneself by the fiction that not the Jewish but the Dutch flowerbed has produced Spinoza; Mahler becomes an Austrian composer, Heine a German poet, Bergson a French philosopher, Disraeli an English statesman, and so on, and so forth. Nearly every year produces new names to extend the long list; and though pronouncedly antisemitic circles attempt at times to detract from the importance of famous Jews, the proof of Jewish inferiority cannot, in view of this acidulate adoption of Jewish heroes of civilisation, be regarded as established by the flowerbed theory.

It may, of course, be objected that all these important Jews have worked amidst, and contributed to, foreign civilisations; that only the accumulated culture of other nations makes the Jewish contribution possible; which therefore, if not strictly parasitic, has a derivatory character. Now it so happens that the Jews have, at the time of their normal life as a nation (the only condition under which independent national culture is possible) produced a cultural treasure of so-to-say anonymous nature which Europe cannot help admiring, as it is one of the main pillars of its own culture. This cultural good is so specifically a Jewish product that its annexation meets with unsurmountable difficulties. Wherefore Professor Delitsch says: In the first place the Bible (that is to say, the Old Testament; Jesus had already been Aryanised by Chamberlain) is not as valuable as one would think; and in the second place, its valuable elements were taken over by the Jews from Babylonians, and by these again from the Sumerians, who were Aryans, or at any rate no Semites. All this seems a joke; but it is in fact extremely probable that the Jews have taken over many elements from other nations and developed them further, as evidenced by the Bible itself. The only improbable thing is that the Sumerians should have produced everything out of the void of their non-Semitic creative power. For history knows of no national culture to which important preliminaries have not been developed by some older nation; except in the case of the very oldest civilisations, where history simply cannot reach farther back owing to technical impossibilities. Especially in the case of the modern nations and their much vaunted culture it is easy to prove the existence of foreign roots; but that would fall outside the scope of this book. For us the question is not so much whether the Jews have produced or still produce cultural values, whether their capacities are creative or rather tend to develop preexisting elements, or even are frankly derivative. What we want is to establish the cause of antisemitic manifestations, and not the attempts at their justification. We must therefore inquire whether that quality of a nation (supposing such a thing actually exists) which finds its expression exclusively in

derivative, one might say secondhand, cultural activity, constitutes an inferiority capable of exciting enmity.

It will have to be admitted that in this general form the question cannot easily be answered; and without deeper insight in
the origin of enmity it even is hard to say why this should be
so. Superficially speaking one might suppose that, if anything,
the "higher" cultural qualities would make for hatred rather than
the "lower" ones, as they might cause presumptuousness on
the "higher" and envy on the "lower" side. But in our case the
issue is decided by a different consideration. The gross of the
non-Jewish population cares nothing for sophisticated distinctions between creative and derivative cultural capacities; they
are incapable of perceiving the difference and therefore unable
to react to it. The man in the street who hears of Jewish inferiority, takes it to mean that the Jews are "bad"; and while he may
have no clear conception of what this badness means, we may
be sure that he does not think of the cultural achievements of the
Sumerians or objects to their alleged adoption by the Jews via
Babylon. These matters only concern a few professors; just like
the question of Jewish productive or derivatory activities in the
field of art interests no one but a couple of critics, and leaves the
bulk of the people cold. So whether the Jews can be accused of
cultural parasitism in the sense of a hateful quality or not is of
no importance for the solution of our problem; and this quality
cannot be that "inferiority" which causes antisemitism in general.
What, then, about economic parasitism?

If we want to employ the term "parasitism" in this
connection, we must clearly distinguish between two
different things. If one wishes to call a person a parasite
because his economic activities would be impossible with-

out those of any other person, then every human being and every group which does not live in a complete state of autarchy is parasitic. From this point of view any group, when considered on itself, may be said to batten on others; trade and industry live at the expense of agriculture to no less an extent than the latter at theirs. Obviously the Jewish groups cannot exist without the economy of the peoples amidst whom they live and with whom they are economically connected. But if this is parasitism, then every trade and profession is parasitic. If, on the other hand, original production is to be considered as of greater intrinsic value, and commerce, for instance, is to be regarded as parasitic (as is occasionally done), then anti-semitism should be directed as much against Gentile commerce as it should leave Jewish industry and the Jewish professions alone. Nor would it make sense that the "Aryan" population throws itself so frantically on so parasitic a livelihood as commerce, particularly where it is possible to elbow the Jews out of it.

But this unpleasant word obtains quite a different implication, as soon as any group is regarded as an isolated foreign body. Then the economy is regarded as a kind of common national property, the use of which by the foreign group—notwithstanding the advantage to the community as a whole—is regarded as a favour, granted half-heartedly or even obtained under false pretences. The enmity to which such a group is exposed is not directed towards its economic activities as such, but against its real or imagined foreignness. But the hatred against foreigners, even more apertly irrational than other forms of hatred (and particularly so in the present case: for behind the Jewish groups there is not even good reason to perceive and fear the influence of other countries) finds its pretext for expressing itself in the economic field.

Now the same objection arises as in the cultural field: the conception of economic parasitism is only current within a certain, comparatively limited circle of anti-semitic theoreticians. Among the people the antisemite naturally finds an echo when he fosters the impression that the Jew in his quality of capitalist exploits the labour of his hosts. This sounds reasonable enough, as there actually exist a fair number of Jewish capitalists, at any rate in Central and Western Europe; according to Sombart, the Jews even have invented capitalism. As for the latter contention, the belief in this invention cannot be the cause of antisemitism, as capitalism was invented rather late, in the most recent stages of the Jewish dispersal, while antisemitism is as old as the diaspora itself. It also deserves some consideration that in those circles which actively oppose capitalism, antisemitism is *comparatively* least pronounced.

Whether exploitation and parasitism is of the essence of capitalism, need not be investigated; for there is nothing specifically Jewish in capitalism. There are innumerably more Gentile than Jewish capitalists; there are innumerably more Jewish proletarians and poor than Jewish capitalists; and among Gentile capitalists one may find the most active representatives of antisemitism. So capitalist activity or lack of activity and its possible component of parasitism cannot be specifically Jewish; cannot be the expression or essence or part of the essence of Jewish inferiority; cannot be the cause of an enmity directed against all Jews, whether capitalists or not, and never directed against Gentiles, even if they are capitalists. So "economic antisemitism" does not either surrender a clue to the nature of the alleged Jewish inferiority.

What we have stated so far might give the impression that we absolutely deny the existence of any collective Jewish characteristics and that we regard the much discussed "Jewish psychology" as a myth. And indeed; specifically Jewish collective qualities in the primitive sense of the word would seem to belong nowhere but to the realm of mythology. One may find amongst us exactly the same characters as in the Gentile world. Exact proof is impossible in this field; but the distribution of vices and virtues (in the everyday sense of the word) appeal's to be by far the most normal aspect of the Jewish nation. Nevertheless, there is doubtless some justification for assuming a specific Jewish psychology. But its characteristics are to be found in fields of the mind which are not overly accessible; the only means of investigation available is a groping closely akin to guessing, and any conclusion must be based on faint clues which may be conditioned by a host of extraneous circumstances. The assumption of particularly Jewish capacities meets with difficulties; it seems somewhat more justified to posit a specific form of conceptional structure, a characteristic way of thinking. The Jewish world of sensations and sentiments is said to have its own colouring: possible, that the way in which volition is influenced and conditioned by thought, and the influence of sentiment on action are in some way characteristic.

Admittedly this is a poor description of Jewish psychology. Conclusions drawn from representative products of the Jewish mind might possibly be far more positive. But anyone who knows what a surfeit of descriptions of the Jewish mind friends and enemies have distilled out of and into the products of that Jewish mind, even if we do not look further than the last century—anyone aware of these facts and possibilities must regard the method with the deepest suspicions. At any rate, Jewish psychology is a question of subtle matters which cannot reasonably be measured with the yardstick of morality.

Cannot reasonably . . . But is it not possible that, nevertheless, they are so measured? That those subtle functions of the mind by which Jewish psychology is characterised, are nevertheless valued, and valued negatively? And that this is the origin of the conception of Jewish inferiority? Let us suppose so. Let us assume that Jewish psychology works by sensory rather than by motor-ic impulses, or that Jewish thought is characterised by an increased tendency towards abstraction, or that the Jewish brain combines at greater speed, or that Jewish emotionality is unusually strong, or that the Jewish mind excels in a positive attitude towards life: is there really anyone who believes that the Gentile population, with the possible exception of a few essayists, is able even to get an inkling of so subtle characteristics? Not to speak of the possibility of evaluating them as good or bad.

After establishing all this, we feel somewhat urgently reminded of the necessity for explaining why, nevertheless, humanity in general remains ineradicably convinced that bad Jewish collective characteristics do exist; for it would be mere stupidity to deny the fact of this conviction. Even the naturally well-wishing Gentile shares this feeling; without accounting for its causes, he is, in his relations to Jews, conscious of a certain dislike which his instincts attribute to bad qualities; though he is, if need be, prepared to excuse them and, also if need be, willing to admit that, by way of exception, a few exemplary Jews may be free of them.

The late Lord Balfour, the well known English statesman and philosemite, who obviously took pains to judge the Jews favourably, wrote in his preface to Sokolow's History of Zionism:

> "Constant oppression, with occasional outbursts of violent persecution, are apt either to crush their victims, or to develop in them self-protecting qualities which do not always assume an attractive shape."

Obviously Balfour must have had qualities in mind which he regarded as so common amongst Jews that, in order to recommend a Jewish cause, he needed to explain and excuse them. Balfour stresses characteristics (unfavourable in his opinion) which he connects with certain forms of struggle. This can only refer to cunning. And indeed, cunning is the only weapon of the weak and defenceless. The Jews have been, and mostly still are, defenceless in the hands of their enemies, who are not always restrained by law. To us, cunning implies lying, dishonesty, deceit, unreliability, immorality. We despise cunning, because we have grown up in the admiration of power; we fail to realise that in times of duress, in war or under foreign domination, wiles and stratagems become highly honoured means of combat, without losing their deceitful character. We tend to forget that for hundreds of years the relation between Gentiles and Jews was permanently and apertly that of a war of persecution and destruction; and that even today the Jew's struggle for existence occurs under conditions which gravely prejudice his chances. So it is only to be expected that the Jew avails himself of stratagems to a larger extent than current morals admit.

All this seems reasonable; but the curious fact is that actually all those qualities which are denounced as particularly Jewish (such as, say, dishonesty within the pale of the law, a tendency to sharp business practices, rapacity; or in private life, a defective sense of honour, obsequiousness, intrusiveness) are as often found in Gentiles as they are missing in Jews. Anyone who takes the trouble to leave the misty atmosphere of unverifiable sentiment and to find himself some actual instances of the characteristics usually considered as the typical results of Jewish misery; anyone who looks with open eyes at his fellow-Jews and-Gentiles, will find himself face to face with a never expected reality: numberless Gentiles behave in the way expected from Jews, and numberless Jews act as if they were anything but that.

The "Aryan" farmers often out-Herod Herod in small-scale swindles in the field of weight, measure, quality and quantity of goods; their greed, which overrides all humane considerations, is notorious, while the Jew reputedly throws away his money for such sentimentalities as the health of a family member. And that same money which he is said to idolise is nothing to him, if it can serve to avert dishonour from his family—while he is reputed to have no sense of honour.

Even the proof of those adverse qualities which are alleged to have been acquired in the course of an unequal struggle for existence fails as soon as it is seriously attempted. So the conception of Jewish inferiority cannot be based on actual conditions. It is quite possible, however, that the "differentness" of the Jew is simply identified with "worseness"; for that is an instinctive process, and even educated persons must take strenuous thought in order to correct this identification and substitute a comparatively fair judgment—to have it blown away by the first surge of emotional stress. It is, moreover, obvious that all conceivable faults, even unto the worst degree of moral turpitude, may be found amongst Jews; that is to say, in the case of individual JEWS. It is hardly just that this fact should lead to the assumption that all other Jews are equally bad. But in actual fact the generalisation is common practice.

These phenomena give us our first glimpse of insight into the way in which the conception of Jewish inferiority actually arises. They lead us towards the field of group antagonies, where they will be discussed at length. Meanwhile it may be established that this remarkable and abnormal generalisation can at all occur, because the Jews are felt as a group, as a unit; and more particularly as a foreign unit. That is why, individually, they draw an undue measure of attention, why their activities are noticed to a disproportionate extent, at any rate as long as they can be judged unfavourably. For the attention paid to them is coloured by suspicion and bad will. And that brings us to the rest of the matter.

We shall never master the impossibilities involved in the belief in Jewish inferiority, as long as we fail to realise that actually *not the bad qualities arouse hatred, but it is hate which causes the qualities of those who are hated to be regarded as bad.*

This is hardly a new contribution to the knowledge of humanity; but the real extent and importance of this fact in human life is not generally realised. One accepts the fact that emotions cloud judgment, but balks at admitting that they have a decisive influence on any evaluation of the human character and that they have an overruling influence in the estimate of group character.

The difficulty arises in part from the circumstance that the broad and really meaningless designations which are currently used to describe group character, are regarded as objectively established realities. But actually, character qualities cannot be observed at all, but only deduced, and only by conclusions from observed human activities. What, with so overwhelming a certainty, we call "character", is nothing but the mere assumption that human acts are the result of mental trends which have a compulsive effect, so that they may be expected to cause the recurrence of similar acts. Strictly speaking, hatred cannot be caused by qualities, but only by the act in which they become manifest. It need not even be an evil act: for not only does the victim of theft hate the thief, but the thief also hates the policeman who pursues him and thereby, surely, acts commendably. But actually the way in which hatred is produced is far more complicated and will have to be discussed at length at a later stage. For the present, an instance from daily life may serve to illustrate the influence of an antipathy of unknown source on the formation of conceptions of qualities.

There are in daily life many cases of dislike to which even popular opinion cannot ascribe a sufficient justification: One speaks of antipathy: one "cannot stand so-and-so". He has never harmed anyone, but one just cannot stand him. Formerly an explanation was sought in the existence of some mysterious antipathetic fluid; for none of the causes of aversion which are generally considered valid could be found to apply. In relation to such people whom we consider antipathetic, we feel the unsurmountable tendency to condemn their actions, to conclude from them to the existence of undesirable qualities or to regard them as confirmation of the presence of such qualities. Not all human beings possess the quality of self-criticism to the same extent, so it is doubtful whether the reader will in all cases admit that his dislike for some antipathetic person has preceded and caused the exceptions which he takes to his behaviour. For the need for justification impels us to believe that the antipathy has only been called into existence by the actions or qualities criticised. But where the reader may not succeed in his own case, he will the readier be able to do so in respect of his surroundings. How often, when a third party is blamed, and in his opinion unjustly blamed, will he say or think: "You just cannot stand the person in question, so he can not please you, whatever he does." In cases of definite enmity this manifestation is even more pronounced and is generally recognised. The hated one may do or not do whatever he may: the one who hates him will only find bitter condemnation for his actions, and will ascribe even the most noble deed to base motives.

In the case of collective enmity relations, such as anti-semitism, the possibility of injury inflicted in the past can be definitely excluded. Of the many millions of Jews whom the antisemite hates indiscriminately, he is personally acquainted only with a few hundred, and even of these he can only blame a few isolated individuals for any injurious activities.

Hatred of, for the present, unestablished origin is directed against millions of human beings who can be proved not to have done any harm. But hate, once present, causes evil qualities to be imputed to the hated group; enmity lurks, prepared to condemn every action and to regard it as confirmation of presupposed vices.

It would be desirable to explain why this process meets with so little hindrance; for our feelings are committed to

the belief in objective judgment, whether reason admits its theoretical possibility or not. Therefore it is so difficult for us to regard
judgments of character merely as a product of our sentiments. But
we need not even recall that character is nothing but an assumed
complex of supposed dispositions, so that its very description may
be nothing but the purest imagination. For even the evaluation of a
concrete action, which is subject to proof in its every phase, actually meets with insuperable difficulties, as soon as it is attempted
to establish an objective standard of absolute validity which
would enable us to establish any action as good or bad beyond
cavil. Even in clearcut cases of crime there remains the eternal
question whether it is the deed or the motive which should be
judged; and even where the darkest intentions seem evident, the
actions condemned may suffer a sea-change when the impulses
which have driven the criminal on his obscure path are considered. In the millions and millions of less extreme cases it is, if
we disregard senseless superficialities, impossible to obtain two
identical opinions at all. It becomes possible to understand this
as soon as we realise that each action can be described both in
terms of praise and in terms of blame. So judgment appears as an
expression of sentiment, and unfavorable judgment, or condemnation, as one of enmity; and instinctively we realise that it is
just that. The problem lies not in the nature of human qualities
as such; doubtless the mental dispositions which determine our
action are of decisive importance; and doubtless they differ
from case to case. But only the greatest of artists, employing the
full gamut of his intuition, is able to depict a human character; the
rough-and-ready designations which we use for the coarse
generalisations we call character qualities, are valueless not only

because of their superficiality, but also because the designation itself implies our judgment and therefore the feeling which determines it.

Language goes far to meet us in our need for terms of praise and censure to describe one and the same complex of actions. What the friend calls liberality the enemy may describe as wantonness; domestic modesty may also be called narrow-mindedness; enjoyment of life, sensuality. Freedom of care and thoughtlessness, wise economy and miserly avarice, circumspection and pedantry, discretion and cowardice; distinguished reserve and snobbish affectation, sociability and intrusiveness, forbearing and lack of character, strength of will and obstinacy or pigheadedness; all these are nothing more than the respective ways in which one may describe traits of character, according to one's like or dislike of their owner. In the same way industry becomes careerism, business sense is called sharp practice; and when sagacity is to be condemned, it is termed casuistry.

These examples are taken from the domesticated sphere of the individual life of the average citizen; a sphere where an offense against the recognised written or unwritten law will meet with a condemnation which, though further determined by the particular conventions of different circles, is in manifest cases fairly uniform; while actions considered praiseworthy may be suspected as to their motives, but will hardly be condemned in defiance of accepted principles. In relations between groups, praise and blame are not restricted to the onesided interpretations shown above, but what, the one side denounces as the most horrible of crimes, the other glorifies as a triumph of morality. In this way it is of course child-ishly-simple to ascribe to the friendly—normally the own—

group any desired selection of virtues, and to the enemy an exhaustive catalogue of vices; for no reality can disprove what out of its very nature is a mere assumption, while the terms in which it is described only reflect the sentiment from which they derive.

This statement is not based on war experience. The phenomena of collective condemnation which have become apparent in wartime are called war psychoses, and so condoned as diseased abnormalities. In reality this psychosis is nothing but the psychological reaction of masses to an increased potential of hate; and it would be a mistake to believe that at a lower potential the situation differs in any essential aspect. Whether it be a case of antagonism between political parties, or the most ridiculous quarrel between two clubs, the ways of conflict are always the same. They dominate the form in which races, nations, states, churches, classes and parties are wont to judge each other.

As an instance, let us take a case which demonstrates the victory of sentiment over judgment in a particularly striking way, because it concerns the evaluation of men and deeds which belong to a remote past: the writing of history. Only history totally unrelated to the nation of the historian, or any other group to which he belongs, is written more or less objectively and in conformity with the conventional rules which the historian has adopted. But as soon as the author becomes conscious of any connection with the history which he relates, his interpretation favours the befriended and disfavours the opposite side; and the abstract terms in which his bias is couched take the form of praiseworthy qualities of the "friend" and inferiority of the "enemy".

Consider, for instance, the indifference with which the

oldest history of Egypt is written, while peoples who may be Semites are treated with a passionate desire to value, and to condemn; a desire arising from antipathy toward the still living and hated Jewish nation. But in this connection the Jewish case, in which the author himself is involved, will not be considered. In other respects, history written in Germany—and in other countries the situation is not essentially different—is no less instructive. The valuation of Roman history has a strong pro-Roman bias, partly because the sources used are themselves pro-Roman, and partly because Europe regards herself as the heir of classical civilisation. The Romans and all that is theirs are glorified, their enemies denounced. All this changes as soon as a few Teutonic tribes oppose Roman conquest and the glorious hero Arminius makes his appearance. The blessings of the *pax romana* and the splendour of antique culture are heard of no more; the virtue and courage of the Romans change overnight into lust for power and loot; and the Teutons, who now have inherited the monopoly of virtue, courage, and so on, and so forth, are the prospective victims of what once were the blessings of civilisation, but now is called oppression and tyranny. The Teutons are further provided with a selection of praiseworthy qualities, though a less loving judgment could find good cause for exception to their way of life; but their quarrelsomeness is called courage, valour, a warlike spirit; their drunkenness (and their aversion to work) is love of life; and a certain honest and by no means chauvinistic historian explained their addiction to gambling as the desire to expose themselves to moral as well as to physical dangers, in order to educate themselves to indifference against the vicissitudes of life. This general admiration is as the occasion demands transferred from one ruling German tribe or family to the other, till in due course it settles in Prussia. The enemies of the day, without or within the German Empire, are the black sheep; allies, as long as the alliance lasts, may bask in a temporary reflection of the admiration. At the time of the Reformation, the ways separate irrevocably. According to whether the standpoint of the historian is Catholic or Protestant, the leaders of his own party become admirable heroes, those of the other side are at best subjected to merciless criticism. Naturally German history looks totally different in the books of other nations, who have their own standards of right and wrong in history; and in the United States, the textbooks are being revised in order to attune them to the recent friendship with England. All this does not refer to doubtful historical circumstances; we have only considered the evaluation of established facts.

This onesided evaluation should not be regarded as conscious tendentialism; the better works of history are no doubt free from all intention to further any particular concrete aims by the way in which they are written. But historiography consists of a description of group enmities: and the psychological influence of these is so strong that even the historian succumbs to its power.

"Von der Parteien Gunst und Hass verzerrt

Schankt sein Characterbild in der Geschichte . . ." (*) says Schiller of Walleristein; but we must go further: character as we see it is the free creation of favour and disfavour, which they have created in their own image.

The way in which the Gentile sees the character of the Jew is dictated by his aversion, his hate against the

---

(*) "Distorted by the favour and hate of the parties wavers his character in history."

Jew. And if we Jews have allowed ourselves to be infected by a belief in the correctness of the way in which they see us, it is nothing but an instance of the perversion of slavery—but that belongs to a different chapter. At any rate, the conception of Jewish inferiority is purely the product of aversion. The Gentiles' hate against us causes them to interpret our every action unfavourably and thence to infer the existence of unfavourable qualities; or the aversion presupposes our inferiority and judges our actions unfavourably by way of confirmation. Where some Jewish action is, according to the accepted norms, too obviously valuable, it is either divested of its Jewishness, or qualified as an inordinate exception from a rule which is thereby the more clearly abused.

The phantom of Jewish inferiority, which also haunts discussions in Jewish circles as the problem of Jewish qualities, has always stood in the way of any research into the nature of antisemitism; and it was necessary to eliminate it before we could proceed. It had to be shown that it is immaterial how the Jews really are; and that it is not even important how we *really* act; that *in the first* place there exists an aversion to us, and that this in its turn has created the belief in our inferiority.

It will now be our task to establish the so far still unknown origin of these primary feelings of enmity.

Chapter III

The Origin of Enmity

In the preceding chapter antisemitism was interpreted as group enmity. Lengthy explanations were needed to show whence this enmity does *not* originate. The answer to the thorny question whence, then, it *does* originate, is best introduced by the no less thorny but essential counter-question: "Whence do enmities in general originate?".

How difficult it is to answer the last question becomes obvious if we consider that in each individual case the cause is readily and definitely stated, while at the same time the thinkers of humanity have attempted from times immemorial until the present day (so that we are entitled to conclude: have attempted in vain), to explain *in abstracto* what in the single case seems so natural, and in general seems so senseless. In any given case of enmity the explanation immediately takes the form of an accusation. One party has committed an act which is considered unlawful and which provokes feelings of enmity in the other, wronged, party. The answer to the question which party is really at fault always differs according to the party, and often even persons not involved are at variance. But at any rate the enmity appears to be called forth by guilt.

Meanwhile, it would seem that behind the self-assuredness of the condemnation there lurks some vague awareness that human guilt, or what appears as its expression, may derive from a more remote, impersonal cause. This cause has been imagined in the form of a non-human power and called fate or destiny; it has been regarded as the "evil principle" and assigned to the human mind, whether it be the heritage of original sin, the influence of the powers of darkness, or whatever else one wishes to call it. The problem is one which has occupied the thoughts of generations; it embraces all the passions of mankind; and the attempts at its solution are a history of those passions. In dealing with such a problem, there is need of modesty; and next to modesty, of that considerable distance which alone provides free enough a view for us to distinguish the general relations which are of importance to us.

From an external point of view, human history appears to the observer as the coexistence of people who continuously come into conflict with each other. Beginning with looks and words (or the avoidance of words) , these conflicts run the whole gamut of injury (i.e. the psychological effect of inflicting harm) down to total destruction. This aspect has not changed in any essential since the beginning of time. Independent of the political and economic systems in force at any given place and moment, of religions and philosophies, of social orders, of accepted or postulated norms of morals or justice; independent also of the character, opinions and intentions of prominent, leading or ruling personalities at any given place and moment, the form of the struggle between men has remained unchanged. Within the territory where a given writ ran, the most violent forms of conflict were from time to time, laboriously and incompletely, suppressed; but outwards they are regularly organised as mass murder; usually with great care and employing the best of human capacities.

Now the same harm and destruction which result from human conflict may equally befall man without any human influence. The worst of crimes, murder, has no other and worse effect than a killing thunderbolt; the most dastardly form of murder, the assassination of an unsuspecting victim, is mentally and physically far less painful than most forms of natural death; and the most refined torture can cause no worse suffering than many a disease. But while harm of non-human origin is submitted so dispassionately—or at least apparently so—and at any rate opposed dispassionately (*), human conflicts, which have essentially the same effect, are accompanied by a display of the unruliest emotions and the most complicated conceptions of right. It is this congeries of feelings, conceptions, conflicts and injuries which causes the difficulties we meet in our search for a satisfactory answer to the question whence enmities derive.

To the human observer, and certainly to the consciousness of those involved, the conflict by no means appears as the mechanical collision of opposite forces. On the contrary, it seems to consist of two phases: aggression and defence. The aggression is supposed to spring from inimical feelings of unknown origin; evil qualities, malice of character or a free will to evil being substituted for the unknown source of these inimical feelings. To the attacked party, the attack results in harm or in what is felt as such; this, psychologically, causes a feeling of suf-

_____

(*) This is not strictly correct; but where passion intrudes into the struggle against the ills of nature, we tend, characteristically enough, to regard the influence which we are combating as a personal enemy; of which more later.

fering; and in reaction there arises in the injured party a feeling of enmity, a component of which is the desire to repay the injury to the aggressor, that is to say, to cause him equal damage or harm, or to destroy him. While aggression and the feeling of enmity causing it is condemned, and regarded as impermissible and wicked, reaction by the way of inimical feelings or actions is considered permissible and justified.

Curiously enough each party involved in a conflict regards its own enmity as a justified reaction on the enmity of the opponent, and its own hostile acts as permissible, justified defence; but considers that of the opponent as impermissible, unjustified and unlawful aggression. Each condemns the acts of the other party, and condemns the other party itself as evil, debased and guilty.

The question therefore is: how it is possible for each side to regard its own enmity as justified and to condemn that of the other party as unlawful; why parties not concerned are divided into two camps on the question of right and wrong, attack and defence, good and evil, and adopt the obviously onesided and contradictory judgments of the protagonists; and particularly, why feelings of enmity appear both as the result and as the cause of hostile acts,

Attempts to explain the origin of enmity in general terms—insofar as they do not founder on the cliff of denouncing the evilness of human nature which always causes strife—generally take one of two directions, in accordance with the two-faced aspect of enmity (*). O n e

---

(*) The question of the origin of war, the most disastrous of all forms in which enmity expresses itself, has produced a voluminous explanatory literature. The question of guilt, particularly difficult in the case of mass conflicts on account of the lack of recognised legal norms, is usually replaced by attempts at objective explanation; though the objectivity is but rarely main-

school considers conflicts and collisions as more or less mechanical necessities; hostile feelings appear as products of the
conflicts. The other school regards the inadequacy of human
emotions as the source of all enmity and conflicts, and consequently demands a change of heart, so that there may be peace
amongst men.

The first school bases its argument on the doctrine of the
struggle for existence. It may not be superfluous to point out
that this approach cannot but lead astray, because of the purely
economic conception on which it is based. Many conflicts and
enmities do indeed arise in connection with breadwinning; but
only too many others are without any relation to the economic
complex.

The economic explanation assumes that men stand in each
other's way in satisfying the essential needs of life. This applies
to individuals, but more particularly also to nations. A nation which
multiplies rapidly needs outlets for its population and its produce; so
it collides with other nations which do not wish to provide territories
for colonisation or markets for export. Now there was a time when
the earth was far more sparsely populated than now; yet men did
not live more peacefully in those days. Moreover, the actual position
is hardly one in which a shortage of the necessities essential to all
men provokes a struggle for the available balance; for the latter is
not a fixed quantity but subject to unlimited increase; and

---

tained. The conflicts are attributed to political systems and forms of government
or to economic systems of production; others regard the mere existence of armaments and armies as the sole cause (some considering the conscripted others the
professional army as the more dangerous) . Nevertheless, in all these cases a
measure of guilt is in addition attributed to the carriers of the incriminated systems
Some regard enmity as the result of mere misunderstandings which will disappear
as soon as men learn to know each other better. There is no need for the critical
discussion of all these more or less abortive partial explanations: in due course it
will appear that they can be dismissed.

it is the easier to increase production, the less energy is squandered on enmities and conflicts: war devours the fruits of peace. It is true enough that most men must make considerable efforts to secure a standard of living which remains poor if compared with that of an infinitely small number of millionaires. But the very need for this effort is what relatively gives the strongest impulse towards a measure of tolerance. The wealth of the rich means the comparative welfare of the poor; economic necessity unites even the most embittered enemies. Where national expansion, determined by economic principles, leads to conflicts, the cause of the conflict is not the economic necessity, but the menace formed by the expansion and penetration of a nation as a militant unit. If Japanese emigrants could be transmuted into Anglo-Saxons by a stroke of the pen, they would be gratefully received by the populations of countries as poor in manpower and rich in resources as Australia or Canada. But that is a different problem, which will have to be discussed later. Later we shall also see why the economic activities of man seem to be so particularly fertile a source of enmity. For the present we must at any rate establish that human efforts are by no means exclusively directed towards the achievement of a minimum standard of living, or even towards the acquisition of a maximum of property; often enough they are concerned with aims which cannot possibly be regarded as necessary for or even remotely connected with the maintenance of life. We only need remember the madness of passion to which the wish to possess a desired woman may lead; or the unbridled pursuit of pleasures which are as destructive to the individual as to the community. Man is driven by longings which know of no surcease; one wish is barely satisfied, before a new aim is viewed. It is the force of everlasting and self-regenerating Desire which lends its changing objects the appearance of necessities.

Enmities without number spring, to be sure, from the boundlessness of man's desire; but only when we expand our definition of desire, so that it includes not only the will to possess, but also the will to do or not to do, we begin to grow aware of a general and objective necessity of conflict, which is a corollary of the selfish will. In view of what is to follow, it may be as well to recall a few known facts and relations. The selfish will is commonly defined as the integration of those efforts of man which are directed towards the fulfillment of the impulses of his desire. The wish to realise these impulses with as little hindrance as possible is felt as the longing for that most precious of all goods, freedom. As a result of the close proximity in which men live together, and are *forced* to live together, the impulses of the individual will mostly relate to one's fellow-men and their affairs. Therefore, one's fellow-men are obstacles on the road to freedom; less so, to the extent to which *their* will is curbed and constrained by force. The use of force presupposes power; and thus the selfish will becomes the will to power; so that continuous collisions between the units of selfish will are unavoidable.

It would seem as if such conflicts can only be avoided if one desists from the fulfilment of one's own desires and concentrates on the realisation of those of one's neighbour. Such an attitude is called altruism. Actually, altruism can never abolish the necessity of collisions, but only act as an inadequate corrective. For if everyone would make the fulfilment of everyone else's wishes his one and only purpose, the end would be general mass suicide—or possibly general mass murder; for the resulting competition in altruism would result in consequences far more horrible than those of the struggle of the egoists. For the egoist can impose a limit on his will. The ideal definition and strict observance of limits which the egoistic will may not exceed should at least result in a considerable restriction of the conflict potential; while, on the other hand, it is impossible to act altruistically, unless someone else behaves selfishly. If one desires to give, one must needs condemn one's neighbour to receive. Ultimately one would be forced to be an egoist, only in order to allow the others the pleasure of being altruists. In reality, altruism is only possible where an egoistic attitude prevails; and only then is it of value.

Even the strict distinction of these two apparent opposites is illogical. For the most altruistic action is in the last resort the realisation of an egoistic impulse: the egoistic individual experiences the satisfaction—satisfaction of a very high order—resulting from an act of altruism. It is far more pleasant to be the subject of altruism than to be its object. To give is more blessed than to receive. Altruism is a refined form of egoism. Why then does the heroic competition in altruism never materialise?

If we examine the deeper relations between egoism and altruism, we encounter a problem of consciousness. Human consciousness contains our individual conception of our existence. Within the structure of organised life of which humanity consists, the closed unit of consciousness is neither the single cell nor society, but the individual. And as the realisation of life is concentrated within consciousness, and derives its value and meaning only from the processes which it precipitates in consciousness, the individual, which is the unit of consciousness, remains confined within its own limits and limitations to such an extent, that his relations with other individuals, however close they may be, and his consideration of their desires, however much that may be attempted, cannot but be extremely superficial in comparison with the influence of his own existence, his own desires and the consideration paid to them by others. Though altruistic activity provides a higher degree of satisfaction, man acts in the majority of cases in a directly egoistic way. For desire and will spring from a depth which knows no reason nor consideration: they force their way to the surface, with a promise of enjoyment or satisfaction, and determine man's actions, long before halting reason can pronounce on the—actually most doubtful—reliability of the promise, or apply its stammering conclusions based on almost forgotten experiences. Within the lonely prison of his consciousness, man occupies himself a thousand times with his own wishes and desires, before he gives a thought to those of his neighbour; which, after all, have a long way to go before they penetrate, distorted, to his understanding.

It is therefore not only faulty understanding or innate evil which causes man's egoistic behaviour; on the contrary, such behaviour is an unavoidable necessity. And the fact that it is unavoidable results in the creation of another necessity: that of continuous unescapable collision. Even where the conditions of life are correlated with the greatest possible care, a certain effort remains necessary if the individual is to be able to let his will prevail to at least a minimal degree against the intrusive will of other individuals. So the expression "struggle for existence" is possibly not so unjustified after all, though in a rather unusual sense.

Unavoidable as it was to examine this question, the result has not brought us any nearer to an understanding of the connection between conflicts and feelings of enmity; and even less of the origin of the latter. The commonly accepted explanation of the process maintains that every conflict interferes with aspirations towards the fulfilment of wishes or the accomplishment of the will. This interference causes suffering and creates a feeling of hate, directed against its originator. According to this theory, the necessity of conflicts would result in the continuous creation of feelings of enmity, which appear as the *result* of collisions. Another explanation, based on an interpretation of our emotional life, argues somewhat differently. It starts from the correct assumption that an altruistic attitude demands the bridging, even though imperfectly, of the distance between men. Such a process is impossible without consideration for the feelings of other men and therefore necessitates an attempt to understand the nature of these feelings; understanding again requires the identification of one's own feelings with those of the other, at least in the imagination; such an identification is characterised as friendly, and the capacity for it as love. The moral ordinance of neighbourly love therefore implies at the same time an attempt to explain the fundamental causes of hate. For in its ultimate, though unrealisable consequence it ordains that we love our neighbour even as ourselves, as there is no need for hate in order to produce the feared conflicts; mere indifference, which is the absence of love, suffices. It is clear that this conception fails to consider the consequences of the general application to altruism which we have already indicated; but in this conception, too, the conflict, though here it depends on lack of love, appears as the cause of the development of positive hate, which is formed through the exacerbation of lacking love in the course of the conflicts resulting therefrom.

Though starting from different premises, both attempts at explanation arrive therefore at a similar result; which *prima facie* would seem acceptable. But even a superficial attempt to check its applicability to actual conditions gives rise to grave doubts. Countless instances from daily life prove that a sensible delimitation of the spheres within which the individual will is respected can reduce the need for conflicts to a harmless minimum. Moreover nature, in this respect certainly benevolent, has allotted to different individuals widely varying intensities of willpower, so that everywhere we see conditions of unilateral domination supported quietly and apparently without suffering; which goes a long way towards eliminating friction. In addition, the conception of conflicts caused mechanically or through indifference, which in their turn give rise to most positive and by no means indifferent feelings of hate, hardly agrees with actually observed facts. True, lack of love and lack of consideration lead often enough to conflicts; but the impression remains that in each human being feelings of enmity, of sometimes deter minable but more often totally unknown origin, lie concealed, in order to erupt at the first suitable occasion as irresistibly as powers of nature.

At this point it would seem that our ideas meet with an irreconcilable contradiction; and as always in such cases, the contradiction derives from a false premise on which the usual explanations are based and which could not be recognised and dismissed as such before its unavoidable consequences had come to light.

For so far we have accepted the current idea that the

inhibition of the fulfilment of wishes and will is felt as suffering, that the suffering is transformed into enmity, and that the enmity directs itself against the persons from whom the original inhibition originates. But this idea is false. Such a close casual connection between the creation and expression of hate and inhibition of the will is anything but the rule, and cases where the strength of the hostile feeling directed against the inhibiting individual is commensurate with the strength of the inhibited wish and the force of the inhibition, are relatively rare. Only in cases where injury is inflicted unlawfully, or seems to be so inflicted, there occurs a hate reaction which might be considered as "normal". On careful examination even these cases prove to be far less normal than they appear at first sight; but proof of this must be deferred to a somewhat later stage.

For the present we must establish that hostile feelings *are continually directed and discharged against persons who cannot possibly be responsible for their formation.*

For clearness' sake we shall support this statement by an instance from daily life. Let us consider a merchant who has failed to conclude some particularly lucrative transaction. The order in question was given to his luckier competitor. Our merchant has suffered no injustice. But he has been inhibited in the fulfilment of a most powerful desire. So he suffers. His suffering contains at the same time some feeling of hostility which tends, naturally, to direct itself against the rival, probably in the idea that the latter has obtained the order by the use of unfair or not permissible tactics. But in this direction the hostility cannot express itself. For the merchant must remain on good terms with his powerful rival; his behaviour must be friendly rather than otherwise; though, if conditions should change, he may let the other feel his annoyance later, even in a case where the competitor is in no way to blame. The memory of former suffering may remain alive in the form of a justification and as such provide a welcome pretext for the ventilation of an annoyance caused by a totally different party. For annoyance must be vented in some way and in some direction. For the present, at any rate, it cannot be directed against its originator. But the outbreak of a hostile feeling cannot be totally suppressed. It seeks an outlet, at least in part. And in our case this outlet is our merchant's employees, who have a bad day. The merchant discovers a thousand real and imaginary faults. His imagination may invent a way in which they share the responsibility for his failure. He may even go so far as to provoke mistakes of his personnel, in order to find a pretext for ventilating his anger.

Thus far, we have dealt with the immediate, though possibly only partial, discharge of a hostile feeling in a direction other than that from which it was excited. But the old accountant knows that such scenes occur not infrequently. Sometimes he knows the reason, sometimes not. He knows that unpleasantness in the merchant's private life often has the same result as a miscarried order; he knows that harm caused by the merchant's own fault, such as ill-considered speculations, has the same result; he knows that even adversities which cannot be ascribed to any human source, such as illness in the family, may cause displays of temper towards the employees. Not that the relation between cause and effect is always the same: the outbreak need by no means follow immediately and is not always commensurate with the degree of suffering inflicted. The same mistakes which normally would only call for a mild remark may suddenly provoke a roaring rage, though the accountant, who is well informed about the private circumstances of his employer, does not know of any particularly unpleasant happenings in the life of our merchant. It almost seems as if the latter transforms all adversities, all suffering which is inflicted on him, into feelings of enmity which sometimes are in part expressed immediately, and at other times accumulate; from time to time they must find an outlet, which is found in the direction of least resistance; while it occasionally seems that the outbreak awaits the opportunity of a mistake, in order to ventilate itself with a semblance of justification.

Our instance shows that we must free ourselves from the current conception that feelings of hate only occur as a reaction to inflicted harm and that they are directed against the originator of the harm. We must on the contrary assume *that every instance of suffering, every feeling of displeasure, by whomsoever and in whatsoever way it may have been caused, whether it arises from the guilt or from the lawful activity of another person, or through the sufferer's own fault, or without any fault, or even without any human influence, tends to transform itself into a feeling of enmity, to direct itself against fellow-humans and if possible to express itself against them.*

So here we meet a new feature in our picture of humanity struggling amongst enmities. We discern a human world, an accumulation of beings highly sensitive to suffering, who, born in suffering, are by an all-powerful will to live condemned to cling to an existence in which wishes and desires bring only pain, where failure of fulfilment is torture, fulfilment disappointment, a source of new desire and new pain. All happiness, which in essence is no more than the avoidance of suffering, increases again the capacity for unhappiness, the sensitivity for suffering; its very continuation must needs bring its cessation. An insecure existence is surrounded by ceaseless dangers, threatened by unforeseen turns of chance; a body exposed to wounds and disease causes frequent and often unbearable pains; and the occurrence most feared and most repugnant of all, death, is a daily threat which eventually never fails to materialise. In addition to all which, weakness of body and poverty of mind force men to live so closely together that they cannot but be permanently in each other's way.

Not this unavoidable friction alone causes suffering which is transformed into enmity; it may even be said to account only for a small part of all suffering; for unlike the dark powers of fate, human beings are gifted with human feelings and therefore capable of sympathy, and they are far more inclined to save each other suffering than we usually assume. One might even go further and say that in the up and down of joy and pain the main factor is something preexistent within each individual mind, which is only accented by outward occurrences. At any rate, all suffering, particularly also where it is not caused by any human agency, is transformed into hostile feelings, which are projected upon other persons.

All human suffering must be borne into the community of human beings as hate of human beings. Enmity is suffering projected upon other men.

We shall now attempt to arrive at a more detailed view of the mechanics of this process. The transference of *hostile* feelings on men who are innocent of the origin of these feelings is, as we have seen, not unduly difficult. It is only necessary for the notion of some fault, of which the prospective victims of the expression of enmity are supposed to be guilty, to be conceived. Where possible, some connection is established between the cause of suffering and some fault of the elected objects of enmity; otherwise, their actual transgressions in other fields will serve; finally, the belief in guilt can arise without any objective cause, as those to be found guilty may always be accused of bad qualities and evil intentions.

Far more complicated is the expression of enmity. Our merchant can from time to time vent his anger on his personnel; but he must confine himself to hard words, while he possibly would prefer blows; and the necessity of maintaining an efficient staff forces him not to try the patience of his employees beyond certain limits. Expression of hate requires the material power to inflict suffering of others, preferably without risk of retaliation. Normally this power is only available to a small extent, while in quite normal cases the effect of suffering may be overwhelming. Under normal conditions, justice occasionally executes indirect vengeance for the most grievous harm; but all the suffering which arises from impersonal sources remains unrequited and except by abuse, an occasional display of cunning, and to a very limited extent physical punishment, the individual cannot give expression to his hostile feelings. And even the use of these inadequate means requires a measure of power or capacity which is but too often lacking.

The greater part of hostile feelings—and more particularly so when they are most violent,—cannot be expressed, but accumulates. Modern psychology has made us familiar with a mental world in which instincts and impulses are confined below the threshold of consciousness, but maintain their unbroken power and their capacity of emerging at any time. There may be some justification for the conception that all suffering which has been transformed into hate finds its way into some sort of common reservoir; the question whether any further changes occur within this reservoir, for instance under the influence of opposite pleasurable feelings, must be left undecided.

The way in which ideas are popularly conceived rarely excels in consequence of thought, but often in close observation of detail. In common parlance a man is said to have had to "swallow" more than he can "stomach", so that he is "fed up" and must "air" his anger, hate or rage: a simple description of the process which must actually be presumed to occur. All suffering, of whatever origin it may be, is transmuted into hate which can be expressed only to an insufficient extent and by inadequate means. So it accumulates. *Within the human mind there always exists a reserve of accumulated hostile feeling; a reserve which by its very presence causes a strong disposition towards the expression of such feelings.*

Of course this disposition differs individually, just as the sensitivity for suffering, and the degree of skill and method by which the transmutation is effected differ individually. But the disposition is universally present. It must be assumed that an abnormally voluminous supply of hostile feelings increases the pressure within the reservoir to such a degree that the normal small-capacity valves are no longer sufficient and a violent eruption takes place; at any rate, an opportunity for discharge will bring hidden hate to the surface and extraordinary opportunities will always produce an extraordinary and unexpected volume of the most violent enmity instincts.

As man always possesses reserves of hate, their expression can never be directed adequately against the person who originally caused them to come into being, and only in the rarest of cases against any person at all connected with their origin; rather is the expression of hate directed in accordance with an available pretext or occasion. The nature of this pretext and of its particular appropriateness for this function will become clear presently; but it is already apparent that the expression of hate, i.e. the discharge of accumulated hostile feelings, can only in exceptional cases be proportional to the occasion. Therefore the expression of enmity does not only as a rule appear unreasonable and senseless, because it excites reciprocal hate and in the absence of a considerable superiority of power may lead to reprisals, but according to the prevailing conceptions of right also is unjust, as there will always be a tendency to discharge more of the accumulated feelings of enmity than the occasion warrants.

This being established, we can now revert to the case of "normal" enmity, where the expression of hate appears as the justified, or at least understandable, reaction to inflicted injustice, to inflicted suffering, to real or supposed guilt. For it is of importance to establish how this "normal" case fits into the general structure of enmity which has been outlined here. At the beginning of this chapter it has already been stated that in respect of the harm and suffering caused, even the gravest violation of right does not differ from accidents caused by no human agency. It should therefore be possible to regard the violation of right as nothing but an accident which has reached its human victim by way of another human being. This approach may enable us to view the difficult problem of guilt more dispassionately.

In reacting on a violation of our rights, and on the suffering which it inflicts on us, with a strong feeling of hate which implies the desire to retaliate upon the originator, we are led by the assumption that the latter *could have spared us the suffering*. We regard it as the essence of his *guilt* that he has not exercised the free will which we assume in him by refraining from the noxious violation of our rights. This assumption is strengthened by experience, which teaches us that fear or retaliatory suffering, which we call revenge or punishment, has suppressed countless harmful acts before they were committed. And from the assumed existence of guilt we also derive the *right* to inflict suffering on the criminal.

Both our hate reaction and the feeling of its justification are therefore connected with the assumption of free will. This conception is of course not the result of conscious thought; rather does man instinctively regard his will and that of others as fully free; and this instinct is so powerful that essentially he cannot imagine any action, any occurrence, any natural phenomenon, or, in general, any change in any situation of any nature whatsoever, without ascribing it to the volition of a freely acting being. At a comparatively late stage of its development, reason was in many instances forced by contradictory facts to conclude towards the existence of a blind fate; but even this fate bears the lineaments of a human will; and where, finally, strictly logical deduction has no alternative but to deny the existence of free will, the deeper and more important layers of the mind continue to conceive of it with unbroken force.

So all suffering, whether its cause is known or not, is felt as a disaster which without the malice aforethought, or at least without the criminal negligence, of some being gifted with free will, *could have been avoided*. And invariably, whether the originator of the disaster is known or not, this feeling is followed by the desire to apply that method of removing suffering which seems natural against human originators: the production of a feeling of enmity tending to inflict harm upon the guilty person or to destroy him. Obviously the oldest experiences of the human race have been embodied in this desire to remove suffering: in reality the suffering undergone is of course not rendered undone by revenge; but the destruction of the originator is intended as a radical means to prevent a repetition of the injury, and retaliation to have a deterrent influence for the future. And the physical effect of pain loses much of its terror as soon as it is alleviated by the hope that its recurrence in the future is improbable. But as the remote, non-human powers which ordain sufferings caused by no man are on the one hand unattainable and untouchable, yet on the other hand are, in the depths of the mind, regarded as somehow activated by human influences, it is easy to understand that all suffering seeks sorely needed relief in hate against men, who anyhow always are underfoot and who at least *can* be harmed.

This relief of suffering by inflicting harm on people in whom free will is assumed, is accompanied by *conceptions of right and wrong*. They are a product of life in the human community and in their turn cause the *need for justification* which necessarily appears together with any expression of enmity, and even precedes it, for it arises as soon as hostile feelings first find their direction.

Man is naturally inclined to distinguish in the acts of commission and omission of his neighbour between that which is agreeable and that which is disagreeable to himself. His moral algebra attributes signs to them and calls the former "good" and the latter "bad". The disagreeable he attempts to prevent: he does not permit it. The announcement of this withdrawal of permission is called "prohibition", the action of announcing it "to forbid". Anyone who acts contrary to a prohibition, commits a forbidden act and exposes himself to the punishment of him who has forbidden it. If the latter has the authority necessary to lend general validity to his orders and prohibitions, they become recognised laAV, and their infringement violation of law. Now everyone would be inclined to forbid everyone else everything which impinges on the unrestricted exercise of his will, even where such a prohibition would affect his neighbour's working power, the produce of his labour, or his existence as such. Thus the need arises for a certain reciprocal delimitation which establishes the extent to which the exercise of the own will may impede that of the other. The act which confines itself within these limits is lawful, that which exceeds them, unlawful.

Originally these delimitations were always imposed by the strong, and therefore laid down to the prejudice of the weak. In this way the norm of the law itself is made to contain an element which the weak cannot but regard as an injustice. In this respect it is theoretically possible to strike a balance: we can very well imagine a law which gives equal protection to all men by an equal restriction of their arbitrary acts. But out of its very nature the law can only give protection against the crudest forms of harmful acts; unlimited possibilities for conflict remain unrestrained by any law whatsoever, and in billions of everyday collisions opinions differ as to which side is right and which wrong. Even carefully codified laws, elaborated in the most minute details and provided with extensive commentaries, cannot avoid the necessity for disputes about their application between the parties concerned and among the legal profession. This uncertainty does not in the first place arise from the always generalising form of the legal rule, which makes its application to the involved particularity of any actual case almost impossible, but from the *structural injustice* with which the rule is necessarily invested.

For even the extreme ethical principle suitable for incorporation in a legal system can only provide that one should refrain from those acts against one's neighbour which one would wish avoided in relation to oneself; and this rule can only apply *equally* to relations which of their nature are *unequal* and therefore unequally affected by the working of the rule. If the rule is applied equally, he against whom fate has discriminated in comparison with his luckier neighbour remains at disadvantage; and this disadvantage is in itself felt as an injustice. For the same discrimination which, if resulting from human action, embitters us to the extreme, is committed by nature, fate, the Deity or chance with a cruel arbitrariness which within the sphere of human conceptions of right and wrong would be regarded as injustice unparalleled. Inequality of material possession might be attributed to human society; but inequality of intelligence, force, beauty, power of resistance is caused by no human agency; yet to the less gifted it is the gravest of disadvantages, to the lucky *a privilege* which no rule of law or morals can be allowed to undo, while neither laws nor even positively altruistic behaviour in the form of aid or assistance can to an even approximately sufficient extent compensate those *deprived of their birthright* for the injustice of nature or fate.

In our conceptions of social justice, which admittedly are highly developed, we are beginning to realise that justice does not only demand a certain degree of protection, but the maximum of happiness which is supposed to be the share of those most highly privileged. Actually, the instinctive conception of right, which persists even at a high level of development, is orientated egocentrically: it posits the pleasant as permitted, and particularly the unpleasant as forbidden. Therefore each party believes itself to be right and its opponents to be wrong. In full consciousness this equation is applied in all conflicts which cannot be decided beyond doubt by the application of rules of law; but even the convict's psychological reaction does not differ from that of any party which has become involved in a conflict. He may submit to the force of the rules whose violation is forbidden by the all-powerful law of the community; nevertheless he regards his opponents, the officers of the law, as enemies against whom he must defend himself; he considers his deeds the justified re-action against a society which has deprived him of his rightful happiness and which now maliciously attempts to catch him in the net of its insidious laws; at any rate he regards his action as the answer to the injustice done him by an undeserved fate: and as a last resort he shall certainly attempt to deny his guilt by appealing to the overwhelming force of the circumstances which have brought about his act. For such factors, which overridingly condition the action, mean, of course, the elimi-nation of free will, and therefore serve to establish innocence. In the face of such innocence legal prosecution appears as persecution, as an injustice; even though the criminal does not always become fully conscious of this feeling. (*)

Thus neither party is conscious of any guilt, while there is a tendency, at least in the deepest layers of the mind, to ascribe guilt to the opponent. (**)

In this connection it should be pointed out that the description of any act as attacking or defensive implies no objective statement as to guilt. Attack and defence are originally mere tactical conceptions, are still currently used in that sense, and form an objectively demonstrable contrast only in that sense. Where two parties oppose

---

(*) Here the overwhelming power of the selfish attitude, resulting from the nature of human consciousness, becomes apparent. In respect of his neighbour, man as a matter of course applies the conception of guilt in all its inexorability, while in his own case he eliminates it, where necessary even by a flight into the realisation of his own lack of free will, which otherwise remains completely concealed to him. We should never lose sight of the fact that conscious reasoned thought, which would *ex post facto* be able to establish the absurdity of such a one-sided attitude, is completely powerless; and no insight gained by reflection can prevent the psychological reactions from recurring in the way determined by the particular nature of consciousness.

(**) Seemingly, consciousness of guilt does not only follow violation of the law, but disregard of any prohibition or even of a wish which commands respect. This consciousness of guilt is, however, only *fear* of punishment, blame, criticism or even a slight expression of displeasure. It occurs even where the validity of the violated rule or the justification of the impending blame is by no means admitted. The power of human society and its censure is overwhelming; the fear of its inexorability is so deeply impressed upon the human mind that it may bring even the undiscovered criminal to a degree of contrition where he delivers himself unto that vengeance which is called justice, so as to escape its ever present terror; or torture himself purposely; or even take his own life. For the force of the threat is the more terrible, as its realisation is also feared from superhuman powers who avail themselves of so unimaginably fearful weapons as acts of fate and the tortures of hell; and as the human conception of right demands that suffering be repaid with suffering, the timid sinner may attempt to evade the threatened pains by voluntary suffering. How deeply the fear of suffering as punishment has penetrated human consciousness, is proved by the lively barter in suffering which even normally decent men will attempt with Destiny: they fear disaster as punishment for known or unknown offenses and bring voluntary sacrifices, that is to say, incur slight suffering to avert the danger of severe harm. But the operative element in all this is not a spontaneous consciousness of guilt, but fear of threatening punishment; a fear which need not exclude an underlying feeling of real innocence.

each other, the one who interrupts a state of rest and takes action against the other with intent to inflict harm is the attacker. The other party can avoid the intended harm by flight, by the application of passive means of protection or by counteraction. It defends itself. But the description of these relations is a statement as to tactical position and not as to right or wrong. The state of rest interrupted by the attack may have been based on a former injustice; the defence may oppose the righting of a wrong. The police which pursues a criminal is in the attack; the criminal who defends himself against the police, acts unlawfully. Objectively seen, attack and defence are merely a difference in the tactical movement of forces. But as subjectively man desires nothing so much as to maintain his liberty undisturbed, at any rate within the reservation allotted to him by the law, attack is identified with interference with the reservation, called aggression and branded as something abhorrent. What exactly the limits of the reservation are, can only be established from case to case by process of law; but this does not prevent the interfering party from regarding such a decision as unjust and feeling within his inner self that even the infringement of formally sanctioned prohibitions is really his good right. Such an action is then regarded by its author as defence against an injustice, though possibly against a legalised injustice; the real meaning of the designation of the opponent's acts as aggression is only to declare him guilty; and that of one's own deeds as defence, to state that they are justified.

   This curiously subjective approach is possible because an objective decision can only establish whether formal laws have been offended against, but not in how far the law is regarded by the parties as having any inner validity; for the latter is based on conceptions of a minimum of pain and a maximum of pleasure, and no balance based on this principle can exist within humanity, or could be demonstrated even if it did exist. Naturally so; for these sensations are not only the result of human activities, but are largely caused by influences in which acts of man are only of partial, possibly of quite subordinate, importance. *With regard to conceptions of right and wrong, the acts of men are seen within the frame of a larger complex of occurrences of non-human origin; but they are distinguished and allotted exceptional importance, because they are felt to be the result of free volition, and their undesirable effects are therefore regarded as guilt.*

The idea of guilt is the centre round which all conceptions of enmity revolve; again and again its singular position has set the philosophers, and particularly the legal philosophers, unanswerable problems. Comparatively the most reliable standards of judgment are those of modern criminal law, which is beginning to deprive the idea of guilt of its objective validity and to unmask it as an element of purely subjective psychology. In the first instance, criminal law admitted the claim that intoxicants inhibit free volition and therefore exculpate the criminal acting under their influence. But recently other factors, such as his surroundings, his emotional life, his mental world and his past, have been taken into consideration as elements which determine acts of crime. Obviously, one can draw the line arbitrarily; but it is equally obvious that if this conception is carried out consequently, free will, and therefore also the freedom to will evil and its consequence, guilt, disappear. For any act is in this way reduced to the resultant of the objective factors which together have produced volition; and if impending punishment is a factor which often impedes the materialisation of a volition of criminal effect, then the committed crime merely proves of how overwhelming force were the other factors, which caused the action to be committed notwithstanding the usually quite powerful feeling of fear. The insight into this relation, which, incidentally, is by no means new, is not likely to prevail in all its consequences; for it is contrary to the most powerful conceptions of mankind, and society will always need to pro-tect itself against those of its members whose asocial instincts are insufficiently inhibited. But instinctively the true position has always been realised; not for nothing does exoneration consist in a statement of the circumstances which lead to the deed, of its history. It exposes the causative factors of objective nature, and who realises their compelling force feels inclined to deny the guilt of the accused. *Tout comprendre c'est tout pardonner.*

In mass conflicts the impression of the essential absence of guilt is far more conclusive than in the individual case, which is why they are far more frequently chosen as the starting point of an attempt at objective explanation. The objective factors which determine the actions of masses are more easily discerned; and behind human activity there arises, far beyond all guilt, destiny: its signification remains incomprehensible to us, for it is im-probable that it possesses those qualities with which our human processes of thought cause us to invest it.

Nevertheless, the conception of human guilt has not lost all reality; but. its essence is of another order: a psychological reality within the realm of human communal life. It appears to us in that real and eminently tragic sense in which the greatest works of outstanding playwrights have brought it to life for us: as the blame which rests on the man whom fate, which in its thrice-remote indifference uses so many material instruments for the same purpose, has used as a tool to inflict pain on his fellow-man. The idea of guilt, which is the base of the "normal" enmity reaction, and without the conception of which no expression of enmity can ever occur, is now seen as a purely psychological construction created by the necessities of life in human society. For there can be no doubt that the social implications of the conceptions of guilt and right, which form the basis—though a basis of clay—for their application in daily life, are of the utmost importance: the feeling that one is accountable for one's actions is an objective determinant which has caused the commission of so many useful, and the omission of so many harmful actions, that it is difficult to imagine the continued existence of human society without the conception of guilt.

But whatever it may be, *guilt is not the cause of enmity.* Enmity is nothing but transformed suffering, which out of psychological necessity must be projected upon human beings in order to be liquidated. In part this suffering is caused by human action, but its larger part is of non-human origin. It is not guilt which turns the earth into an arena where the struggle with bloodless weapons never ceases, and the fight with bloody arms is only interrupted by those periods of exhaustion which we call peace; it is not guilt, but the psychological need which forces man to transfer his own suffering upon other men in the form of hate. The conception of guilt is merely a construct of the mind; a construct, though, of immense social importance and overriding psychological influence.

For actually the belief in the reality of guilt and in its instrumentality in producing actions which cause suffering cannot be shaken by any process of thought or reason. The character of this conception is so compulsive that man actually inverts the relation: so far from pitying the sinner as the instrument and victim of a blind and disastrous fate, he even regards the visitations of fate as the act of a human author—or an author in the likeness of a man, acting according to human conceptions of right and guilt. Afflicted by suffering which he cannot ascribe to a definite human cause, man first seeks suspiciously amongst his fellow-men for the secret malefactor, to whom he ascribes dark designs, occult powers, a pact with the devil, magic, witchcraft or similar activities. He may be amenable to the assumption that by his own known or unknown sins he has offended an avenging deity who now inflicts suffering on him as a punishment; but he must reconcile his fate, and the pain and pleasure by which it affects his mind, with his human conceptions of right and wrong. An order of things which neither gives regard to human feelings nor concerns itself with human conceptions of right and wrong, is beyond his comprehension. Even though his reason would have him admit such a principle, the first actual occurrence will cause the depths of his mind to deny it.

Therefore the power of the conception of guilt is so irresistible, that every expression, and even every feeling of enmity, is accompanied by the compulsive demand for justification by some recognised, assumed, invented, or at least feared guilt on the part of its object.

So whenever suffering of non-human origin, or suffering which cannot, for any reason whatsoever, be visited upon its human author, or (which is the rule) feelings of enmity accumulated from different sources, demand expression, or demand a direction in which they are to be expressed, justification is provided in the shape of those highly fictitious accusations which struck us when we discussed antisemitic phenomena: the object-elect is saddled with assumed evil qualities and intentions, or even accused of offences which are no more than the fruits of a fertile imagination.

If, however, the human author of some injury can be clearly determined, *then hate, ever present and ever ready to be realised, makes avid use of an opportunity for discharge which is felt as so eminently justified; and whenever it is practicable, the expression of the feeling follows immediately upon its emergence into consciousness.* In other words, we have a "normal" hate reaction. If, moreover, the case is one where *recognised principles* are violated, then even utter outsiders avail themselves of the heavensent opportunity for venting their feelings of hate. The discovered thief is pursued by a crowd panting with indignation; likely, some of the pursuers are thieves themselves, and none of them is in any way concerned with the victim of the theft. And in the Wild West they will empty their revolvers into a hanged horsethief, though the poor devil is already as dead as mutton, just to cool their rage. Often the crowd is not even satisfied with surrendering the criminal to the law, for it longs to give immediate effect to its hate; and when the passions of the multitude are more than usually excited, when in disturbed times extraordinary opportunities for expression have called the most concentrated feelings of hate out of their concealment, then a victim who has committed some particularly offensive crime is not even immediately killed by the excited crowd, but slowly tortured to death: for in this way the intensive expression of hate can be made to last longer.

Even where there seems to be a normal hate reaction, there is no just, or even fixed correlation between the undergone suffering and the intensity of the expression of hate. Not only does the same infliction of harm which causes the one to react violently, leave the other practically cold; but one and the same person will on one occasion react strongly, and on another not at all, to the same injury. For the reaction depends far less on the nature and degree of inflicted suffering, than on the state of the inner store of hate and the *possibility of expression.* It is determined by the nature and force of the feelings of hate which happen to be, so to say, available for issue; and these in turn may be mitigated by pleasurable feelings. But hate ready for expression finds in the case of injury inflicted by clearly discernible persons a satisfactory direction, as the clumsy process of applying fictions, to which in any case reason always takes some degree of exception, becomes superfluous and the will to express hate finds a recognisable object ready to hand, together with a most legitimate conception of guilt; if, moreover, recognised rules have been violated, the apparatus of justice provides ways and means of expression which, if usually indirect, are free of risk.

So it may occasionally *seem* as if the reaction of hate is approximately commensurate with the inflicted suffering and that a direct, so-called "normal" hate reaction has taken place on a short circuit, without the participation of the hate reserve. But this is a mere semblance; actually, the reaction nevertheless takes its way through the domains of the mind where suffering is transformed into hate and undergoes the influence of the conditions which rule there. In the "normal" like in all other hate reactions, undergone suffering is transformed into feelings of hostility and forms part of the reserve of hate ready for expression; but the easy identification of the person responsible for the suffering, facilitating formation of a conception of guilt, singles him out as a ready target for the immediate expression of hate already available. Doubtless harm of human origin contributes to the substance of the reserve of enmity; but it is to be doubted whether its share is considerable; *its real importance lies in the unimpeded creation of a legitimate conception of guilt* which it makes possible, and in the facilities for finding a direction which it provides for the reserve of hate.

The impression of the origin of enmity which we have formed is far less beset with improbabilities than the commonly accepted theories. In general, human hate seems senseless; an evil arising from causes which ought to be avoidable. Again and again one comes to the conclusion that men, however much they may be in each other's way, are interdependent; and with some good will they should, it seems, be able to live together peacefully. But all attempts to attain this modest ideal have been doomed to failure, and have even themselves become abundant sources of enmity and strife. It is man's tragical fate that the suffering from non-human sources of which he would rid himself, is multiplied instead, because he attempts to avenge it on his fellow-men; human nature appears to us as always charged with hostile sensations which seek a direction and opportunity for discharge.

The *availability* of a direction and opportunity depends on the *circumstances* which have been discussed. These circumstances are what determines the *occasions* for the expression of enmity. And as it is part of their essential function to provide a *motive* for the expression, the *occasions so often appear to be the causes of the ex-*

pression of enmity and are therefore so freely and naturally confused with the deeper and real causes.

Thus it could happen that economic life, and more in general, human desire, is so often taken to be the cause of all enmity. For they form the background for innumerable collisions which are felt as harmful interference and can easily be ascribed to definitely discernible individuals, so that they provide easy possibilities for the formation of satisfactory conceptions of guilt. The limits imposed by fellow-men on unlimited desire; the threat to the owner implicate in the desire of him who would own; these provide hate with a most reasonable justification for its existence, with a direction for the needed expression, and often enough with an opportunity for expressing itself. Both are furthermore found in the clash between egoist units of will in general. The tendency of the will of another to suppress the own will and the permanent necessity for submitting to the wishes of others form a welcome possibility of direction and opportunity for expression for ever-ready feelings of hate. Far beyond all established rules, the imputation of selfish lack of consideration remains a potential accusation, always available and often used, against easily discernible persons; more than that: it is the justification which hate needs in order to find direction and expression.

In view of the aims of this work, the problem of hate as such had to be investigated (*) ; but as we are more particularly concerned with a case of group enmity, the direct, so-called "normal" hate reaction is of no further

(*) Investigations into the nature and function of conceptions of right and wrong in relation to the phenomena of enmity, fundamental though their importance is, had, naturally, within the frame of the present work to be restricted to the barest essentials.

special importance for us, as, strictly speaking, it only occurs in the course of relations between individuals. We are rather interested in cases where there is not even a semblance of direct hate reaction; where existing feelings of hate *find no, or only insufficient, possibilities of expression.*

We have instanced the case of a merchant who uses his personnel as that animal of biblical fame, the scapegoat. Scapegoats are those unfortunate beings who, wherever possible, are blamed for any harm which may have been incurred, and who at any rate are the victims of any annoyance which happens to be in the air, whether they can be blamed for the suffering which predominates at the particular moment or not. The defenselessness and dependence of the scapegoat favour such abuse. But, as we have already demonstrated, its practicability is comparatively confined. Legal restrictions, the censure of society, and selfish interest keep the possibilities for expressing hate within usually close limits. Moreover, not everyone has scapegoats ready to hand. Only a small minority is in a position of authority over others; and the members of one's own household make in general but poor scapegoats. True, the closeness of family life causes continuous friction, which would seem to favour the expression of unfriendly feelings, because the apparent justification needed for expression is always provided in abundance. But on the other hand there exists a necessity for consideration which is not only realised by reason but also finds its expression in the realm of sentiment as friendly feelings of often considerable strength.

We may recall that human society is based on the helplessness of the isolated individual. Reciprocal aid and assistance are therefore one of the most important tasks and elementary needs of men living together. This assistance is not always rendered in the degree desired by the individual at the moment of his need; but in reality men do assist each other; not only in normal or exceptional cases of total helplessness, but also for purposes of bread-winning, in order to avert dangers from non-human sources, and towards the proper fulfilment of nearly all essential functions of life.

In these relations of reciprocal assistance the closest sur-roundings of man play a special part. Those fellow-men who are bound to the individual by the close ties of special assistance in the most intimate needs of body and mind, usually embody for him the best and most precious gift which human society has to bestow. They give him—and he gives them—the richest senti-ments of friendship, affection and love; the purest instances of charity and self-sacrifice find their expression within this circle; here the abyss isolating the individual has been as far as possible bridged; the multitude of common relations causes the joy and pain of the one to be the joy and pain of the other.

Many of the slighter and slightest unfriendly feelings find, of course, by preference their expression within the intimate circle, because the close connection between its members does away with certain considerations which are unavoidable in respect of strangers, if tolerable relations are to be maintained; the less the degree of affection and the more frigid relations in general, the greater weight is attributed to even the slightest expression of unfriendliness and the more prudence is neces-sary to avoid conflicts. It is even possible for hate to insinuate itself into the closest relation in its most deadly form; then it finds daily and hourly food and finally leads to a catastrophe or to a separation. But in general the necessity and the attractions of a protected life within a circle closely united by sentiment prevail; *then it becomes imperative to keep the reserve of hate remote from contact with this circle and its intimacy, even to the extent in which it arises from relations within the circle.* This again increases, of course, the sum total of hate which cannot be expressed. Failing a possibility of expression it finds at least its *direction ivhere there is some imagined chance of expressing it without punishment, and therefore without danger; it must be diverted from the closer circle and directed outwards.*

In this way we automatically arrive at the conception of a circle of human beings which has an inside and an outside: the *group,* as an immediate consequence of the desire to enjoy the advantages of human society—love, sympathy, friendship, consolation, protection, assistance, succour—and at the same time the possibility of directing (and where possible expressing) accumulated and ever present feeling of hate outwards.

We do not consider the group as a collection of human beings with similar characteristics, established for scientific or other purposes, but as a functional unit within human society, charged with the distribution of feelings of affection and disaffection according to certain principles.

Seen superficially, the following should be stated in the first instance:—The prophets and moralists have ever found their ideal of humanity in a brotherly community of all men, where all separating influences so obviously connected with the existence of the uncounted group combinations according to race, nation, tribe, language, religion, caste, trade, class, and so forth, will have disap-

peared. The role played by these distinctions as separating influences will yet have to be investigated; at any rate, the ideal of a
brotherhood of all men has never been realised or even approxi-
mated. On the contrary, we are forever witnesses of a process in
which men assemble in countless large and small groups; that
is to say, set up partitions between each other. Groups come
into being, increase and decrease, unite and separate, disappear,
combine with other groups for the purpose of closer cooperation; but the process of group formation as such never ceases.
Groups are formed according to almost all principles imaginable;
sometimes it seems that they are meant to serve some objective
purpose—though even in the case of such groups the struggle
against men who oppose the attainment of the material purpose
seems to be by far the most important element of the aim; but in
many cases even the semblance of some sensible purpose cannot
be discovered: at first sight they often seem devoid of all sense
and even useless for the very members of the group. Only one
purpose seems to be common to the formation of all groups: to
provide a scheme of division of the opposing masses in conflicts
amongst men. The principle of grouping is obviously of subordinate importance: in the case of the most violent clash, war,
the principle which provides the characteristics of the division
may be political, ethnical-national, geographic; it may take its
clue from ruling dynasties or from chance leaders. Some forms
of groups appear principally in grave, armed conflicts; others in
the minor collisions which are fought with unbloody arms.

But *whenever groups are formed, the most remarkable
characteristic is some latent or apparent conflict:* even
the most harmless of clubs is essentially a closed unit,

closed, that is to say, towards the outer world. And there is always a more or less manifest lack of good will towards those outside. For how much some of the more harmless groups may solicit new members, admission to the group is only possible on the group's own conditions; and to the members the outsider is always, more or less consciously, a potential enemy, or at least someone who, in respect of those who belong to the group, lacks some valuable and important quality.

For to the member, membership of the group is always an advantage; just as the more or less unfriendly attitude towards the outer world is always contrasted by more or less expressed friendly relations within the group itself. Amongst group members there always exists, though in different shape and degree according to the nature of the group, a feeling of solidarity, in the first place in respect of the enemy outer world, but also in the form for a particular obligation to assistance within the group. For the sake of the group man often displays an uncommon measure of unselfishness, in the interest of the group he is comparatively often, and with comparatively little effort, able to attain a high level of moral accomplishment. Acts of total self-sacrifice, rarely seen where the interest of a single individual is at stake, often are committed on a large scale for the sake of certain important groups.

The group appears to be a curious form of extension of the individual. It seems as if under the influence of the necessities of human communal life, human beings who need love and produce hate combine into new, collective and collectively selfish individualities of a higher order; directing their love inwards, their hate outward, their social instincts towards the insider, their anti-social tendencies towards the outsider. The group becomes apparent as a functional unit and as the organisation which cannot be foregone if the enjoyment of all advantages which human society can provide is to be combined with the possibility of expressing the hostile feelings which always clamour for discharge.

It will now be attempted to show more clearly that this utter abstraction really enables us to distinguish the essential element in a multitude of occurrences which seem to defy analysis. In passing we shall have to arrive at a series of findings which do not particularly refer to group *enmity* but which cannot very well be disregarded if we are to arrive at a complete understanding of its nature.

Chapter IV

The Group

1. *Distribution of Functions*

An essential element of any relation of friendship (which of its very nature is an alliance) —in fact, the one from which it derives its value—is its implication of a degree of lesser friendship in respect of all outsiders. Persons united by friendship commonly devote to each other, by tacit or, occasionally, by express agreement, those socially advantageous feelings which lead to mutual consideration of desires and therefore to mutual aid and assistance; which finds its practical expression in the overcoming of impediments, the averting of dangers and the avoiding of injury of non-human origin. But the relation will also be directed against the ever obtrusive wishes and desires of surrounding humanity and the threat of its ubiquitous enmity. A state of preparedness against expected attacks, however much regarded as defensive internally, cannot but make an impression of hostility and aggression on the outside world. Armaments, of their very nature, are no demonstration of friendship, though peaceful intentions be proclaimed ever so loudly. An alliance always constitutes a threat.

Thus we meet, in its simplest form, that process of group formation by which even the most noble, charitable and honestly altruistic of men creates a boundary between humanity as a whole and an—always comparatively small —number of individuals who within the sphere of his friendly feelings enjoy preferential treatment.

Before the process of group formation is discussed in more detail, it may be of advantage to point out that even if one does not realise the true causes of enmity, an overwhelming preponderance of hostile over friendly feelings must be admitted as an established fact. *Homo homini lupus.* This does not in itself invalidate the assumption that man is fundamentally good, or capable of some change of nature; but about the fact as such there can be no difference of opinion. Without the explanation of the origin of hostility which we have attempted, most of the phenomena of group antagonism would have to remain unexplained; but the process of group formation as such might be satisfactorily derived from the mere fact of the preponderance of inimical sentiments. If some higher purpose is to be attributed to this process, one might say that it serves to bring some order and direction into the otherwise disorderly confusion of little love and much hate, friendly sentiments being reserved for the inner circle and hostile feelings as far as possible for the outer world. This distribution corresponds to the overwhelming preponderance of the unfriendly feelings; and it almost seems as if group formation, however undesirable it may seem at first sight, is useful in isolating and salvaging the obviously small volume of friendly feelings, so that they may remain available to the full extent for a humanity which so obviously needs them.

Of course, hostile feelings are expressed even within the group, to the very limit tolerated by the purpose and necessity of its existence; for *qui a compagnon a maitre* and the closer a relation of friendship, the greater the sacrifices of freedom with which it has to be bought; and these sacrifices cause suffering which naturally tends to direct itself against its originator in the form of enmity. Usually this direction is barred, in order to maintain the friendship undisturbed, but the tendency persists and only waits for a favourable opportunity; which appears the sooner, as friendly relations are far more tolerant against the expression of a minor degree of unfriendliness than an attitude of correct indifference. The consequences are those internal disputes and quarrels so frequent amongst friends; and no less natural a consequence the sudden and violent change of face when a friendship is terminated: then not only those hostile feelings which have been created by unavoidable friction are expressed in the previously barred direction, but the exceptional opportunity is exploited for the utterance of hate arising from totally different sources.

So far, all our remarks only refer to the principle of group formation; actually, group functions are distributed over a whole range of various and variegated group types, while the criteria of distribution are discerned with even greater difficulty as the interrelation and interaction of groups of different character causes additional difficulties in discerning the underlying rule. But it must be regarded as established even at this stage, that *the described distribution of functions, namely the outward direction of hostile and the inward expression of friendly feelings, is an exhaustive definition of the cause and purpose of group formation.*

It is generally realised and admitted without more ado that numberless groups lack any reasonable purpose which might be regarded as a sufficient cause for their formation. In the case of those important groups which are distinguished according to descent, language, religion, etc., the fundamental differences between the individuals united in and separated by those groups are commonly considered a valid motive for group formation; while it is not further investigated in what, actually, the validity consists. At any rate there is no material purpose; for no one will seriously contend that national groups are formed with a view to the improvement of national qualities, or that a linguistic group is created as a means of furthering the development of the language concerned. In the case of many political, numerous religious and uncounted other groups, the feeling of objective superfluousness cannot be dismissed, inasmuch as no material purpose appears to be served by their formation. Where the group, an instrument for the expression of enmity, is confused with the cause of enmity, the impression created is that of definite harmfulness; for many people regard the group as the cause of human conflicts instead of the mere scheme according to which the parties arrange themselves. Moreover, many minor group formations appear harmful to the observer, because they weaken a greater unit, and therefore their own members. Especially in political life, where a maximum of power is to be reserved for the state, the weakening and apparently senseless formation of parties is again and again deplored; a complaint which is repeated on the party level when subsidiary groups, whether in the form of organisations or not, arise within the parties themselves.

Nevertheless, in the case of political parties and other groups with an alleged material purpose this might be taken for the real cause of group formation. But on closer inspection the purpose always proves to be a mere pretext; though, of course, founders and members are of a different opinion. Where the material purpose aims at a change—in the eyes of the founders, an improvement—of any conditions in any field, it nevertheless subordinates itself to the main end: the struggle against the human exponents of the conditions to be improved. It is remarkable how much difficulty such groups, even after a long existence, often experience in establishing their real purpose, and how great a part of their discussions must again and again be devoted to its, if only approximate, formulation.

More readily than in other cases this fact may be overlooked in the case of those groups which aim at exercising such activities as sports and games. But here, too, we can establish (the easiest way being that of historical comparison: consider for instance the blue and green parties of the Roman circus) that there was primarily a need for the formation of groups, and that time and circumstances merely dictated the material purpose which formed the pretext for it.

In the later stages of adolescence, for instance, the demand for combination and differentiation according to groups is particularly pronounced: the absurdities to which undergraduates are wont to go in this respect are only too well known. According to time and circumstances, this demand expresses itself in the field of sport, politics, literature and art, or even mere amusement. The irrelevancy of the material purpose often remains clearly visible; obviously it rarely is more than a means to occupy and amuse the members at their meetings.

In an even more remarkable way does the dominant character of those group functions which have here been described as primary become apparent in the fact that often groups of absolutely similar nature, between which there exists not even a contrast in interests or aims, which frequently acknowledge the same purpose and which have merely been grouped artificially for technical reasons—that such groups often live in relations of a totally senseless tension, to which internally there are corresponding feelings of solidarity. Weapons and bodies of troops, down to the smallest units, maintain the most absurd relations of tension, of mutual enmity, even of mutual contempt. The inhabitants of neighbouring villages, of suburbs, and even of single streets, live in by no means always harmless group enmities. Schoolboys, who, like children in general, express their hostilities with even less restraint than adults, are divided into enemy camps according to schools and grades. On the other hand, the members of even the smallest, most casually composed groups own to a most pronounced feeling of solidarity. And all this though no one, even within the limits of the reasons for hate usually regarded as valid, could show cause why the soldier of one regiment behaves as an enemy to his comrade of another formation, and why a soldier of the own regiment is entitled to altruistic treatment in a way by no means conceded to members of other units of the same army.

The function and distribution of functions so far described is to be discerned in the case of all groups; its most obvious demonstration is possibly the state or state-like structures. Properly speaking, the state is not really a group, but the organised superstructure within which gimips with different bases exercise their most important group functions. This exercise demands the existence of an executive equipped with overriding powers, called the government. Many groups assume an essentially similar structure; but their executive cannot avail itself of armed force in order to impose its decrees; and where it attempts to appropriate armed force, it comes into conflict with the state and its organs.

The continuation of society demands that the selfish will be subjected to at least those restrictions which where properly observed, guaranty to the members of the community a minimum of security: an existence not continuously threatened by their neighbours. Each member is surrounded by a reserved territory which must be respected by all other members.

The free decision of the individual has never yet been sufficient to guaranty the observation of this restriction; it is therefore necessary that there be an institution of a higher order, equipped with overriding powers, which enforces respect of the law by its threat of punishment and which takes revenge for acts against the law out of the hands of the injured individual and its relatives, thus preventing the occurrence of those feuds which so gravely prejudice the peace of the community.

In many cases the laws were of set purpose discriminatory, or at least affected different parts of the community unequally; and so provided a means for continuing the domination of one section of the population over the other. But that does not change the fact that legislation and jurisdiction, the writing and the implementation of the law, form the major element of the justification for the existence of the state. In higher stages of development the state has in addition taken over numerous activities which are intended to protect and facilitate the existence of the citizen; these activities are not characteristic for the state as such; but insofar as they are taken over by the state, this is always done under the consideration that the function in question is too important to the community to be left to the nearly always selfish mercies of the individual. Internally, the state therefore ministers to the welfare of its citizens, principally by providing the most essential conditions of security: legislation and jurisdiction.

While in complicated state structures the judicature may be wholly or partially entrusted to subordinate groups of the population (though usually in the sense of a delegation of powers), the state has always reserved for itself the direct exercise of the other aspect of its function, the organisation of the most violent and dangerous outbreaks of hate and their direction on *external* targets by means of armed force. For the preparation and execution of this task (the complementary part of the *justification,* and in this case certainly the *condition* and *cause* of its existence) the state often avails itself of a complicated diplomatic and military machinery; which, at any rate, has the advantage of preventing a permanent state of war. Seen from inside, outbreaks of hostility appear, of course, invariably as defense, at least in the legal sense: for even the state which tactically takes the offensive believes that it is defending its existence, either by destroying an enemy who may endanger it, or because within its present frame existence has become too difficult and its maintenance therefore demands more favourable conditions, which naturally cannot always be realised without action against those who stand in the way of their realisation. The conviction of justified defense arises the easier in the case of states, because laws defining right and wrong as between states are lacking in all essential respects. In the individual case, the claim to existence is regarded as fairly well established; but there is no general rule as to which groups within humanity are entitled to independent state existence. Nevertheless, struggles between groups are of course also accompanied by conceptions of right, and what to those involved seems to be a just war of defense (exactly as the individual expression of enmity is regarded as a justified reaction on inflicted injury) is none the less an outbreak of mass hate.

Even more arbitrarily, but also far more extensively, than by law, is that what is permitted and forbidden within a given community determined by custom, morals, and conventions which often are not even based on any discernible standard.

Unlike the law, generalising, admitting of exceptions and ethically often reduced to mere negation, custom and morals can prescribe attitudes and relations in positive detail; while the very fact that convention is not based upon any general standard gives it access to even the most intimate details of daily life. Its frequently offensive illogicity and the injustice inherent in its very nature are compensated by the restful balance which it lends to the life of the community. The sanction by which custom and convention are enforced is social proscription, which often enough also follows the punishment of the law and lends it greater force. The latter, however, ceases to be the case as soon as the social circle to which the condemned belongs does not recognise the moral basis of the judgment. Laws provide punishment for offences which are regarded as permissible and even as honourable in the best circles; while those classes who come most often into contact with justice regard crime as their lawful breadwinning, justice as their natural enemy and condemnation as a normal trade risk which entitles the victim to the aid and assistance of his colleagues. In these circles, the support to be given to the authorities in the discovery and apprehension of criminals, laid down by the law as the duty of every citizen, is regarded as base treachery characteristic for a contemptible mentality. Which goes to show that conventional morals are not connected with the community which we call "state", but differ according to class, trade and even locality.

Now the protection of rights and the maintenance of conventional morality form a most valuable support rendered to the individual by, and exercised through, the group; but they can only be fully implemented through additional social prestations of definitely positive implication. The group provides aid and support in need and emergencies of non-human origin; it serves the satisfaction of those intellectual and emotional needs for which man needs society no less than for his material requirements. Even the most violent outbreaks of hate do not, on the other hand, even approximately satisfy the need for expression of hostility. A whole range of non-violent, but yet fairly powerful feelings of enmity seeks an outlet and a target. The individual belongs simultaneously to a number of groups—its relation to them will be discussed later—over which the sum total of group functions is distributed. As may be realised from the function of the state groups, the scheme of distribution is neither haphazard nor arbitrary; it follows a certain gradation; for each group is, naturally, given that share in the general group functions which is most germane to its structure and extent. It goes without saying that this allocation must not be regarded as a systematic and considered arrangement; in respect of certain welfare institutions the adequacy of the group which is to undertake responsibility is sometimes given careful consideration; but in general, the distribution of group functions has developed automatically from the needs of the community.

The largest and most important groups are those organised in state form or at least tending towards state formation. Racial, ethnical-national and linguistic-national groups take the first rank; only under—strategically— particularly favourable conditions does this function devolve on local-geographical units; while at certain times in the past, religious groups have formed the basis for state organisation. These groups generally function as instruments for the direction and expression of the most violent, brute and elementary hate instincts. Again it must be stressed that occasionally bloody fights for life and death also occur between the smallest groups, and even between individuals, but where this happens within a higher order of group organisation, the general purpose of the distribution of functions is interfered with, and the larger groups accordingly attempt to suppress such individual outbreaks—and succeed to a comparatively large extent. (*)

Notwithstanding all questions of right and guilt laboriously introduced into the conflict, the most violent outbreaks of enmity seem to the disinterested observer wild and senseless; too rarely they are to any extent a proportionate reaction to an injury; too visibly they have outgrown the smallness of their occasion. Medium degree enmity feelings usually seem far more reasonable, as they can at any rate to some extent be traced back to some injury; the immediacy of the reaction makes them appear more acute and caustic, but in reality they are far less dangerous. Feelings of this kind find their principal opportunity for expression and direction in class and party conflicts.

(*) Historical development seems to tend towards a monopoly for mass murder for ever larger units.

The slightest and comparatively harmless everyday feelings of unfriendliness are directed and expressed by means of small groups such as clubs, societies, lodges, *cliques* etc. The tension between such groups often evokes derision: the enmity prevalent between football clubs, Dorcas guilds or Venerable and Ancient Orders naturally lacks that semblance of motivation by grave and important conflicts of interest which lends an odour of respectable necessity to class and party struggles.

A similar gradation may be discerned in the complementary function of the group, directed towards the activation of social instincts. The most important groups provide the frame and the source for man's most exalted feelings of human solidarity and his heroic realisation of a community of destiny; they are the background against which, in the culminations of group life, he experiences the festal awareness, sometimes elevated to the realms of ecstasy, of being part, and therefore also exponent, of an entity of world-wide importance; they grant him the feeling of being protected against the mortal dangers with which remote enemies may threaten his life and good; they invest him with a sensation of strength and power the more welcome as it cannot be derived from pitiable individual weakness. These groups moreover are what gives the individual the larger part of the importance which, else a lone and nameless being, he may have in foreign parts; there, they protect the otherwise defenceless. Even man's awareness of his own value and importance derives largely from his belonging to the more important groups; but this aspect will yet be discussed in connection with group ideology.

These functions of the group are made possible by the activities undertaken and feelings harboured by men for their groups. The members of a group are bound together by a feeling of solidarity which results in a recognised obligation to mutual assistance; a feeling which in the large and important groups is principally activated when grave dangers threaten, and which in normal times is rather localised in the minor groups. With regard to the outside world, however, this feeling is nearly always strong; particularly in cases of conflict it causes an unconditional identification with the standpoint of the own group and a preparedness to take up its quarrel, even where the justification of its cause may seem doubtful: *right or wrong, my country.* The group as a whole is so closely related to the individual, is to such an extent an extension, and even an intensification of individual consciousness, that the group occasionally enables the individual to escape from the locked and barred dungeon of his individual loneliness. Individual man is lost and yet preserved; the impulses of his will no longer benefit himself, but the multiplication of his own self which is the group—and therefore nevertheless his own self. He acts for the good of his neighbour, and so at the same time for his own good. He even may go unto self-destruction; which, in the service of his nation, for instance, may still aim at the fulfilment of his most ardent and essentially strictly selfish desires.

What man does for the sake of another *individual* can never be anything but an altruistic action, unavoidably tainted with a taste of vanity, presumption, and would-be superiority; for altruism needs an object which by its selfish acceptance of the altruistic service debases itself in the face of him who serves. This unpleasant taste is lost where the interest of the group is concerned; for then the unselfishness also benefits the unselfish individual. Selfless work for one's own group is therefore justly regarded as one of the most highly valued human activities. True, the same psychological mechanism allows the group to permit the individual at the same time the expression of less highly valued instincts; but that is a welcome favour readily accepted. Vanity, the admiration of the ego and its qualities, is in the individual case always received by other men with unpleasant feelings, even where it may seem objectively justified. Even the most famous man cannot sing his own praise without annoying his fellow-beings: self-praise is no recommendation. But the man who praises himself by extolling the qualities of his group, flatters all other members of that group, thereby earning their grateful appreciation. The group gives, in the form of group praise, an opportunity for gratifying expression of vanity which if concerning an individual would meet with hostile derision. Virtues may be paraded freely, provided they are labeled as those of one's nation.

To a lesser extent these functions of the group are also found in the case of smaller formations; they can be demonstrated even in the smallest; but it is in groups of the first rank that they find their most apparent and vigorous expression. The medium groups form the framework for the representation of weighty social-economic interests for those forms of social assistance which require the cooperation of more considerable numbers. These groups also provide man with the lion's share of his ideas, opinions and valuations. Men who, in reflective conversation, do not produce a phonographic record of their newspaper (and the newspaper is the visible precipitate of the opinion of the medium group) are exceptional phenomena. Moreover, the medium group provides a backing for man's daily work and enriches its return beyond that of mere subsistence by a conception of its social importance.

The smallest groups are those in which, admittedly, heroic sacrifices of life, such as are brought to the nation, do not often occur, but where the absolute obligation of mutual aid is felt most clearly and where support in that state of absolute helplessness which, at any rate, man is never spared in childhood, is a matter of fact. And if the great group provides the feeling of protection against the threatening violence of remote enemies, the smallest groups give a sensation of security against the changing fortune of life and fate. In these groups man finds solace and encouragement, rest from the tribulations of the day and strength for renewed work. They satisfy his need for the warmth of intimacy, for laughter and good cheer. In the small groups man has an opportunity for the exchange of opinions, and therewith the ardently desired escape from the loneliness—which is the emptiness—of his own mind; for man fears nothing as much as isolation in the horrible void of mental poverty. And real intellectual life finds within these groups the stimulus which it always needs, be it only in the form of expected understanding.

The more particular function of groups as instruments for the expression of enmity will find detailed discussion later; in respect of the group as vehicle for the expression of friendly and unfriendly sentiments these general indications will have to suffice.

We shall now consider the categories according to which the formation of groups occurs.

2. Group Categories

Approach between men always demands to a certain extent the bridging of the intervals which separate them in their individual seclusion, To this end it is necessary that men become acquainted to some extent. Acquaintance as such need not cause pleasure. As man, naturally and essentially selfish, must partly suppress, partly at any rate conceal many of his selfish instincts, the eye of an intimate observer may reveal many an unpleasantness which remains concealed to the stranger. But this revelation, especially if it uncovers less flattering aspects of mentality, removes the darkest and gravest threat which can emanate from any individual: the threat of the unknown; which possibly is most menacing where no outward sign justifies the muted warning of diffident intuition. The unknown person, of whose mental life one can form no impression, whose wishes and desires remain concealed, whose standards of right and wrong, of the allowed and the forbidden are inscrutable, evokes fear and distrust; particularly because behind the impervious mask of a face there may lurk that malice which, more than anything, renders man dangerous. Actually, the insight into a man's mind and soul which is gained on acquaintance is vague enough, but this inadequacy is usually masked by a benevolent illusion; which is sufficient, for subjective fear is cancelled by the subjective illusion of its unfoundedness. As soon as one believes that one knows a given person, much of the feeling of danger issuing from him is dispersed. One feels strong and safe with regard to him: *homme averti en vaut deux.* A closer acquaintance produces feelings of rest, trust and security; feelings which render the narrower and wider circles within which man moves pleasant, and at any rate indispensable. The connection between men who combine to form a group is therefore in the first place based on the principle of mutual acquaintanceship.

The latter is determined by two conditions: proximity in space and the presence of sufficient elements of similarity. In order to become acquainted with a person one must be close enough to be able to observe him; and as our thoughts and understanding move exclusively in analogies, we can only recognise as much in others as introspective self-analysis allows us to understand. Therefore we understand that person best who is most similar to us. And therefore we also believe that we know an unknown person, even if he lives far from us, as soon as we *know* that he has characteristics of importance in common with us. We consequently see that the smallest groups are in the first place formed as a result of local proximity; which, as a matter of course, also involves a large number of significant resemblances. In the smallest local circle such primordial similarities as those of descent, language, religion, customs and traditions, ideas and notions, and even of class and trade, often concur. On the other hand, proximity also is the first prerequisite for that *friction* which, through the conflicts resulting from it, creates opportunities for expressing enmity; wherefore groups based on similarity often cross those determined by locality.

The more so, as the element of similarity has the definite advantage of providing knowledge of others without postulating their proximity in space. For it is not so much real knowledge of others as the belief that one knows them, which banishes fear; so the awareness of a similarity in others, though they be remote, suffices completely; and possibly favours the establishment of a group connection the more, as the idea of unity is not disturbed by the correcting influence of experience and the friction of close contact. Groups based on similarity are therefore capable of far wider an extent and actually prove more important.

At first view it would seem as if every and any element of proximity or similarity may be the basis of group formation; but it appears that we must make an exception for those character qualities which mark degrees of willpower. In fact, the group requires considerable differences of willpower amongst its members, this being the easiest way of avoiding internal conflict. For it is the principal function of the group's organisation to provide expressly agreed and often scrupulously elaborated relations of subordination, intended to prevent the possibility of collisions within the group. Accordingly, one is not likely to find groups constituted on the base of obstinacy, indecision or compliance. In this connection it should be remarked that by no means all groups have a formal organisation: organised groups play the most important role in human history, but occasionally unorganised groups may, in the form of trends and tendencies, be of considerable influence.

The elements of group formation, however, are not its cause; just as differences as such are not the cause of group separation. The possibility of communication between people who differ greatly is not to any significant extent less than that between those closest and most similar. As soon as it comes to fighting a common enemy, the most significant differences, which seemed to constitute so wide a gulf, lose their separating power; and we often find groups facing each other as enemies, while they have the most important characteristics in common. The *primary* factor is the need for expressing enmity, which leads to group formation; this often occurs on lines of similarity; and so the semblance arises as though similarity were the cause of group formation, dissimilarity that of group enmity. (Amongst would-be world reformers this error has led to many attempts at creating artificial similarities, attempts which could not but fail: where similarity between men is so great that they can find no more visible differences to serve their demand for group distinctions, a flag, badge or ritual will do to create them artificially.)

The principal group categories might be summarised as follows:

a) Biological categories: Family, clan, tribe, nation, race; occasionally also sex and age-group.

b) Local categories: House, street, suburb, village or town, district, country, continent.

c) Cultural categories: Language, religion, philosophy of life (or what of late has come to be called "way of life"), similarity of conception and aim in science or art.

d) *Social-economic categories:* Social circle (clique), club, trade or profession, class; also party.

e) *Purposive groups:* All groups where an expressly stated material purpose or aim appears as the reason for group formation. Purposive groups of course are also based on a similarity of conceptions; on the other hand, nearly every organised group adopts an aim of sorts, even if it is only defined as the protection of group interests. Political parties may in a certain sense also be defined as purposive groups, though their programme is usually formulated from case to case and their basis is either social-economic or founded on a common philosophy of life.

Our catalogue of group categories fails to account for the state. We have already indicated that the state is merely an organisational structure which the principal groups tend to assume; where they succeed, the demarcation line of the state will, admittedly, rarely coincide in all respects with that of the groups which have constituted themselves into it. Strategical considerations, often of a geographical nature, will commonly cause foreign groups to be pressed into the framework. But such, so to say, accessory entities are subjected to more or less consciously purposeful attempts at absorption by the ruling groups.

The several groups over which man distributes the exercise of his group function assume in his eyes different degrees of importance, due to the different nature of their categories. Obviously groups differ in their relative extent, in their constancy of form, the degree of their permanence, their activity; these differences determine from time to time the share of any given group in the group function of the individual, that is to say, its qualifications for satisfying the needs which the group function serves; a qualification depending on the elements of similarity on the basis of which the group is formed, or which have developed within the group in the course of its existence, and which therefore *characterise* it: the group *characteristics*.

First amongst them ranks the conception which the group forms of its import and purpose: the group *ideology.*

3. Group Characteristics

As group characteristics we must therefore qualify those elements of similarity which characterise all members of the group and which distinguish them from members of other groups of the same category. The dark skin of the Negro, the light complexion of the white, are the predominant characteristics of their respective races; the French language unites the Frenchman and the Walloon, the English tongue the American, Englishman, Irishman and Scot within one language group; the Roman creed and rite are group characteristics for the Catholic, the Protestant tenets and devotional practice for the Protestant; the free trader is hallmarked by his belief in the advantages of free trade, the protectionist by his conviction of the efficacy of tariffs; and the group characteristic of the Blankshire football team is a blue jersey with red shorts, while that of the Botherhampton club is a red jersey with blue shorts.

Obviously, these characteristics do not rank equally. We may distinguish those which men bear with them from birth, which are inherent in their blood: these are *invariant group characteristics.* They include all those mental and physical qualities which determine a man's place in his biological groups. In respect of religion, language, manners and customs, the situation is somewhat different. Man can learn a foreign language, and sometimes even achieve command of it; at not too advanced an age he may acquire the manners of a different social class: his religion (*) he can even change with a certain degree of facility; and the man who throughout his life maintains unchanged opinions on politics, science and art, is probably something of an exception. The relative groups can therefore be said to possess and confer variable group characteristics. The hallmarks of the football club, again, are not only variable, but artificial.

_____

(*) Or his religions community; which is all that need concern us here.

Artificial characteristics have a great attraction for groups, particularly for those whose natural marks cannot readily be recognised at sight but whose members wish to display their group solidarity in a way that strikes the eye. For the group characteristic is the distinguishing element: it is the banner and uniform of the group struggle; and where the individual has not received any visible mark from his group, a distinctive badge must be found instead. Intended as marks of recognition in battle, the artificial group characteristics become objects of ostentatious adoration; they become the focus of all those sensitivities which are implied in the psychological elements of the struggle. For the essence of the struggle is often far less the actual fighting than an attempt to prejudicate its results by a threatening display of force and power, by demonstrating a contempt of the adversary's might intended to weaken his self-assertion, in short: by intimidating him. Prestige and honour are less the belief in one's own power than the fearsome impression of it which is to be made on the opponent; wherefore any doubt of the efficacy of this power—and abuse is such a doubt—is felt as an insult. All these sentiments which accompany the struggle are by preference centered on the artificial group characteristic, which symbolises the purposes of the group: the struggle. And on this symbol the principal justification of the struggle, the consciousness of the group's value, is transferred. The group takes pride in its emblem and its flag. The symbol becomes the embodiment of the principal means of intimidation, the group's authority: the flag is the incarnation of group honour. An insult of the flag is therefore no mere incident, but wounds the whole of collective group sensitivity in its most sensitive spot; in group struggle, the artificial group characteristic is of no mean importance as a cause of conflicts, and of overwhelming weight as a tactical means of recognition. But it cannot decide the importance of the group as such; it derives all its value from the group for which it serves as an emblem.

The inner importance of a group is the greater, the more invariant group characteristics it confers upon its members and the more essential are the factors of human personality which it does so confer.

Each human individual is of course a separate entity, distinct from all others; individual differences exist, though one may attribute little weight to them. But they appear, in fact, remarkably insignificant as soon as one observes a sufficient number of people who have several of the main groups in common. In an ethnically highly homogeneous nation with only slight variations of type like the Dutch, let us, for instance, consider the boys and girls of undergraduate age, the men, the women of say, the higher middle class: they all have the same looks and manners; speak with the same accent (with slight vocal variants), have the same inclinations, feelings, interests—, morals; they all approximately think and say the same things. Mentally, the uniformity is possibly even more pronounced than physically: there are of course differences of opinion on all and every subject; but they are the same kind of opinions and the same kind of differences. The individual presents itself as no more than a representative of the group average, as some sort of sample card of group characteristics. So we come to realise the importance of groups for the individual, who owes to them the greater part of his personality.

Those groups which are characterised by invariant qualities naturally rank first: for their characteristics are a man's heritage from his birth; they are an integral part of his mind and body; he cannot change them even if he should wish to do so; *with or against his will,* he must fight under their sign. His fate is unalterably bound to that of his biological groups. And as, for tactical reasons, it is the ethnical group which is particularly appropriate for large mass collisions, it is the ethnical group which has achieved so outstanding a historical importance. It has a great stability and power of resistance, for its members always remain at its disposal. It persists throughout history, for its characteristics are automatically transferred from generation to generation. Groups with variant characteristics are less stable; their extent may change with comparative suddenness; but they are capable of deriving the energy for a great development of forces from a vigorous group ideology, and if this ideology fulfills certain requirements they may persist for a considerable period, even by historical standards; of which more presently, when group ideology will be discussed.

The group characteristics are those elements in which man sees the embodiment and symbol of the advantages and amenities offered to him by his own group; they are—and this is particularly important in the case of large and widespread groups—the passkey to these advantages. The group's consciousness of its own value, summarised in the group symbol, is also transferred to all other group characteristics. The group member takes pride in them. The instinct of group preservation, a continuation and expansion of the individual preservation instinct, finds its expression in the zeal with which variant group characteristics are maintained and in the embittered resolution with which, without regard to their practical value, they are defended against all comers. If, on the other hand, the will to preserve a certain group is lost, that is to say, if its members conceive the desire of belonging to a foreign group (not too rare an occurrence in cases of slavery, whether actual or mental), then there arises an inner loathing against the invariant, and a conscious suppression of the variant group characteristics of the own group. The invariant characteristics of the foreign group become the object of nostalgic admiration and of comical imitation, the variant characteristics are greedily adopted.

But apart from the degenerate symptoms of slavery, the characteristics of *foreign* groups are the first and foremost target of group enmity. In them the conception of enmity finds its focus of attack; to them hate applies its destructive tactics of derogation and deprecation which are still to be described; *even as the own characteristics are objects of pride, so do those of the foreign group evoke contempt; they are regarded not only as symbols but as actual evidence of the foreign group's inferiority.*

When we shall discuss single group categories and group antagonism, we shall yet have to refer to group characteristics; so far, they have mainly appeared to us as passive elements, of importance for the coherence and resistance, and to some extent for the historical persistence, of the group. But this persistence is in part co-determined by an active element from which the group derives to a considerable extent its qualifications as a fighting organisation and which determines the extent of the development of power of which it is capable: *the group ideology;* which is to some degree present in all groups, highly developed in most, and demands separate discussion.

4. *Group Ideology*

In our chapter on the origin of enmity we have discussed the conceptions of right and wrong which occur in connection with the expression of enmity and without which it is actually impossible that any unfriendly feelings are directed against a person. The need for the justification of enmity is so compulsive that man would vindicate his very existence, which he must maintain by struggle. And vindication he finds in the consciousness of his own *value,* for his value is the expression of his importance for any cause in particular and for the community in general. And even as unfavourable valuation—the notion that he is bad or dangerous, or at any rate useless-stamps a man as the object of permissible enmity, so favourable valuation becomes for the individual that would struggle for his existence, a justification for his struggle and for the expression of enmity which it needs involves.

No need to stress that, here as much as, and more than, elsewhere, judgment is the prisoner of self-centered consciousness, so that man cannot but be convinced of his own value. As long as the will to live is not wholly broken, no experience, be it ever so bitter, is able to uproot this conviction from the primordial depth of the ego. Man's conviction of his own value springs from the preference—understandable yet often absurd to objective judgment—for his own self and the chance complex of his qualities. He may often and in many respects desire to become different from what he happens to be; still he is obsessed by the irresistible inclination to regard his own qualities as in some way excellent and to adorn all that concerns him closely with a special nattering valuation. The poor man would fain be rich; but as long as he is not, he discovers in his poverty a thousand virtues which he denies to opulence. And should opulence become his share, then he will discover that the poverty which before was merely unpleasant is now wretched; while the riches which formerly seemed wicked are now in his eyes adorned by ennobling dignity. The unsophisticated, little aware of the effect of their words, speak by preference of themselves, of their qualities and conditions, and argue their excellence. But even the less simple-minded often lack the self-control which should have prevented the revelatory expression of self-admiration.

The form in which the consciousness of own value appears is, one might say, activated: expressing itself in the exercise of its function as the conception of a task, a mission which man has to fulfill within and towards the community. And as in its sublimated form consciousness of value grows into a conviction of being chosen, so the idea of a task is occasionally heightened to the conviction of a special destination, of a function exclusively imposed on the individual by virtue of the excellence of his qualities. Usually, though, there is little more than the feeling that one takes a more or less important place within the community; the modest ambition of the average man consists in the desire that on his sudden decease he may leave a gap which is at least felt for the moment. But at any rate he wants to believe that his life does not benefit only himself, but some greater entity.

The same premises on which the individual ego is enlarged and absorbed into the group also determine the transference of the individual consciousness of value and belief in a mission to that of the group. Here, too, the group assumes the exercise of that part of the function which is too hard for the individual. The belief in own excellence and in the importance of the personal mission is too ready a target for the criticism of reason and experience; the belief may persist in some obscure sphere of emotional life, but it dare not face the light of controlling thought; it must go without the so ardently desired confirmation by that mental function of little fertility but great repute: reason. And it is this confirmation which is provided by the group. Only an infinitely small minority of people are so gifted that they can find sufficient authority in reason for the belief in the outstanding value of their contribution to the welfare of the whole or any considerable part of humanity; and therefore for the belief in the greatness of their own value and their own mission (incidentally, these are the people who tend most towards isolation, as in this respect at any rate they do not need the group; just as richness of mind generally favours individual isolation). The group, however, is large enough to obviate the invidious comparison which in the individual case so often causes disillusion, and to draw its sting even for the most modest. In respect of the groups to which he belongs, particularly the larger and more important ones, man can freely and uncontradicted by cavilling reason form any desired conception of superiority. The foreign groups which might furnish the disillusioning comparison, are always remote; moreover, the standard of comparison is provided by the own group, so that otherness is in any case regarded as inferiority: *the irresistible inclination to ascribe superiority to all that is one's own can find its unimpeded expression in the group.* Likewise, it is far easier to ascribe a mission towards humanity to the group. The sudden disappearance of a group of any considerable extent would indeed leave a noticeable gap and create a disturbance; so that its very existence fulfills a function of importance. Also, the concept of a positive mission of universal scope, highly speculative as it must of its nature always be, is more readily connected with a whole which survives the span of individual life, such as the group.

And indeed: *we* actually find in every group an ideology which has developed consciousness of value into a feeling of superiority. It corresponds with the special preference of the members for their group and its characteristics; it corresponds with the conception of a mission amongst and for humanity; even with comparatively unimportant groups the idea of a mission forms an ideological superstructure of quite universal scope. For not only the world religion and the empire regard it as their task to build a better world; in the last instance, even the football club wants to serve the brotherhood of mankind, while the choral society works for the betterment of the human soul.

Working for improvement presupposes that there are all kinds of things to be improved in, about, or amongst humanity. The mission idea is therefore based on some dissatisfaction. Now dissatisfaction is a form of suffering of which we believe that we know the cause; which therefore becomes a focus of attraction for feelings of enmity which demand discharge; and which in the discerned cause find the more readily their justification, as their discharge can direct itself against those guilty of and responsible for the abuses concerned, whose removal would be to the general benefit of humanity. Thus the idea of the mission not only justifies defensive self-preservation, but most vigorous deployment and even a powerful struggle for expansion. The war is not only just, but holy. To reach its aim, no sacrifice is too great; particularly if those to be sacrificed are those who, actually or allegedly, stand in the way of its attainment; hostile action which otherwise would meet with general condemnation becomes a sacred charge; for the group's mission ordains a relentless struggle against all who resist the benefit of the mission. In this way the group develops its group ideology into an idea of justification which supplies it with the psychological prerequisites for the expression of enmity to any desired extent.

The power of the mission idea and the sublimity of the mission are commensurate with the depth of the feeling of superiority. An important, powerful, and therefore militant group will ever develop an important mission; and an important mission, again, is capable of assembling around its banner the militant elements from numerous groups of other categories and to transfer upon them a consciousness of superiority deriving from its exalted idea. In groups of the biological category the group ideology therefore has the appearance of an ideological superstructure, while in groups which can be selected at will, such as those of political or religious nature, the group mission appears as the element which determines the attraction, and therefore also the impetus of the group. With groups of the latter type, ideology also becomes a determinant factor for the continuity of the group. For the more concrete the aim of the mission, the easier can it be attained; or the sooner does it become evident that the chosen aim cannot be realised by the recommended means. Thus political parties, which expect the salvation of mankind from the introduction of certain forms of government, from the enforcement of certain distributions of power, or from similar measures, often perish by the very realisation of their demands, because the expected salvation does not materialise. Those groups, on the other hand, which defer liberation from what they regard as the evils of this world to some beyond (which at any rate is beyond control) , or make it depend upon demands on man which cannot be realised, may be expected to last long; if only because the insufficiency of the measures applied can be proved by no experience. The importance of a well-developed group ideology is so great that no movement of any considerable extent can deploy itself without it, and that even biological groups must frequently be inoculated from outside with a vigorous group ideology.

The sufferings of a certain group may have stultified its sensitivity, impaired its consciousness of value, paralysed its capacity for acting to such an extent that it is no longer capable of any vigorous expression of enmity. The masses which now are the carriers of the socialist idea have not themselves produced the conception of their mission; it had to be inculcated into them from outside; the mirror of their misery had first to be held up before their eyes, their consciousness of value had to be awakened from the stupor of slavery, they had to be shown ways of liberation and a responsibility for themselves and humanity, before they could gird their loins for battle. The renascence movement of an ethnical-national group, for instance that of the Jews, follows the same lines. Physical and mental misery of a probably unprecedented degree had had so stupefying an influence that considerable parts had lost all trace of the will to group preservation, and that even today many members of the group are only prevented from the flight into a foreign group by the inherent difficulties, which in an ethnical group are, of course, formidable. The ideology of this renascence movement is of Jewish origin; but it had, strictly speaking, to be brought to the nation by one of its sons who had traveled far on the path of alienation. And even so the deeply buried consciousness of value has again and again to be uncovered with endless pains, the normal sensitivity to suffering has again to be evoked. Only when this has been done, the imposed historical task can take hold of the people's minds and give the impulse to a deployment of energy which at times even astonishes its carriers.

In order to energise the idea of universality, the group ideology must invest its aims with the character of a definite purpose, a purpose which must naturally derive from the category; the social group will find a social, the religious group a religious purpose for its ideology, and the struggle against other men is directed against the enemies of the ideological aim; the battleground lies therefore in the field of the same category in which the group ideology has originated; wherefore *a group always fights another group of the same category.*

Finally, the group ideology is a co-determinant of the rank taken by several groups within the consciousness of the individual which belongs to all of them. This rank follows from differences in the degree of domination exercised by the groups upon the individual which is part of them. But this phenomenon had better be discussed after some of the more important group categories will have been dealt with in detail.

5. *Biological Categories*

The biological categories, as far as they concern our investigations, consist of the family, the *gens* or clan, the tribe, the nation and the race. (Occasionally, sex and age-group also provide demarcation lines for group formation, but such groups rarely attain organised form and are of subordinate historical importance.) The *dan* has lost much of its former influence; though a degree of coherence between cognates and agnates often persist beyond the strict family level, it rarely exceeds sentimental associations and preferential treatment in matters of mutual aid; and except on the dynastic and pseudo-dynastic (e.g. Krupp) level, its influence on the affairs of civilised humanity is now negligible (*). The term *"tribe"* is also best reserved for primitive conditions: there it means a community held together more or less closely by common descent and an internal rule based on some principle of relationship, and readily recognised by distinctive customs.

But if these categories are easily defined, the terms *nation* and *race* cause quite inordinate difficulties. To some extent this is due (and possibly no one is more aware of the fact than the author of this book) to the different ways in which these expressions are used in different languages; and as writers dealing with the subjects in question must needs use sources written in foreign tongues, much confusion would arise even from this cause alone. Worse, possibly, is the effect of the multitude of categories to be defined and named, and the paucity of words to name them by: the term *race* has to serve as the denomination of anything from the sub-species of *homo sapiens* (if that still has any precise scientific meaning) to larger tribes; "nation" may, *inter alia,* mean a

---

(*) It may be as well to stipulate that "civilised" and "civilisation" refer exclusively to what may be more precisely termed the European-American civilisation, unless the context demands otherwise; and that these terms are not of necessity to be constructed as implying any valuation.

group of more or less common descent organised as a state, an immediate sub-group of such a group, a group of this character aspiring to state organisation or to separate organisation within a state, or a host of other variants. "People", another word of the same family (and one which we studiously have tried to, and shall try to, avoid unless by its use we may escape a *petitio principii)* is, except in "We, the people" and similar phrases (where it means the constituents of the state as distinguished from, and as constituents of, the government), still less precise; being usually nothing but a much vaguer synonym of "nation", whatever that may from case to case signify.

But the greatest difficulty in the application of all these terms is a psychological one, caused by the very nature of definitions. We have had occasion to make some remarks on the subject before; and will now merely point out that it is the unfortunate but common practice amongst controversial writers on these matters (and which writer is not, after all, controversial?) first to decide on the conclusion which they wish to draw and then to adapt their definition to their aims. This would be fair enough practice, if the different actual usage would not continuously confuse the reader, and if this confusion would not, consciously or unconsciously, be utilised to force false conclusions. No need to quote instances: the technique is a favourite one in war literature and opposite loci can be found in any ten chance books excluding mathematics and chemistry.

For our purposes, "nation" may be best defined as a group characterised by a community of descent and history, which forms, or in the relevant past has formed, a political entity, and inhabits, or has in the relevant past inhabited, a common territory. As for "race", we would prefer to see the expression confined to the use of stockbreeders and biologists not concerned with the primates; but as we shall hardly be able to escape its application to human relations, it had best be reserved for those major groups which are most readily recognised by their pigmentation. For though it is not uncommon to designate, for instance, the whole of the nations of Teutonic descent as the Teutonic race, contrasting this with, say, the Celtic and Slav races, we seem to discern biological entities of still wider scope; skin pigmentation used to be regarded as their distinctive characteristic, but intermediate forms are so frequent as to cause insurmountable difficulties; while attempts to use other body characteristics have led to no result (*) and the historical conclusions drawn from them are purely arbitrary. But though inadequate as a theoretical basis, similarity of colouring is in the actual realm of group formation liable to function as a uniting element wherever it is supported by obvious contrasts. The effect is proportional to the strength of the contrasts; for their function is that of a uniform distinguishing between friend and enemy: one of the principal requirements of the group, which, being an instrument of strife, gravitates towards the conditions most favourable for strife. All other considerations are of subordinate importance. If the most favourable conditions for struggle are to be found in other fields, even the most fundamental differences of pigmentation may of course lose their separating effect.

There can be no doubt that the biological-ethnical cate-

_____

(*) Anthropologists never lose hope. Comparatively recent research calculates a factor from a combination of the facial angle and blood ratio indices; but the method seems to be applicable to distinctions between tribes rather than on the larger scale.

gories are historically the original ones. Where their pattern is at a later stage modified and interrupted by other categories, (sometimes, for instance, determined by language and quite often by religion), these categories originally coincided with them. Their influence is so strong that groups of other categories which extend over several ethnical groups are from place to place subject to characteristic modification by the underlying ethnical category, as can be easily observed in world religions like the Islam and the Roman Church. This strong influence is to be attributed to the many important and invariant characteristics which the ethnical group confers on its members: identities and similarities which are inherent in the blood and cannot, therefore, be changed at will. Man can, if he so desires and if the circumstances are favourable, change groups in all other categories; but into his ethnical group he enters by virtue and at the moment of his birth, and at no later stage can he leave it. Man can neither choose nor change his biological groups. At most he can, by marrying a member of a foreign group, leave it indirectly; then his descendants may, after a few miscegenerations, submerge in the foreign group, unless the original differences are too great. This, consequently, is the only form in which, technically, a declining ethnical group may be absorbed by a foreign group. The individual as such is for the duration of his life chained to his ethnical group.

Since the characteristics of the ethnical group are inherent in the blood, they also determine the most important qualities of body and mind. For the individual, these characteristics are therefore a signal part of his individual personality. In momentous attributes of the body and in the most minute ramifications of the mind, the ethnical group finds its expression. Thus it becomes of even more positive importance to the individual.

Probably, it is only due to natural defects in our capacities of observation that we often meet with certain difficulties in describing the group characteristics of ethnical groups. In the case of the largest and, notwithstanding all intermediate forms, obviously very old ones, the racial groups, the physical characteristics are immediately apparent. It may very well be impossible to establish the existence, limits and extent of a general Negro race; but it is a fact that the Northern European belongs to another major ethnical group than the Central African, and that the differences in the physical characteristics of the two races can be easily described. On the other hand, we cannot gain any precise insight into the psychological structure of the foreign greater ethnical groups; for the observation of such a structure demands a certain nearness and understanding. In the case of our own race, again, we lack the oversight needed to perceive mental traits of general validity on account of insufficient distance and of interference by the differences between subordinate groups which obtrude themselves to the eye. In respect of minor ethnical groups nearer to us, on the other hand, we are highly sensitive to their psychological structure, while the distinction of definite somatic types is less easy. There is some belief that it is possible to discern a French, English, Spanish, American somatic type; but even in a comparatively much older entity of common descent such as the Jewish one, there is, at least in Southern Europe and the Near East, a plenitude of cases in which the physical type does not suffice to establish the ethnical group to which they belong (*).

When we discussed Jewish qualities we already drew attention to the difficulties encountered in *describing* mental characteristics, even where clearly discerned. Here, we only would point out the fundamental difference between psychological functions and mental contents. Psychological functions are obviously innate; their exercise can be improved by training, but the improvement is subject to limits which are likewise innate. For the very conception of psychological characteristics presupposes—contrary, by the way, to the idea of free volition— their invariability. Mental *contents,* on the other hand, that is to say, the *objects of thought and feeling,* seem mainly to depend on external circumstances, though it may be claimed that their selection is to a certain extent determined by the mental structure. Man is born with the tendency to think precisely or vaguely, swiftly or slowly, in abstract concepts or in concrete images; he is gifted with serene or violent, subtle or obtuse, deep or superficial feelings; but the objects of his thinking and feeling, be its nature whatever it may be, are supplied by the external circumstances of his time and surroundings. And because within a general cultural frame mental functions

---

(*) In fact, the situation is even far more complicated. To keep for a moment to the Jews: Jews living, even for one generation, amongst any given nation assume to a certain degree the superficial characteristics, even the physical ones, of that nation. The result is possibly nowhere as apparent as in present-day Palestine: for the Jew from Western Europe it is difficult and occasionally impossible to distinguish between Arabs and Jews from the Arab countries; and even for the Palestinian Arab (who, in his way, is as much of a mixture as the Jew) there are occasional difficulties. But if neither the Dutch Gentile nor the Dutch Jew can distinguish a Salonican Jew from his surroundings, the Salonican Jew and Gentile are perfectly able to do so. And we may rest assured that, though even a Lebanese or Iraqi Arab may be in doubt whether he has to do with an Arab or a Jew from the Yemen, both the Yemenite Arab and the Yemenite Jew will be perfectly certain.

produce, as it were, a corresponding precipitate in the realm of contents which is capable of being transmitted and particularly of being communicated to the younger generation through the channels of education, the mistaken impression arises as if, together with the mental contents, the psychological functions can also be taken over or even acquired at will. Thence the belief in the possibility of a voluntary change, or at least adaptation, of psychological *functions;* a belief which plays so strange a part in internal Jewish discussions. No one can escape the realisation that the Jewish facial type is an invariant element of the Jewish individual's group heritage; but Jewish mentality is by preference regarded as an empty container which may be filled with any desired group culture; and it is supposed that the filling process implies the taking over of the relative group mentality in all the peculiarities of its functions. But actually, the fact that we find the Jew as the exponent of some fashionable idea of Western provenience is no evidence as to the nature of his mentality; for the idea is merely mental content. What is of importance, is his tendency to acquire such contents; the ease with which he incorporates them; the obstinacy with which he champions them; the often peculiar and characteristic nature of the process of mental integration. In the particular case of the Jew, incidentally, the combination of close contact in space and a great mental distance creates outstanding possibilities of observation and understanding.

As the ethnical group cannot be abandoned by its members, it possesses, more than any other category, those passive qualities which invest this category with so prominent a share in the severest group conflicts in history. The groups of this category can only be made to disappear by the annihilation of all their individuals; the ethnical group can always command the services of its members, and they, in turn, take a natural interest in the fate of the group which is so closely linked to theirs. They are forced, willy-nilly, to fight in its ranks, for any enmity directed against their group involves them personally: their honour, their repute, their life and goods are welded to the fortune of the ethnical group. Throughout history the scheme of division for group collisions has often been furnished by totally different groups; in fact one could hardly mention a category which has not at one time or another served that purpose; for expression of enmity is the purpose of group formation, and feelings of hate sometimes grow riotous enough to find a way even where conditions for struggle are comparatively unfavourable. But in all struggle throughout history one can discern an ethnical pattern as substrate, and even where ethnical groups have for a time been split up between enemy camps of other categories, they have always shown a tendency to unite according to their own category. States always tend, in the interest of their stability and fighting power, to base themselves on a homogeneous ethnical group which becomes the principal, or at least dominating, element. Finally, the qualification of the ethnical group as the historical element of conflict also derives from the readily distinguished emblems provided by its many momentous and invariant characteristics. The flag is the symbol and signal of preparedness for battle; an emblem immediately stamps the member of a group as such. And though the overriding influence of the urge to find expression for hate may create antagonies between groups which are distinguished by nothing except the mere fact of their separate existence;

though it makes it possible even for the most dissimilar races to unite against a common enemy; yet the natural tension will, in the absence of influences which point another way, always be greatest where ethnical categories with the most considerable differences in characteristics come into contact. America has its fair share of antisemitism; but the hate of the Negro exceeds that of the Jew by far.

In the ethnical group the group ideology expresses itself in both of its aspects; usually it is highly developed. Unless an ethnical group has sunk into a condition of mental serfdom, one discerns a strongly emotional feeling of superiority which strives to become conscious as an often immoderate contempt of other groups and which is not infrequently exalted into a conviction of being elected. Verily, not only the Jews regard themselves as the chosen people; if the attempt were made, it might well prove easier to enumerate the nations which do not believe that they are chosen than those which do. The Arabs regard themselves as the chosen people of the Islam; and as they, naturally, regard the Islam as the chosen religion, the restrictive clause is hardly operative. The German believes that the German way of life is to be the salvation of the world (*) ; the Frenchman regards his nation as the leader and pioneer of all civilisation; the Englishman is convinced that Providence has appointed him to bear the white man's burden. In milder cases contempt for other nations is accompanied by the conviction that they are to be pitied for being different and that they ought at least to attempt to render themselves more similar to the ideal conception of the own nation; though at

---

(*) "Am deutschen Wesen wird die Welt, genesen."

the same time there is a no less positive conviction that such an attempt must lead to an at least partial failure. Expansive nations have a way of incessantly stressing their belief in their own superiority, of which they would forever convince the whole world; but even more quiescent nations foster a thorough admiration for their real or imaginary national qualities and regard them as a most definite advantage; amongst themselves they may indulge in some mild mockery, but woe to the stranger who spits into their ocean: irony at one's own expense is often nothing but a self-conscious expression of vanity.

The practical importance of being conscious of one's own value is fully realised by the ethnical group. The education of the younger generation aims at the reproduction of consciousness of value in its most pronounced form. This purpose is served by the way in which the group history is conveyed. The very existence of a long historical record is regarded as proof of excellence: what could maintain itself for so long a time must needs possess exceptional qualities: a long history is regarded as a good cause for glorification. Furthermore, leading personalities are transformed into heroic figures, and the whole history is (unconsciously) subjected to that cosmetical operation by which persons and actions regarded favourably are shifted into the foreground; while these embellishments are yet underscored by painting the group's enemies in correspondingly black colours. For valuation is an expression of love and hate. When we discussed Jewish inferiority, we already drew attention to the curious circumstance that the writing of history is nothing so much as a meting out of love and hate, projected backwards and consisting in the attribution of positively valued facts, actions and qualities to the own, and the opposite to the enemy group.

The most invigorating food for the ethnical group's self-admiration is commonly found in that precipitate of the group's mental life which we are wont to call "national culture". Strictly speaking, it forms a group category in its own right; for the national culture's substrate of forms and thought contents is capable of being taken over—and is indeed often enough taken over, in whole or in part—by members of foreign ethnical groups. In Western and Central Europe, for instance, the cultures of the nations concerned have to all intents and purposes been assumed by the ethnically quite different Jewish groups, which may without any reserve be regarded as belonging to the German, English, French, etc., *cultural* groups. The boundaries of cultural groups need not, therefore, coincide with those of the ethnical entities. But that ethnical group which sets its imprint upon the national culture regards it as its own product; and so the cultural characteristics become variable, but highly valued characteristics of the ethnical group. So high is the regard in which national culture is held, that by far the greater part of the nation's consciousness of value derives from it: while its suitability for being transferred upon other groups makes it an unparalleled catchword for expansion, as it enables the ethnical group to envisage its lust for domination and desire for expansion as the praiseworthy impulse to communicate to other nations the blessings of its own, highly esteemed culture: in fine, as something which ranks high in the generally accepted scale of values, as a *cultural mission.* And to such an extent does consciousness of superiority depend on the pride which derives from the possession of an own group culture, that oppressed and enslaved nations are rarely able to cast off their shackles unless they have first regained an awareness of their own value through a revival of their national culture, and thus found force and will for deeds of liberation. A cultural-literary renascence often precedes political liberation movements.

Formerly, and to a certain extent even today, the ethnical group was wont to identify itself with a group based on religion or on a philosophy of life; for these criteria are usually also of high repute, suitable for providing the idea of a mission, and even more readily taken over (and therefore suitable for export) than a national culture.

Languages do not share the general appreciation as products of culture which, for instance, the arts, literature and science enjoy. They only participate in the cultural aspect of the group mission because they give access to the most important products of group culture. But the propagation of a language also creates important relations, mainly of an economic nature and favours contacts which, by way of penetration, may lead to the subjection or even to the absorption of the foreign group; it is rather a technical means of expansion, and only in a subordinate sense of content of the group mission. It is, incidentally, not without interest to observe how the U.S.S.R. today uses a group ideology of originally social-economic provenience in exactly the same way as formerly the Christian, later the Catholic and in some cases the Protestant states, yet later monarchies and republics, and at present more particularly totalitarian and democratic states have used and still use ideologies which were to be or have been incorporated in the anatomy of the body political. Like them, the U.S.S.R. also propagates its ideas abroad and attempts, through the adherents gained for them in foreign parts, to exercise an influence which is to serve the state's need for expansion. (*)

In general, the ideology of the ethnical group has the advantage of being primitive: consciousness of superiority will not be denied, and the idea of a mission which derives from it, whether in addition relying on national culture and religion or not, will not lightly fail by reason of the mission's partial realisation. For there always remain nations enough to be made happy by cultural and religious blessings; and a culture can rarely, a religion never, be convicted of being unable to bring about the salvation of mankind.

We would, therefore, expect the primitivity of its group ideology to guarantee the ethnical group a long life in history. If we find, nevertheless, that religious groups not infrequently outlast the ethnical ones, we must reflect that the struggle between ethnical groups may mean a decisive loss of power, and even slavery, for the vanquished. Moreover, ethnical groups are subject to ups and downs ruled by purely physiological influences; they may even be totally annihilated, like the American Red Indians. A group based on a religion or a philosophy of life can, however, if its ideology is sufficiently attractive, again and again recruit new members amongst all possible ethnical groups; and as the psychological needs which are satisfied by such ideologies are of a highly universal nature, they may find their adherents at all times and amongst the most heterogeneous elements. Particularly when an ethnical group is declining, when its consciousness of value has diminished and its missionary idea has suffered a

---

(*) And, looking back after 25 years, the same may be said of the "Western Democracies". — 1949.

commensurate loss of power, these remaining elements which have still retained their vitality tend to gravitate towards other groups of a non-ethnical nature to which they have access; there they are attracted by a group ideology which promises their individual need for struggle that satisfaction which the ethnical group can no longer provide.

6. *Cultural Categories*

More than any other element, a common language promotes that reciprocal understanding amongst men which favours the formation of groups; particularly so, because a common language is an immediately effective means of communication in any place, and therefore is favourable to the development of groups which extend over a wide area. But as language groups are closely connected with the principal ethnical groups, often coincide with them, sometimes outreach them, but rarely run counter to an ethnical group pattern, the independent importance of language groups is inconsiderable. The case of the Jews, where the ethnical group has been dismembered into countless language groups, is an exception as abnormal as the Jewish diaspora itself. The language problems which occur in a number of countries are actually due to the struggle of rival ethnical groups within one state structure.

As a result of the great distance which differences of language create among men, language is an excellent means of delimitation between groups. Where different language groups meet there usually exists, therefore, a tension as pronounced as that commonly found on ethnical frontiers, even where the case is one of ethnical groups which are closely akin and cannot, or not easily, be distinguished by their characteristics, but which use different languages. The German-Danish border tension is a characteristic instance.

Quite different from the importance of the language groups is that of the groups based on religion or philosophy of life. Originally, religious conceptions have probably arisen from ethnical groups, and even now they are continuously influenced by the ethnical substrate. But the psychological function of the religious mind— which, incidentally, is subject to far-reaching individual differentiation—finds its concrete form in concepts which readily become uniform and which, being mental contents, can readily be transferred. The rites and customs which symbolise these concepts and which are the means of communicating with the godhead in the most important moments of life, are artificial and variable but by divine sanction strongly vested group characteristics, and even more suitable for transfer. In addition, it is the easier for the individual to change his religious group, as it is hardly feasible to examine his real religious convictions; wherefore acceptance of the ritual, accompanied by a formal endorsement of the creed, must needs suffice. History therefore knows religious groups of outstanding importance which have dissociated themselves from all ethnical connections and exist as independent groups. When we consider how difficult it is for men to understand each other, be they ever so close, and how deep clefts can be created by differences of opinion on comparatively trivial matters, we realise the advantages for group formation provided by a common religious conviction; advantages supported by common rites and customs which leave their imprint on the most important and usually even on the most intimate aspects of daily

life, and by the urge for communal religious exercises. Consequently, the religious groups take an important part in the exercise
of the human group function, both in its inward aspect of embody-
ing loving-kindness, and in its outward aspect of expressing hate.
In times of pronounced predominance of religious conceptions,
the religious groups temporarily supplanted the ethnical groups
in the exercise of the principal group functions and provided the
scheme of division for the most enormous mass conflicts. In such
times they even showed the beginnings of a tendency to form independent states; but these, sooner or later, always reverted to the
frame of ethnically determined political entities, though within
the state religion often became the dominating characteristic, as
it provided a highly attractive group ideology.

It would seem that the ease with which group characteristics
are transferred tends to have an adverse influence on the dura-
bility of religious groups. And indeed, their extent and limits
fluctuate to a considerable degree, except where the religious
group is closely linked with an ethnical one. Nevertheless, the
religious group characteristics have a stronghold in the psychological needs from which they have arisen; and a group ideology which originates in the most fundamental and ubiquitous
necessities of existence is the more certain of finding adherents
ever and again, as its ideology contains the more positive and
authoritative consolations and promises of relief from the evils
of life and death. Such an ideology is practically indestructible as
its inadequacy can never be proved in reality; and the objections of the critical mind are eventually always overridden by
the force of the need for the satisfaction of which the ideology has been evolved. We may, moreover, remark that the far-

reaching inner similarity of religious ideologies does little to make a change of group attractive; wherefore such changes are rarely the result of an inner urge, and are usually caused by direct or indirect compulsion. Conversions are, in the overwhelming majority of cases, either imposed by force or due to the attraction of economic and social advantages.

As an instrument for the exercise of group functions the religious group differs in no way from groups of other categories; and the predominance of this exercise is no less than elsewhere. Internally, the religious group serves the satisfaction of many social, and particularly religious, needs; externally, it is an instrument of struggle, and as such sometimes expansive, sometimes exclusive. Exclusivity as a strategical measure is in the case of ethnical groups of lesser importance, as there the intrusion of foreign elements is in any case difficult; for expansion, the religious group has a particularly suitable weapon in its ideology. Out of their very nature, religious conceptions must claim universal validity; and their extension to the whole of mankind appears as the natural consequence of their essence, as soon as the urge for expansion needs justification. Some religions expressly ordain expansion; but it would be an error to ascribe the expansivity of these religions to such ordinances. The urge for expansion is inherent in all viable groups, as long as expansion is expected to result in an increase of power; which for ethnical groups is not always, and for social groups almost never the case, wherefore they seek their strength in *exclusivity*. And religious groups may, notwithstanding all divine ordinances, *cease* to be expansive, if the superior power of rival groups forces them into a defensive position, or if, as in modern times, they have lost their strength by a partial devaluation of their ideology. The Christian religions, for instance, may be regarded as having ceased to be expansive at the end of the nineteenth century, with the minor exception of some colonial missionarism—which, moreover, was by no means free of a secular-imperialistic odour; and Protestantism, in particular, confines itself to laborious attempts to maintain its present scope. Philosophies of life of not explicitly religious nature have in the past rarely given rise to the formation of major organised groups; unorganised, but occasionally most powerful, movements have, however, regularly coagulated round any idea which could be elevated to a general principle. Such complexes of conceptions are, as we have seen, by preference incorporated in the ideologies of other categories and tend, like, for instance, the idea of religious tolerance, of democracy, or of emancipation, to become part, or even the nucleus, of ethnical group ideologies. Of late, trends of thought have tended towards the formation of organisations in their own right. It is their nature to extend to individuals who live far apart; and only recent transport facilities have made it possible for them to become regularly established in the form of international organisations.

Opinions on matters of science or art usually affect too few people to cause the formation of large groups. As *movements* or *schools* they usually lack formal organisation; a shortcoming which does not, however, prevent them from engaging in the most vicious group strife. It does not matter whether the issue is the contrast between impressionism and expressionism or the restoration of a iota subscript. The great advantage of such group formations is the circumstance that the gathering of congenial minds at the same time provides the difference of opinion which forms a pretext for enmity: some scientist need only invent a theory about the presumable shape of the moon's surface ten million years ago, and immediately two enemy camps are formed, one favouring, the other opposing his theory; the members of each of these enemy groups will regard those of the other as idiots ("an unfavourable valuation resulting from unfriendly feelings") and acquaint each other of this opinion in terms of more or less cautious circumscription ("the expression of the unfriendly feelings aforesaid").

7. *Social Categories*

Groups of the same category are almost never in a state of complete equality; as a result of group struggles (which continue even where there is no open enmity) relations of one-sided dependence develop, ranking from a slight degree of unilateral consideration consistent with the fullest formal independence to conditions of complete subservience. The legal terms which define the various forms of dependence and sovereignty reflect the real situation only in a most superficial way; even sovereign states are not equally independent; differences of power give some of them an excess of influence which in its practical effect may not differ to any extent from formal domination. For the annihilation of an enemy group to the very last member is but rarely the aim of the group struggle, as it is disadvantageous to the victor himself; and even when hate is so powerful that some group desires the annihilation of its opponent against its own interest, this aim can but rarely be achieved. Destruction of the enemy group by absorption is attempted where it is admitted by the group category (in the case of ethnical groups absorption is notoriously difficult) and where no permanent loss of strength is feared by the absorbing group, which after all must find its main force in homogeneity. If absorption also seems undesirable, *domination* of the opponent becomes the aim which, when achieved, may at the same time render him harmless and make his productive power available for exploitation by the victor.

All this had to be mentioned here, because the social groups, which are now to be discussed, exist almost invariably in conditions of obvious unilateral dependence. They therefore seem to form a vertical structure, and the upper social group usually dominates those beneath it to a considerable degree. Of late it has become fashionable to designate the social groups as classes.

In recent times the social group pattern has invariably run counter to the ethnical formation: social groups tend to connect with corresponding groups amongst foreign ethnical units. European aristocracy maintained, and still maintains, close international relations; monarchs—formerly a prosperous profession—frequently had lost all connection with the ethnical groups from which they had sprung and formed a social group which, like all social groups, kept itself closed to outsiders. At present the tendency to seek international contacts is most pronounced in the case of the lower classes, who have indeed achieved some degree, however loose, of international organisation. In olden times it was indeed the rule for the economic potential of vanquished nations to be exploited by the victor; the ethnical group was annexed in the form of a social group of slaves. Today such relations are still found in colonial countries. The inner distance between social groups which in addition are ethnically different is of course particularly large; the hostile tension as such need not be greater than that between any other two groups, for the degree of tension is not determined by the degree of difference in characteristics; but in the case of an external conflict the danger to the dominating group is larger, because it cannot enlist the solidarity of the slave group by a plea of common ethnical interests. How old this problem is, is proved by the history of the Jewish exodus from Egypt: in persecuting the Jews, the Egyptian ruler was also motivated by the fear that this ethnically foreign slave group might turn against him at the first conflict with outside forces.

Though highly interdependent, the social groups, like all groups of the same category, live in a condition of more or less pronounced tension; a fact which inescapably follows from the very purpose of group formation. Social conflicts, which are frequently regarded as characteristic of modern times, are in reality half as old as the world, and it would even seem that in the past they used to lead to sanguinary collisions more often than they do now. Social conflicts differ from those between groups of other categories in the first place by an often remarkable divergence of aim; the lower, insurgent, class often strives for the complete annihilation of the upper class, while the latter, which needs its opponents as a source of labour, only wants to dominate them. And in contradistinction to wars between ethnical groups, the social struggle never ends in the establishment of an independent state by the victorious party, but only in predominance within an ethnically determined state group. Until now it has not been proved possible for a group

consisting of one homogeneous social stratum to exist as a state
(*) . Social groups provide their members with pronounced, but
not quite invariant, characteristics. Theoretically, the individual
can change his social group, though the practical difficulties may
be great. The characteristics of the social group: habits, manners,
customs, are at the age when man commences to consider the
desirability of changing his social group usually so fixed that it is
rarely possible to achieve more than an inadequate and ridiculous
imitation of the foreign group characteristics. For the individual
as such the successful change of class must always remain the
exception; but appropriate education may even the path for his
descendants. Favoured by considerable economic changes (the
basis of social groups is mainly the economic one of similarity
of trade) extensive shifts in social grouping are with comparative
ease accomplished in the course of a single generation.

There is yet another reason for the difficulty of individual
changes of social group: the social group structure is highly
exclusive. It resists penetration by strange elements. Essentially,
of course, all groups are exclusive; they are closed to outsiders, let the admission of strangers depend on the fulfilment
of various more or less difficult conditions, and even where
their expansive tendencies are most pronounced, they regard
new members with diffidence and do not admit them to the
full enjoyment of membership rights for a long time. But some
groups, particularly those which are based on a philosophy of

----

(*) Recent Russian history and—at the other end of the scale—developments in
communal settlements in Palestine seem to warrant a more definite conclusion:
a group which at the beginning of its separate existence has no class differences,
tends to develop them. — 1949.

life and whose characteristics consist of spiritual contents, are by virtue of the nature of those characteristics better equipped for absorption; when sufficiently conscious of their own strength, they therefore admit new elements, provided these are willing to assume the new characteristics and divest themselves of the old ones. The social group, on the other hand, seeks its strength exclusively in inner homogeneity, the more so as it cannot in general expect any increase in power from an influx of new members; its force is to such a degree based on tradition and habit rather than on numerical strength, that the highest authority is always held by a minority group. Inner homogeneity is maintained by exclusivity. This, naturally, is mainly directed downwards and strongest developed in the case of the upper classes, for penetration of foreign group elements is rarely to be expected from above; where this nevertheless occurs, the lower classes also treat the intruder with the utmost reserve and distrust.

The different power position also results in fundamental differences in the ideology of social groups; for it is obvious that at different class levels the necessity for struggle will assume different forms.

The ideology of the upper class derives from an unbounded consciousness of superiority, the right and the task to lead, i.e. to rule, the lower classes. Often this task is given a religious foundation which bases the right to rule on divine sanction; but even without such a conception the feeling of superiority suffices to support the group mission; and the need for its deeper motivation is only felt when the preferential position of the ruling class is attacked.

A certain consciousness of value is also present in the

lower classes; it is based on their awareness of their indispensability, which finds its demonstration in cessation of labour, be it in the classical form of the Roman secession to the Sacred Hill or in the modern sit-down strike. But this consciousness of value, in any case somewhat negative, must first be awakened before it can express itself demonstratively; as a rule it is, like in all enslaved groups, more or less deeply buried and exists only under the surface of a jealous and hostile admiration of the upper class. The member of the lower class therefore develops, if his personal consciousness of value is not stunted, the understandable desire to leave his own social class and to join a higher one. This is called the urge to improve one's social condition.

In the large masses of the enslaved class oppression causes a loss of sensitivity for suffering which results in a life of thoughtless vegetation; suddenly increased pressure may cause a sudden, wild and unorganised explosion of rage, which rarely has a lasting effect; but a group ideology which liberates consciousness of power and gives the multitude a mission cannot ordinarily be developed by the enslaved class out of its own resources. The ideology must come from outside. The Jewish slaves in Egypt were given their ideology by a man who had been educated at the Egyptian court; the French *tiers état* received his from the *salons* of the nobility; and the socialist gospel was brought to the industrial proletariat of our days by the intellectual middle class. But if a missionary idea of great scope has once conquered the minds of the masses, then it is able to unleash the enormous power which finds its nourishment in misery made conscious and its immutable direction in the set goal: then the group ideology may even have a magic attraction for members of strange groups whose own satiated class can no more give them the great ideological ideas needed for the development of their militant energies.

The ideology of the lower classes therefore stresses their value and importance, makes them aware of conditions which in view of this value must seem a mockery and derision, and gives them a mission which aims at ending their miseries, and at the same time those of all humanity. This ideology must contain as precise as possible an indication of the means by which the end is to be attained: for in its ultimate aim the ideology of the large movement differs but little from the dull longings of the dormant masses, which find only occasional expression in ineffective revolt—the ultimate aims are always as similar as the natural limitations of man's imagination and capacity for desire inevitably cause them to be; the difference rather consists in the explicit statement of rights claimed and in as lucid an exposition as possible of the means by which the aim is to be attained and can with a reasonable degree of probability be attained. For the passive attitude of the unconscious masses and the loss of their awareness of value are the result of a despair which dares no more hope for a chance of betterment; they cannot but regard the ruling group, which holds its own though it is an infinitely small minority, as superior beings; so lost hope must be shown an unmistakable way which promises possibilities of overcoming what could not be overcome before. Thence the infinite pains commonly spent on the theoretical elaboration of group ideologies, also those of religious groups.

8. *Local Groups*

After all that has been said so far it is self-evident that group patterns based on locality often clash with those built on simi-larity lines, and that they are therefore of decisive importance only when they coincide with one of the principal groups. With ethnical groups this usually is the case: closed settlement is one of the main elements in the definition of a nation. From it derives a most effective factor of the group ideology; for the love for one's country, particularly in a defensive position, strengthens and justifies the will to fight (and, lest we forget, even in the case of tactical attack the fatherland is in danger) . Real sentimental relations usually exist only in respect of the district in which a man has grown up; but with larger nations part of this glamour extends to the whole of the nation's territory.

9. *The Dominating Category*

When we regard individual man as a group being and at-tempt to establish his relations to his own and other groups, we are in the first place struck by the fact that in respect of each group to which he belongs he lives in an attitude of enmity towards another group of the same category. This seemingly somewhat curious relation may be clarified by any amount of examples. Let us consider the comparatively simple case of an American worker of Anglo-Saxon descent. As a worker he is, of course, anti-capitalist (social category) ; as Anglo-Saxon, he is in opposition to what we, politely, call "Latins" and he, less politely, probably "Dagos": the descendants of Mediterranean nations (ethnical category), who, incidentally, usually are American citizens like himself, and frequently workers, also like himself: as a white man, he detests Negroes (racial category), and as an American he hates the Japanese (national-political category) . If, *in his enmity conception,* the stress does not so much lie on the political *contrast* between the American and Japanese empires, but rather on opposition to Japanese living in the States, this enmity is better also classified as racial. In addition, our American worker probably belongs to some Christian religious community; and even if his loyalties in this respect are not of the strongest, they arc sufficient to cause some dislike against other religions (*) . We italicised the term "enmity conception". In the next chapter we shall yet have to establish why group enmities can find their *direction* only through the group ideology. For the moment it must suffice that it is the group ideology which, in the absence of actual collisions, furnishes enmity with the pretext which makes it possible to give hostile feelings a definite direction. And as the enmity conception must always be drawn from the ideology characteristic for a group category, it results that the groups which face each other in a state of tension invariably belong to the same category. As a member of his social group, the worker is dominated by its ideology, which causes him to regard the capitalist as his enemy; as Anglo-Saxon he shares the pride of this ethnical group and its contempt of Latins; his mind is saturated by the ineradicable conviction of the White Man's

---

(*) To avoid misunderstandings: We are interested in religions as groups, not in their creeds; and the violence of struggles between groups is not determined by the *degree* of differences in criteria. Myriads were killed in the fights between Arians and Athanasians, whose creeds differed by literally no more than a single iota. From the standpoint of group behaviour, we can and must regard Presbyterians and Lutherans as no less discrete than Moslems and Shintoists.

superiority and his destiny of ruling the world, wherefore he detests Negroes; he believes in the glory and prominence of the United States as the most important country in the world; so he hates in the first place those countries which compete against the United States, and foremost Japan, the nearest and most threatening amongst them. All this really belongs to the next chapter; but it seemed desirable to show at this stage that hostile tension always arises between groups of the same category, because it becomes at the same time clear that in not quite primitive conditions man always belongs to several groups which rarely coincide and whose interests often clash. The resulting relations of the individual must needs be complicated and pregnant with conflicts; and we are interested to see how he works out his salvation. For, to keep to our instance, our worker will in the eventuality of a war against Japan see himself in the necessity of fighting his own class comrades, that is to say members of his own social group; in the struggle of his social group, on the other hand, he opposes his fellow-citizens and fellow-Christians; together with his white brethren, including the bourgeois among them, he lives in relentless opposition against his black fellow-citizens, fellow-Christians and almost certainly fellow-proletarians; together with his Anglo-Saxon capitalist brethren he excludes his fellow-whites, fellow-Christians, class comrades and, by and large, fellow-citizens from obtaining employment. In fact the complication reaches even further, as our friend would be either a Catholic or belong to one of the Protestant sects, is probably a member of some political organisation or trade union, and in addition may have committed his soul to yet other movements, clubs or schools.

In a dispersed people like the Jews the interrelation of group allegiances is still far more complicated; we are an ethnical-historical group, but belong individually to the most diverse state, language, social-economic, cultural and philosophical groups; officially, we are regarded as a religious community, while the specifically Jewish religious ideology does not, to say the least, dominate the larger part of the ethnical group. In this case, at any rate, the conflict of claims between the various groups to which the individual belongs has reached such a degree that it cannot but express itself always and everywhere as an internal conflict of the mind; daily and almost hourly the individual is pressed into different ranks and forced to regard the same person now as friend and then again as enemy in an alternation too rapid for sanity; the loss of balance of the personality is yet furthered by the circumstance that even such characteristics as are normally supplied by the ethnical group, as language and culture, are here drawn from heterogeneous groups; also, because in his case the struggle of the categories for the allegiance of the individual is not interrupted even for short periods (*) . For individual balance is obviously commensurate with the degree of coincidence of the principal groups to which the individual belongs.

The better to understand these facts, we should consider that all the groups to which the individual belongs compete for the domination of his soul: obviously so: for the group, being organised for struggle, must make sure that it can always rely on its members, lest, for instance, the worker whom his state has called to the

---

(*) This struggle of allegiances probably explains the important function of the family in Jewish diaspora life, even where other Jewish connections are already largely neglected; the family is the only undisrupted group still available to the Jew.

wars lower his arms when he faces his fellow-worker on the other side; even as, on the other hand, the proletariat does not want its solidarity to collapse before the barricades between nation and nation.

The question therefore arises which group allegiance is decisive in case of conflict, which category predominates within the individual and on what this predominance is based. At first sight one might think that the ethnical category, objectively the most important, would rank first on the domination scale. This, however, need by no means be the case; for the order of domination is not determined by objective importance, but by the influence which the group ideology exercises upon the individual—and the group ideology may even be borrowed from a foreign group. That group category which through its ideology most completely saturates the individual mind, takes the first place in order of subjective importance. Therefore the leaders of the group, who are charged with organising its struggle and consequently with maintaining its fighting potential, continuously strive to convince the individual of the outstanding importance of the ideology concerned. The process, called internal propaganda (*) or education, is familiar enough.

The struggle of the categories is a struggle of ideologies for predominance within the individual.

Now it is often most difficult to distinguish at first sight which category actually dominates. The individual

---

(*) In recent years, the word "propaganda" has come to be identified with a certain lack of truthfulness and has fallen into disrepute; during the war, American parlance introduced "indoctrination" in the place of "internal propaganda", but the new word soon became tainted with the unpleasant flavour of the old one. Man, priding himself on his largely illusory independence of judgment, tends to suspect all vigorous attempts to convince him; and often falls for that very reason into the opposite error of leaning over backward.- 1949.

concerned is not in all cases clearly aware of what passes in his own mind. At first sight one is inclined to regard as dominating the category in which the individual exercises the largest and most important part of his group functions. The socialist, wholly absorbed in the life and strife of his organisation, would seem completely saturated and dominated by the relative ideology. The misleading element lies in the fact that at the given moment the social category is, among all the groups to which the individual belongs, the one which is in the most violent state of antagonism; and therefore its attraction for the individual is the strongest. The real decision of predominance only occurs when another group enters into an equally violent state of antagonism. In Holland, for instance, there occurred, shortly after the first world war, a recrudescence of the Catholic-Protestant antithesis. The social-ist workers remained totally unaffected by this development; which proves that in their case the religious group ranks low on the predominance scale, a fact which must be attributed to the obvious indifference of the worker in matters of religion. When, however, where in some country relations with a neighbouring nation become strained, the result is that within the country social contrasts are overruled by a certain feeling of unity, and when more particularly solidarity with members of the own class in the neighbouring nation is replaced by bitter enmity between the two peoples, then the ideology of the ethnical group, however often denied, has proved to be actually predominant.

The most important part of his group functions man ex-ercises within the one of his groups which lives in a state of intensified antagonism and ranks first within the scale of domination. Therefore the real relations of predominance do not become apparent except in the most acute stage of antagonism, that is to say, at the outbreak of hostilities with the employment of organised armed force.

It is hardly astonishing that that group which is organised in the form of the state almost invariably takes the first place in the order of group predominance; practically the only exception being the case of a suppressed group within a foreign state fighting for its independence. Better than any other group is the nation organised as state able to indoctrinate the individual with its ideology. For the ideology, being a complex of mental contents, is transmissible and, above all, can readily be implanted in the child's mind in the course of education. The state avails itself for this purpose of its all-powerful educational system; the national language contributes its mighty aid; national culture acts in the same direction; and the instruments of state power often serve not so much to keep other countries (the potential enemy) in awe and terror, as for the internal purpose of strengthening within the own nation the element which carries the group ideology: its consciousness of value and excellence, of power and superiority, of importance and preponderance.

Moreover, the state tends to ally itself with one of the categories from which it has to fear but little competition; in these days, the preponderance of social group ideologies makes the religious group with its leaders, the hierarchy, the ally of choice in the struggle for the allegiance of the individual.

Formerly, when the church occasionally attempted to displace the state from its dominant position, the latter also used to conclude alliances against the church with ethnical and social categories. But not only the state searches for allies in its struggle for dominance in the soul of the individual; groups which have been relegated to the background tend quite generally to pool forces against the successful competitor. In this struggle, even conquests are often attempted, inasmuch as powerful groups often set out to subject other groups of all kinds to their exclusive domination. Thus, for instance, the religious group tries, not without success, to break up the natural structure of social groups by lending its exclusive support to parts of social bodies which separate themselves from other parts of the same bodies according to a line determined by religion, and acknowledge the domination of the religious group. In this way there arise those social organisations affiliated to a church which no longer establish their *organisational* group limits according to the precepts of the category to whose power they are subject. Nevertheless, certain contrasts, such as, for instance, those between a proletarian and a bourgeois body equally dominated by the same church, unavoidably continue to exist.

As within the mind of individual man the domination of the categories is reflected in the form of the notion that he *feels* himself in the first place as a member of one group, in the second place as belonging to another, there arises the almost general error that personal feelings are of any importance in such a matter of objectively established fact as group membership. This error is favoured by the transmissibility of the group ideology, whereby a group of lesser or no importance may take first rank in the scale of predominance; the individual may even appropriate a totally foreign group ideology and so fall prey to the domination of a group to which he in no way belongs. Particularly in the case of groups which live in a state of mental serfdom, the assumption of foreign group ideologies may result in the passing of the domination over the whole of the group by a foreign group; which in, such cases, is the first step on the way to absorption.

Where, however, absorption cannot be effected on account of excessive difficulties (absorption of ethnical groups, more particularly, often meets with insuperable impediments) , such cases of "emigrated" group ideologies usually lead to tragic consequences. In the decisive moment of bloody struggle, the ideology of the social group, for instance, can no longer command the allegiance of its members; domination is achieved by an ethnical group, which repudiates the ethnically foreign element. The adopted foreign group readily accepts aid in the actual battle—in fact, if the need be but dire enough, assistance is welcome wherever it may come from; but whether the outcome be victory or defeat, the necessity of submitting to an alliance must be revenged on the foreign group: to the disappointment of those who in their own minds had already been translated from slaves to members of the admired group of rulers, who sincerely believed that this change had actually been effected, and who now again see themselves expelled into a camp which they are no longer accustomed to regard as their own.

To illustrate these abnormal relations of domination, let us consider a Jewish instance: a young Russian Jew in the days before the first world war, member of a Zionist organisation of socialist character. The principal groups to which he belongs may be defined as follows: —

1)   State: Russian;
2)   Ethnical-historical group: Jewish;
3)   Social-economic group: lower middle class;
4)   Philosophy of life: socialist;
5)   Jewish political group: Zionist,

It would seem that the accent of predominance lies with the fourth group, the socialist philosophy of life. And as this philosophy is in actual fact the ideological superstructure of the proletariat, our Jew has assumed the ideology of a group to which he does not belong; he has assumed it and convinced himself that he is a proletarian, while in fact, though quite probably poor, he belongs socially to the middle class. In the second place he is aware of the circumstance that for him personally, part as he is of the Jewish ethnical group, the realisation of his social ideals is only possible within a Jewish, normally producing society; and as he regards its creation in his land of residence as impossible, he is also Zionist.

He considers himself a very indifferent Russian citizen and is a violent opponent of the Czarist regime; nevertheless, the ethnical group of the Russian people, with its language, customs, art and literature, in short, with all those characteristics which the state has appropriated and which form the propagandist, element of its ideology, has completely conquered his Jewish soul; and though he is fully aware that ethnically speaking he is no Russian, he yet often enough feels as if he were one. And indeed, when the war breaks out, the Russian state group suddenly appears in predominance absolute. Our Jew feels himself as a Russian subject, and nothing else; with his blood he would buy the love of the real Russians, who hate him: his international group interest is summarily sent packing; and the Jews in the enemy armies, even those together with whom he wanted to build a Jewish state, are to be destroyed, enemies of his Russian fatherland as they are.

Not much later, however, there arises a painful inner conflict. The ethnical group of the Russians, which rules the Russian state, begins to persecute the ethnical group of the Jews. Our man is a Russian soldier, and as such threatened by the outside enemy; but he is a Jew, and as such much more gravely threatened by the Russians. Here we see domination at work in the fulness of its power. One would expect the Jewish group now to become preferential for struggle, because it is in the more intensive state of antagony. But while he is lying in hospital, more dead than alive, he is far less concerned with the Jews who are being deported to death in cattle trucks, than with the Russian armies which fight on the frontier; his enmity is not directed against the Russian hangmen, but against the unknown, and individually uninteresting, enemy regiments and the nations which stand behind them. The Russian state group maintains its domination over the Jewish soul, even while expelling its Jewish subjects as its worst enemies.

There may, of course, in such cases occur a temporary shift of predominance. The Jew may recall his own ethnical group to which he is held by never breaking bonds; he may direct his efforts to the achievement of a better future for it. The change is rarely complete; for the binding elements of the foreign group ideology, instilled into the mind in early youth, do not lightly lose all their influence later. As soon as defeat makes it possible for our friend to regain the recognition of the Russian citizen as a socialist, he will the sooner yield to this temptation, the more socialism had already before predominated in his mind over the Zionist ideology.

And a new wave of antisemitism is needed to remind him that for all changes of state form and state ideology the Russian remains a Russian, the Jew a Jew. It is of no account where he feels that he belongs; the only important thing is what he actually is. Group membership is an objective fact, and in the case of ethnical groups an invariant fact, not affected by notions without reality and constructs of fiction. Where there is a real shift in the predominance of group ideologies, there occur revolutions of the utmost historical importance; the preponderance of a given category as the criterium of delimitation in group struggle may temporarily or permanently be transferred to other categories. But the question why, for instance, religious ideologies achieved for a time absolute predominance, would require research far beyond the limits of the task here undertaken; and we do not intend to answer it here.

10. *Apostates*

In the individual case, the group member who falls prey to the domination of an absolutely foreign group ideology becomes a turncoat or apostate. Not only is he then wholly possessed by the foreign ideology, but he becomes its most fervent apostle; by his zeal he would compensate his lack of more objective connections with the adopted group; but his attitude nourishes rather than eliminates the real group members' distrust, and often enough the apostate sees himself expelled from his self-chosen paradise.

A special case of apostasy, curious but by no means rare, is presented by the foreign group leader. Oppressed groups — which, given an appropriate ideology, may become highly efficient instruments of struggle — are often unable to find capable leaders within their own ranks, and at first willingly accept the help of a stranger; whom his own group has endowed with the quality of leadership and who, being a stranger, can more readily command obedience. To him, on the other hand, the foreign group offers the opportunities of struggle denied him by his own. His position, though, remains precarious: no devotion can quite overcome the group's distrust of the foreigner, a distrust yet reinforced by the natural enmity of the ruled against their rulers; an enmity which even the chosen leader, covered though he may be with gratitude, never wholly escapes.

This raises the problem of group leadership, to which we can give here only a few words. The organised group needs leadership; and this, if it is to accomplish its task, must be invested with special powers. Within the group we therefore find relations of dependence, a small leading minority ruling, with a lighter or heavier hand, the majority. This domination is submitted to as a necessary evil, but remains felt as an evil and, like all domination, as an expression of hostility. In fact, the leading group has all the characteristics of a separate formation; it distances itself, distinctly and often pronouncedly, from the masses which it leads, and as a rule is actively opposed by the latter. Thus the group is divided into two sub-groups, leaders and followers; in addition, the leading group may again, amongst the followers, have its more particular supporters and adversaries; and if the parent group is sufficiently large, the subsidiary groups may in turn develop an organised structure, though they often remain unorganised and then are termed trends.

This process of progressive subdivision often makes it particularly difficult to recognise the real distribution of the group's functions, because it seems as though more enmity is expressed within than without the group. This is never more than a mere appearance; though it must be realised that large groups live in a state of intensified antagonism more rarely than small groups, while the expression of the less violent, but often quite pronounced, feelings of unfriendliness is a daily need, served by the smaller groups, amongst which the sub-groups play a prominent part.

Chapter V

Group Enmity

1. *Neighbouring Groups*

Once we have recognised the group as a form of organisation and as an *instrument* which does not only from time to time appear as the carrier of collective feelings, but whose main task is the expression of love and hate, we can also envisage group enmity, which we met when considering antisemitic phenomena, in the light of a new understanding. Then, we found ourselves faced with the difficulty that the so-to-say normal enmity reaction which we usually seem to discern in the individual case could almost never be established in collective relations; while, on the other hand, quite insufficiently motivated expressions of enmity, regarded as abnormal between individuals, form amongst groups a rule which offends all reason and sense of justice.

But in the light of what we have meanwhile established the Abnormal and apparently Paradox is realised as self-evident. For group enmity arises precisely from accumulated inimical feelings of varied and often non-human origin which are ready for expression but cannot be applied, and must, by means of the group, be directed towards an external aim from which they certainly have not originated. And this external aim is again a group, a plurality; for thus the transference of hate, the finding of *pretexts* for enmity can more readily override the voice of reason, ever objecting where individuals are concerned: it is much easier to justify enmity by crying havoc against the dangerous turpitude of unknown foreign masses than against a perfectly familiar individual. Therefore the objects of group enmity will be totally unconnected with the real causes of the inimical feelings.

It is a fundamental and decisive characteristic of every group enmity that primary enmity feelings of varied origin are directed collectively against groups which have had no share in their creation.

Obviously, the expression and direction nevertheless requires a justifying conception, a *pretext*. The oddest and most improbable fallacies will serve; but they must at any rate be made to connect with people who, while not so remote as to exclude any possible relation, are near enough to make it possible for conceptions of conflict to arise. The fear of expected injury cannot, for instance, bear upon a far-away group with which there are no actual or possible contacts. The appropriate objects are, on the contrary, found in the nearest neighbourhood; for the neighbouring group, even if not organised, is also self-contained, and within it there act the same forces to create outwardly directed tendencies towards unfriendliness. Neighbouring groups, therefore, direct feelings of unfriendliness against each other, thereby causing a more or less pronounced inimical tension.

In the previous chapter we already had the opportunity to explain that, failing concrete reproaches—which with some justification can only be made against individuals—the direction of these feelings of enmity must find its justification in a complex of conceptions provided by the group ideology. As the latter is always derived from the group category, i.e. from similarities which have determined the formation of the group, it is always between neighbouring groups of the same category that we find enmity tension. The complicated interrelations of the groups to which one and the same individual often belongs make it occasionally impossible to establish this fact at first sight, but closer examination will always show that fighting groups are of the same category. Thus it could seem as if, after the French revolution, the social group of the Third Estate was at war with the national state groups without; actually, the fight was against the armies of another social group, the nobility.

The relation between neighbouring groups of the same category is always one of more or less pronounced inimical tension.

The importance of this fact must be fully realised, for it forms the key to the understanding of collective enmity relations.

It is *the mere local proximity* which, for the reasons stated, is accompanied by a state of tension; which, therefore, *causes* this state of tension. All other apparent causes of hate and enmity are mere incidents which are called upon to provide an at least somewhat plausible pretext for their so ardently desired expression.

2. *Collective Characteristics*

We now must make a closer examination of the ways in which the conceptions of justification arise. When we discussed the group ideology, which has to furnish these conceptions in the first place, we distinguished consciousness of value, and its active expression, the mission idea. The reason why these are so particularly suitable for the creation of justifications of hostility is that they assist in the overcoming of certain psychological difficulties which stand in the way of materialisation of the justifying conception. For, as we know, group enmity can never base itself on the one thing which could make it appear normal and justified; condemnable actions by all members of the enemy group.

In the best case, the attitude of the group executive may cause offence, or some isolated group member may render himself guilty of objectionable conduct; but in order to impose the responsibility upon the whole group and all its individual members, it is necessary to expand the scope of the hate reaction to an extent not easily approved of by a strictly objective sense of justice. And as it is precisely the hater's sense of justice which has to be satisfied, there invariably arises within the parties concerned an auxiliary concept: the *collective characteristic.*

The general principle behind this generalisation is more conveniently discussed at a later stage, when we shall deal with collective responsibility. Meanwhile we might recall what we recognised as the main constituent of the group ideology; the consciousness of value which everyone derives from the group to which he belongs. This, of course, corresponds to a conviction of the *lesser value* of all who do *not* belong to the same group. With the ease permitted by the already extensively discussed mechanism of valuation of character qualities, this conviction is expanded to the assumption of pronouncedly unfavourable, i.e. *inferior,* collective qualities in all numbers of the foreign group. This explains why the existence of collective qualities, so difficult to establish objectively, is nevertheless posited and believed in as self-evident in everyday life, which is a life of group enmity.

The conception of the existence of collective characteristics is a first necessity for group struggle.

The presupposed evil collective qualities are conceived of as a potential source of evil, condemnable, and therefore also harmful actions. The undesired action of the individual group member is the sooner regarded as confirmation of this assumption, as the possibilities of unfavourable interpretation and valuation of an action are practically unlimited, and as attention, in itself suspicious, is in any case focused on notoriously undesirable, and disregards notoriously praiseworthy ones. The intuitive expectation of harmful actions, the potential presence of which is presupposed in the evil collective qualities, is to be found in every enmity relation in the form of *fear,* present even where it seems to be contradicted by pronounced consciousness of power or confidence in victory. Consciousness of power and expectation of victory serve to maintain the psychological fighting potential; nor do they render the prevention of the feared damage by hostile action superfluous. And herein lies the significance of *fear,* which plays so important a part in all enmity relations. Fear furnishes the justification for *preventing* the feared action *before it has taken place.* Thus arises *preventive warfare.* The word is commonly used only in the case of actual warlike clashes; but the same phenomenon occurs in all enmity relations.

The belief in the collective inferiority of the foreign group finds its complement in the positive part of the group ideology, the missionary idea. The inferiority, then, does not merely appear as an accumulation of faults of all kinds, but its manifestation is particularly seen in the resistance offered by the foreign group to the group mission and the acceptance of its contents. Thus the inferiority must seem the greater, the higher the fighting group values the universal importance of its mission. The representatives of expansive religions, philosophies of life, and even ideologies of general or particular scope, react with embittered indignation to any resistance offered to their mission; to them it proves the inferiority, and even the depravity, of the resisters.

Colonising powers fail to understand how the natives can be inferior and anti-cultural enough to reject the blessings of so exalted a culture. And it is obvious that from beings so depraved as to be incapable of appreciating such cultural goods, all and any atrocities are only to be expected. It should, incidentally, be noted that the non-expansive, merely defensive, groups act essentially in exactly the same way. They want to preserve their own nature, their own opinions and ideas, because they regard them as valuable and their maintenance as a mission of culture; in the fulfilment of this mission they are hindered by the expansive group, and this disturbance causes precisely the same notions of the baseness of the mischief-maker who is incapable of comprehending the value and importance of the threatened institutions, cultural circles, or worlds of thought and feeling.

The conception of the existence of collective qualities, therefore, provides the possibility for a general diffusion of feelings of love and hate.

Within the own group, every member becomes, as a bearer of the valuable group characteristics, indiscrimi-

*nately the subject of friendly feelings; every member of the for-
eign group, as the carrier of the collective inferiority, becomes
as indiscriminately the subject of the enmity feelings directed
against his group. Individual activities and inactivities remain in
either case without influence upon the group feeling bestowed.*

This somewhat abstract statement demands the following
reservations: the expression of friendship tends far more to
differentiation in the choice of its objects than the expression
of enmity, for which blind generalisation is the rule. Feelings
of friendship, always scarce, have to be used with far greater
economy than the always plentiful enmity sensations. The degree
of tension also is not devoid of influence on the generalisation.
At high tension the process is most complete in either direction.
At the outbreak of war, the most indifferent fellow-countryman
whom chance brings within reach of an eruption of friendship
is overwhelmed by often pointless favours; the foreigner who,
but yesterday an honoured friend, has been changed into an enemy, becomes the target for all the bitter hostility now directed
against his nation. In lesser states of tension there often does
not remain much more of the collective friendly attitude than a
certain awareness of the obligation to relieve private indigence.
The hostile generalisation has a much tougher life; but where
tension is slight it still admits, at least, of favourable exceptions
in individual cases.

At high levels of tension the conception of collective inferiority of the enemy group may proliferate into an abysmal obsession
which turns the very name of the hated group into the epitome of
fear and disgust. The most horrible criminal tendencies are ascribed
to all members of the group without discrimination (one may

remember the "Huns", as the Germans were called in the first world war), the case is no longer only one of malevolent interpretations and generalisation of individual actions: brains afever with hate invest the detested group with every vile and destructive intention which the wildest fancy can but imagine. And in the same measure grows the horror of a fear which can see no other hope of protection than in the total destruction of the enemy.

3. *Antipathy*

At first, in conditions of lesser tension, the fear of the foreign group's inferiority appears as antipathy, which is the emotional precondition of flight from the object of enmity. Where the degree of tension is low, the antipathy may assume so mild a form that the bearer himself is not always clearly aware of it; in which case it is often not recognised or not acknowledged as an expression of enmity. But an expression of enmity it is, as is proved by its capacity for developing into the most intensive hate and by the fact that this development actually takes place as soon as the tension between the groups concerned increases. It is self-evident that the increasing tension causes no change in the nature or character of the group members which would even seem to justify such a development of antipathy into active hate: it cannot be made sufficiently clear that this groupwise antipathy is neither objectively warranted nor objectively determined. It is nothing but a hostile group feeling, projected upon an opposite group; its intensity depends on the degree of tension present, but in no way upon the nature, the behaviour, the activities or non-activities of its objects. *The victims of such antipathies who attempt*

*to overcome them by a show of personal excellence fail to realise
this situation.*

At times the fog of emotion is penetrated by the realisation
that the assumption of the inferiority of foreign groups is as
unfounded as the antipathy against them. Where this insight
dawns, the attitude objected to is excused as a *prejudice.* This
designation has a great disadvantage: it raises the expectation
that levelheaded thought may, as a result of acquired understanding, correct the prejudice. Such an expectation cannot but prove
deceptive; for the emotions have ever remained all-powerful,
and to look for a change of the strongest and most instinctive
feelings through the operation of reason is to misjudge its power,
and possibly its task.

In the more extensive groups, which contain large masses living in close community, the antipathy against the neighbouring
group can, at least in the contacts of individual members, only
express itself at the group perimeter; in that case there arises
the so-called border tension, which will demand our attention
particularly in connection with the minority group and the hate
of the foreigner. In groups with a large area of contact, however,
that is to say in the first place in the case of social groups, dislike of
individual contacts is the constant form of enmity expression, which
never rests and is only from time to time interrupted by more violent
outbreaks of hatred. Where local conditions result in groups of other
categories having larger areas of contact, there will be antipathy
against these as well; religious arid general-cultural groups
are sometimes in extensive contact; but where ethnical group
fragments are in their whole extension in touch with ethnically

foreign groups, we face the problem of minority groups, where that antipathy which otherwise is only possible at the group perimeter affects the group as a whole.

Antipathy, as already stated, is graded according to the level of tension; and accordingly expresses itself in degrees often reflected in the most subtle shades of which human relations are capable. Where tension is slight, for instance, all contacts except actual family relations are admitted; next follows exclusion from the domestic circle, and only thereafter from the already less exclusive *salon.* As the process continues, first social clubs, then sport clubs, then professional, and thereafter political associations close their doors. When tension increases the mere presence at public entertainments, in hotels, and even in all localities accessible to the general public, is shunned, and finally even business contacts are avoided, though it is their nature to overcome even relations of strong antipathy.

Antipathy is the emotional basis of exclusion, boycott, isolation; it is a form of escape, inasmuch as the danger is not liquidated: it is hoped that it can be made harmless through the isolation of its focus. But as the relations interrupted in this way often existed between groups of which the one was dependent upon the other, the exclusion may in its actual results well bear the character of routing and expulsion. As the persons between whom antipathy manifests itself are the closest neighbours, the possibilities of escape are naturally limited; and though strictly observed exclusion may be a weapon of considerable effect, enmity will take to stronger arms so soon as it exceeds a certain degree of violence. Then it resorts to forcible expulsion and murderous annihilation.

4. *Contempt*

Antipathy is accompanied by contempt, an apparently simple, but actually rather complicated notion.

At first sight it would seem that contempt only means lack of respect, based upon the assumed lack of value, qualities, in short, upon the assumed inferiority. Thus the term "contempt" would express nothing but the emotional precipitate of the inferiority conception by which in group enmity every foreign group is branded. But the only emotion justified in respect of worthless individuals is sovereign indifference. Enmity and hatred, which manifest themselves as antipathy, prove on the contrary that the object of hatred is regarded as the more important, the more pronounced the expression of dislike appears. For conceptions of value and importance do not only, and not even in the first place, relate to ethnical qualities; which in theory are highly appreciated, without however transferring much of this theoretical appreciation to their bearer. Much more important appear the qualities with the aid of which man conquers nature, and most important those by which he conquers his fellow-man: strength, courage, presence of mind, coolness, cleverness, intelligence, versatility, cunning. All values are, after all, determined by necessities, and the value of a general consists of other qualities than that of a Sister of Mercy. Enmity may therefore value the ethnical qualities of its opponent as low as it will; by its very existence it admits his importance and moment. This unwilling recognition is painful to the own mind of the hater, for it betrays fear; while he not only desires to believe in his own moral worth and his enemy's moral worthlessness, but also in his own fighting power and strength, and in the unimportance and weakness of his opponent. Therefore he is angry with himself for the importance which his hatred lends to the hated one, and for the weakness which he thus reveals, also to his enemy. Both must be compensated. So the hater appeases his feelings by persuading himself that the enemy is not really worth spending so much emotional energy or time on. Outwardly he attempts to display his disdainful indifference towards the other, and so to give an obvious demonstration of his consciousness of superiority. Towards oneself contempt is a mask for one's own fears, a pretext for lacking consciousness of power, a veil before the insight in one's own vulnerability; towards the enemy, contempt is a means of intimidation, a threat intended to undermine the qualities most valuable to him in his struggle: courage and self-confidence. For in enmity relations all means of deceit are widely used; and it is only the question whether self-deception does not take far larger a place than that of the enemy. Self-praise and slander of the enemy, in order to justify enmity; bragging about the own power and demonstrative disdain of the opponent's fighting qualities, in order to encourage the own and discourage the other side: these are regular concomitants of every enmity. Therefore the verbal insult takes so eminent a place: the invective attributes to the enemy either a specific moral shortcoming (which suggests a more general ethnical inferiority), or a lack of fighting qualities proving inferiority in struggle: one way or another, the insults used can always be paraphrased to mean scoundrel, coward or weakling. And there has never yet been a struggle which has not been accompanied by these apparently so purposeless wars of invective.

In group enmity all these things assume fantastic proportions; the enemy group upon which at any given time is concentrated with particular tenacity is, as a rule, simply indicated by a single insulting name which summarises all notions of contempt.

5. *Friction, Contrast, Collision, Conflict*

Notwithstanding collective relations of dislike in the personal contacts of group members—and we should not forget that this dislike is a *demonstration* of enmity rather than the actual avoiding of contact—the antagonistic groups are in so close touch that their wishes and desires interfere with each other, and therefore lead to collisions. The contact thus proves to be a permanent source of *friction.*

In the collective far more than in the individual case this friction is induced by the circumstances that groups have *a priori* the task and function of assisting hostile feelings to express themselves; far clearer than in the individual case can the objects to which the discrepancy of wishes and desires relates be recognised as mere pretexts, with the only purpose of making the expression of enmity possible. This observation is supported by the curious fact that in group conflicts not only and not in the first place contrasting economic interests appear as the occasion for friction, but that differences in qualities, in nature, in language, in religion, in opinions—in short, all characteristic differences between two groups—are regarded as legitimate reasons for an opposition which thus, in turn, gives the impression of being the cause of the enmity which so apparently always accompanies it. As the real meaning of these differences is regularly misunderstood, and as this misunderstanding is a worse stumbling block in the way of true understanding of group enmities than any theoretical error, this point must be dealt with at some length.

Dispassionate consideration must make it seem curious that one should hate one's fellow-rnan, merely because his skin has another colour, he speaks another language, or confesses another religion than oneself. Hatred based on nothing but the existence of such differences cannot be regarded as legitimate by any current conception. For the fellow-man concerned cannot help his skin, and its different pigmentation cannot harm us. Nor can we in justice regard it as Injurious that still other languages besides our own are spoken; and while difference of opinion about, say, ways and means to attain a common purpose might still pass as a reasonable cause for conflict, there seems to be no ground why we should take exception to the different religious opinion of another, which is of importance to no one but himself. The realisation that such differences form no admissible cause for enmity is not voiced since today or yesterday; but this fact cannot change a reality which in any case is none too readily influenced by cool reason, and which in this particular case, moreover, is not envisaged correctly.

For not the differences excite enmity, but the common factors form the basis for agglomeration into groups; and some common factors, such as, for instance, skin colour, do so most imperiously. And as similarities become the principle of combination, the differences must of necessity become the criteria of differentiation: of differentiation between units which of their very nature and purpose are instruments for the expression of enmity. So the appearance arises as if the differences are the cause of conflict and enmity, while they actually are no more than different uniforms distinguishing between friend and enemy, and no one would conceive of the inane idea that the difference in the uniform of enemy armies is the cause of the war between them. It is, however, correct that existing enmity may finally even be transferred to the uniform of the opponent and make it a symbol of the hated enemy: the French *kepi* was as hated in Germany as the German spurred steel helmet in France, when those pieces of equipment were still in use, and in English-speaking circles the word "jackboot" has an unpleasant sound quite undeserved by so useful a form of footgear; for even the external and artificial group characteristics do not escape the process of degradation and devaluation which hostile sentiments impose upon them.

In reality differences lose their apparent capacity for exciting enmity as soon as the struggle is directed against a third, common opponent; that is to say, as soon as the temporarily allied groups can exert their function of expressing enmity together, against a third group. On the other hand, even the most painful lack of most minute difference cannot prevent either group formation or group enmity, as soon as they become a necessity; in that case the characteristics needed for distinction are simply created artificially.

In this connection we may recall what has previously been said about the domination of categories. Man belongs to numerous groups, but he gives preference to some of them for the exercise of his group functions. This preference shifts when a group which ranks high in order of dominance passes into a state of heightened antagonism. When, therefore, violent class struggle is replaced by war between nations, the social difference, though it continues to exist unchanged, loses for the time being its capacity for exciting enmity and gives way to the most harmonious unity. If, on the other hand, social enmity predominates, national contrasts lose part of their usual keenness. The same may, *mutatis mutandis,* be said of all group categories, for the ruling and determining factor is solely the need for enmity expression; a need which for its purposes selects the groups which from case to case seem to offer the most favourable conditions. In the groups employed to a lesser degree, differences are consequently accompanied by almost no hostile contrast. In differences of nature nothing more can be determined than the bare fact of the difference; its degree cannot well be measured: it is hard to say whether the Mongol differs more from the European than the Red-Indian. In differences of conception we deal with formulated ideas, whose distance can easily be measured. Therefore such differences are by preference connected with the fallacy that they cause the stronger an enmity, the greater the contrast between the conceptions represented is. Actually, one could rather claim the opposite, and say that two groups based on conceptions are the more violently opposed, the *slighter* the difference between their ideas as such. One need only remember the enmity between the former right and left socialist movements in (imperial) Germany, or the contrast between socialists and communists everywhere (*). This fact should, of course, not be constructed so as to mean that the degree of enmity varies in inverse ratio with the degree of difference. But where groups are particularly close in conceptions, this

---

(*) Again: this was written in 1923; and the years gone by since have added numberless instances. — 1949.

circumstance acts as a particularly favourable condition for conquest and absorption; one group grudges the other its continued separate existence and refusal to be absorbed, and answers the resistance against its attempts at incorporation with correspondingly acrimonious enmity. In this case also, the conceptions and aims laid down in the group platform do not constitute the cause of the enmity, but only a circumstance favouring its expression and direction.

In another sense it might admittedly seem as if differences of conception would form a real cause of enmity. Like all group characteristics, the own conception is highly valued and forms an integral part of the consciousness of value which we have found to be the basis of the group ideology. In view of this consciousness of value, the contrary opinion of an opposite group is not merely a deviation to be dismissed with indifferent ease, but a doubt of the justification of the own consciousness of value. And such a doubt insults: it attacks the group's honour. Honour and insult are characteristic concomitants of enmity relations, and are only understandable as such. In reason it should be immaterial what anyone else thinks or says about us; for it does not change us, and if it differs unfavourably from actuality, it can only illustrate the other's stupidity. And what can it matter to us if others disagree with our opinions in theological matters— only of theoretical importance, and only important to us—as long as we are convinced that ours are right? But in the hard world of actual facts it is not reason which rules, but the enmity relation. There, the value of a person is a legal claim, entitling him to preference at the expense of others, and to protection against this preferential position being endangered by others.

Worthlessness and faults are regarded as permission and justification for hostile treatment of the unworthy, inferior other
party. Amongst the qualities valued highly we count intelligence
and cleverness; amongst those regarded as faults, stupidity. If,
therefore, I differ of opinion with someone, I cast doubt on his
intelligence, and criticise his opinion; an activity which, in contrast to friendly approval, is generally regarded as an expression
of unfriendliness. For the criticism and the implied doubt of
the intelligence of the person criticised insults him, as it makes
his value dubious; he feels insulted; and it only depends on the
relative strength of the parties concerned, which side is the most
sensitive to insults. Of the group it may be said that this sensitivity
is heightened to the utmost because struggle is so exclusively its
reason of existence. Individual man, who personally is able to
display a certain indifference to doubts of his value in general
and of the correctness of his opinions in particular, becomes hy-
persensitive as soon as the criticism is directed against one of his
groups, and particularly the one which ranks first with him.

If, therefore, it is comparatively easy to establish that differences of nature are not the cause of group enmities, and some
consideration will prove the same of differences of conception, the situation is slightly less clear in the case of so-called
conflicting interests. Diversities of race and creed have since
long been discredited as valid causes of enmity, at least in
theory; but the conflict of interests is still, with a certain fatal-
istic resignation, admitted as such. It is, for instance, a favoured
assumption that modern wars have their cause in the economic
competition of national capitalism or national economies.
Capital, like all social-economic groups, has, on the con-

trary, pronounced internationalistic tendencies, and we see continually how the state must forcibly guide the activities of capital in the direction of national special interests. And indeed, it seems unreasonable for international capital to send its valuable "slave material" to mutual capital-devouring slaughter—in which the capitalist moreover risks his own life and property, while he could peacefully prosper, with his international fellow-capitalists, on the common exploitation of the international working class. But against its natural tendencies international capital is split up on national lines and subordinated to national, *non-economic* antagonisms; its special technical qualifications turn it into a strategically functioning vanguard of competing states. If oil were nothing but an article of exploitation, there would be no threat of oil wars, for all capitalists concerned could easily combine in one common trust. As things are, however, there are a number of competing trusts, whose competition is of course against the advantage of the interested parties, but becomes unavoidable because they must secure, to the greatest extent possible, the use of oil *as a weapon* for the imperialist states which they serve. In the case of other raw materials the profit arising from their exploitation goes to strengthen the *financial war potential* of the State; and in any case economic activities abroad can create spheres of influence which are of importance to the state as strategic positions. To what extent strategy is essentially the only consideration, is proved by the rivalry in the field of archeological research, which differs from the struggle for oil concessions only in being economically unprofitable. But both the manager of a commercial undertaking and the research scientist occupy national advanced positions;

and it is pleasant if advanced positions are at the same time lucrative, but it is not the main consideration (*) .

In respect of the opposed interests of national economies the main points have also been made already. Overproduction of men and goods is not in itself a cause of enmity, but only becomes so because behind the overproduction there stands the closed group, drawn up for struggle, depending for power and strategic position on the export of manpower and goods, and meeting with opposition against this export for that very reason. How obvious this becomes in the case of the emigration problem has been shown before. One of the clearest examples of a seemingly economic conflict was the case of Danzig. Danzig is a German city. But Poland needed an outlet to the sea. Such an outlet is generally recognised as an economic necessity, and enjoys the best of international reputations as such. Actually, it is purely a strategic necessity. But for the national, quite non-economic Polish-German conflict; but for Poland's consequent fear that she would not always be able to avail herself of the port of Danzig, and particularly not when it would be most necessary to her, namely in the case of war; but for these considerations it could have been a matter of supreme indifference to Poland to whom her principal

---

(*) National research also serves another strategic aim, namely the increase of *prestige*. What to the own mind constitutes that consciousness of value from which the claim to the right of existence or expansion derives, must also be forced upon the recognition of the outside world by an appropriate demonstration of qualities. Thus the group does not only display as much wealth, glory and power as possible so as to show its strength and to intimidate the world (fortune in general means power, because it stands for independence; misfortune causes dependence and so means weakness; wherefore fortune is shown ostentatiously) , but it also likes to display prestations highly valued by general opinions, such as research and football. *For in group strife proof of value is a claim to rights* and therefore strengthens the strategic position. A nation which has given the world famous scientists or famous football players has thereby established its *right* to exist.

outlet to the sea belonged. Only the presence of opposed groups turns the port into an instrument of power, into a weapon; and thus into an object of strife and an occasion for war. And so one might go further and say that in the possible absence of the Danzig problem other questions, such as that of Upper Silesia, would have provided the necessary fuel for a conflict.

For if differences and contrasts are not the cause of enmity, they are the more suitable as subjects of conflict from which conceptions of justification for the enmity can be derived. And therein lies their importance. Even if one wants to accept the existence of purely economic contrasts between groups one must admit that they only excite enmity if the will to understanding is lacking, if, therefore, hostile feelings prevent understanding. For where the economic contrast seems most acute, there are actually the strongest common economic interests; at times they are so strong that they are even able to suppress existing enmity feelings, though these have usually worked their will before the force of economic necessity can make itself felt.

Where, on the other hand, hostile tension is strong, the economic contrast is particularly prone to furnish the pretext for the expression of enmity; for economic activities engage, after all, the major part of the human interest, and pretexts for enmity born from a sphere so pregnant with passions work strongly on the imaginative power. And for a pretext for enmity that is a distinct advantage. For the assumed inferiority of the foreign group is sufficient to justify the direction of enmity feelings and their expression in comparatively mild forms to the conscience of the hater, *but for the expression of enmity by more violent means the mere concep-*

tion of inferiority is usually not felt as sufficient. In that case there arises the need for a more *concrete* accusation. This is most readily derived from the numerous collisions which arise from the contact and friction of groups; they often occur in the economic field, but particularly in group life they are also found in many other spheres; and the conflict between two football clubs who quarrel about the contested decision of a referee need essentially not be less violent than that of the greatest economic organisations in the struggle for wages.

Now these conflicts of collisions are always accompanied by conceptions of right. Each side believes that it is in the right or that it is threatened by the other party with injustice and iniquity. The expression of enmity can therefore occur supported by the indispensable conceptions of justification. These are the more important in group struggle, as in mass conflicts there usually is a total lack of any rule of law which would make an at least formally authoritative decision possible; and because they justify an expression of enmity which nearly always occurs *directly.* For supreme instances which could enforce the law or exact vengeance as punishment are totally lacking in conflicts between nations, are usually disregarded in internal commotions, and are hardly relevant to the struggle between the minor groups, which is conducted by unbloody means. The group which wants to express enmity by means of direct action feels therefore an increased need for regarding its enmity as justified; the conviction of be-ing in the right is for the group an indispensable factor of moral fighting power (called *morale* for short) ; and so every party involved in a conflict does its utmost to prove that it is indeed the right.

Thus, as a result of the conceptions of right connected with it, the collision has become a contention of rights, a conflict, and therefore an occasion, a pretext, which permits the expression of enmity under satisfactory conceptions of justification. It becomes the ardently desired opportunity, grasped by an enmity which has long been lying in wait; it is the more readily provoked by the primary enmity, the stronger the pressure of the existing hostile feelings is.

In the consciousness of the antagonising groups themselves the conflict, the occasion, *appears* naturally as the *cause* of the enmity, for it must justify its expression. And it is felt as the cause, be its objective unimportance ever so apparent. One would expect that the outside world, at least where the occasion seems obviously immaterial, would realise the true relation between the cause of th. enmity and the occasion for its outbreak; and in particularly demonstrative cases this actually happens: as soon as the term "occasion" or "incident" is used, the secondary and only mediate character of the occurrence which allows the outbreak of enmity in the form of a conflict is recognised. Where it is realised that the conflict is being sought for on purpose, it is even characterised as a pretext; but generally even the unconcerned spectator allows himself to be seduced into regarding the conflict and the opposition or friction from which it derives as the real cause of enmity. He will often admit that it is difficult to decide the question of guilt, but he will not readily be prepared to consider the possibility of an outbreak of hatred ultimately caused by anything but the assumed guilt of the other party;

his own life is too much bound up in a world of similar notions, and the need for an explanation cannot escape the seduction of the obvious and apparently rational, as long as further penetration is barred by conceptions which, like the conception of right, are rooted in the strongest needs of the human mind.

Nevertheless, the relation between the occasion and the expression of enmity, which in individual cases often seems not unjust, is in group enmities necessarily so abnormal that the eruptions of hatred ever again make an impression of elementary unreason. Beside the violence of the outbreak and the fierceness of the struggle the occasion appears insignificant; and therefore the aim of the struggle is always horrendously disproportionate to the sacrifices brought for its dubious achievement. Who would seriously justify the waste of good and blood demanded for the possible conquest of a town or district; and who would have the courage to calculate the real value of a seat in parliament, for the by no means certain gain of which an enormous expense of work, time, money, passion, strife and bitterness has been squandered?

The case becomes most curious when the group enmity expresses itself between man and man, between individual and individual; and that, after ail, is always the ultimate result. Then enmity must necessarily attack people who personally are completely harmless and innocent. No occasion for the expression of enmity can be found in relation to them; and the justification which we had characterised as essential seems to be totally lacking. Actually, of course, it derives from the conception of inferiority, which imputes to each member of the enemy-group the evil qualities which, as first condition for harmful actions, permit preventive warfare. But where the conception of inferiority is not quite satisfactory for expressions of enmity of a factual nature, it becomes exacerbated to the imposition of *collective responsibility,* which holds all group members responsible for real, imagined or invented, but in any case credited, harmful actions of other group members or of the group leadership.

6. *Collective Responsibility*

The process of generalisation is technically made possible by the curious changes to which human *observation* is subject. For we do not register the world with the cold objectivity of a photographic plate; every change in distance and in the frequency of our observation causes a variation in the result, while moreover the inner world of our thoughts and sensations is of decisive influence on our observations and findings. We are often surprised at the sight of a photograph of even our closest acquaintance, which seems but a poor likeness. And thus we who, notwithstanding all mirrors, have not even an approximately objective idea of what we look like, are also unable to retain a true general impression of our nearest daily surroundings. We do not see them in our mind in a uniform image, and when we see them unexpectedly from afar and in unfamiliar surroundings, their appearance surprises us. To us, the individual variation and its impression, which moreover continues to be modified in our consciousness by personal associations, gains a preponderance yet increased by the closeness and frequency of contact. To a lesser degree are close acquaintances dissociated from the approximate objectivity of the general impression; only the indifferent stranger leaves us with a fairly objective picture determined by his individual characteristics. Thus we might remember him, for instance, as that man with the thin gray hair, watery eyes and a rather broad nose. With very remote persons who belong to a foreign group the process is precisely opposite to that in the case of our nearest surroundings; in the stranger we only discern the typical *group characteristics;* individual traits become subordinate and escape our observation; in the case of ethnically far remote groups it becomes at times impossible to distinguish individuals at all. And just as in the sheep we only recognise the species, a woolly animal with thin legs which belongs to a flock of similar animals, so we see in the Negro only a dark-skinned, snubnosed being with thick lips, one out of millions of similar beings. In Rotterdam's Chinatown the police has more than once been hampered by being unable to distinguish the individual faces of Chinese. And even the German, ethnically so closely related to the Dutchman, makes in Holland definitely the impression of one of a group, and is easily recognised as a group type.

The foreign group appears as an agglomeration of similar beings., the foreign individual as an accumulation of average group characteristics, so to say as a representative sample. *Therefore the stranger appears representative.* His group is judged by his appearance and behaviour. And the group, accordingly, demands exemplary behaviour from its members abroad, for there they are regarded as representative for the group.

And thus, as in any case and *a priori* unfavourable collective characteristics are imputed to the foreign group, the attention with which its doings are observed is malevolent and full of suspicion, and the eagerness with which it throws itself on any undesirable or under the accepted rules condemnable act, understandable; as is the satisfaction with which such an act is regarded as *symptomatic* and considered as a *confirmation of apprehensions entertained* and a *justification for antipathies felt.*

The evil act of the individual becomes the potential evil act of his community: it appears as the unavoidable expression of a malignant group character., which only by chance has availed itself of the chance individual concerned, but has issued from the community as a whole.

The judgment of reason is always subjected to the potent rule of the instincts, and subordinated to their needs; nevertheless the approval of its control is always sought for, even if it has to be brought about by highly fictitious notions. Therefore the misdemeanour of the individual is always so welcome a confirmation of the foreign group's depravity; therefore nothing less will suffice as justification for an enmity thirsting after expression. Then what is easier than to regard, instead of the undiscoverable or unattainable guilty or at least accused individual, his available group comrades as objects of revenge? Or to vent an excess of hate which is not satisfied with a single victim upon all who can be reached?

Thus collective responsibility is imposed in group relations: the group is made responsible for the member, the member for the group, and every member for every other member. *The attribution of collective responsibility,* however offensive it may be to the normal sense of justice, *dominates group enmity.* Particularly correct behaviour, often laid down in a special reglement, is demanded from the officer and the official, because his fault is reckoned against his whole class; even before the first world war, the German in France was made to pay individually for the hatred felt against his nation since the defeat of 1870; when the "Lusitania" was torpedoed, London mobs looted the shops of Germans who individually were the most harmless of persons; and Jews are being killed to this very day because they are held responsible for the crucifixion of Jesus, ascribed to Jewish influence, and the treason of Judas Iscariot two thousand years ago.

In practice, the principle of collective responsibility is also made to serve further purposes: parties are discredited by recalling that their leaders or individual members belong to hated groups; unpopular persons are made impossible by being, often falsely, accused of belonging to unpopular groups; until recently (*) every undesirable politician in Europe was accused of being a bolshevik: that is to say, hostile feelings fostered against this group were directed against the individual and the latter thereby made to share the responsibility for everything for which the bolsheviks were blamed. Tendential literature is constructed on the principle of collective responsibility. The essential point of the method is not so much that the representatives of favoured groups proclaim the theories of those groups, but that they are equipped with noble qualities and commit noble actions; the representatives of the opposite group are scoundrels, and act as such. The technique is based on the well-founded speculation that the public will assume that the group concerned has in general the same qualities, and that it will tend to ascribe the

---

(*) And now again — 1949.

actions of the fictitious representatives to the whole group. In war literature the hate of the crowd is of set purpose excited by letting representatives of enemy nations commit all sorts of outrages in novels and plays.

By means of the imposing of collective responsibility it becomes possible for isolated clashes and the conflicts resulting from them to become the occasion for an outbreak of enmity which directs itself against all available members of the enemy group, even where all individual victims of the outbreak are apertly innocent.

This possibility is of such eminent practical importance because in group struggle never all, and often only very few, group members clash personally. The clashes often occur only between the group executives, or are, at least, transformed by them into conflicts, while the groups themselves notice little or nothing: thus the imposition of collective responsibility is absolutely necessary in order to create the conditions for a struggle in which anonymous group beings who, of course, personally have nothing against each other, jump at each other's throats under the influence of mutual conceptions of justification. For these reasons there usually is, in addition to the accusations in grand style which act as introduction to the actual hostilities, some single incident which gives the signal to die beginning of a real fight. For an incident acts far stronger on the imagination of the group masses than the complicated argument involved in an accusation; and generalisation renders it possible to make the enemy group with all its members responsible for the incident. Most wars and revolts begin with a single clash, usually a murder; and in the (first) World War the concrete justification concept had to draw not upon the alleged appetite for conquest of the enemy, but upon (largely invented) outrages of individual participants.

For the suitability of an incident for purposes of collective responsibility does not in the least suffer by its being invented. It is sufficient if the crowd believes in its occurrence. So the group executive, which by entering into the fight merely executes the will of the masses, but at the same time exposes those same masses to the gravest dangers (for one would like to annihilate the enemy, but does not want to be annihilated by him) would rather provide the demand for justification with more substantial nourishment than can be extracted from the always highly problematical White Paper which is supposed to established the guilt of the enemy. It will therefore invent accusations which act upon the imagination of the masses. In group war coldbloodedly fabricated accusations are standard tactics, which are held to be hallowed by a purpose regarded as overruling minor ethics; but then, these tactics can only succeed because the most improbable incrimination is most readily believed by masses who need it as justification for instincts of hate clamouring for expression.

The artificially invented accusation responds to an urgent demand and is met halfway by an imagination heated by fear and suspicion; where the potential of hatred is sufficiently high, generalisation is not only most complete and uninhibited, but the incidents can then assume a fully imaginary character; unsolved crimes are imputed to the enemy group; if the crime is solved, they are accused of intellectual authorship or direct instigation; economic emergencies which seem somehow to be due to human activities while the actual connections remain unclear, are by preference attributed to alleged machinations of the hated group; even epidemics and other unmistakable "Acts of God" such as famine, flood or earthquake, are blamed upon the enemy by the common people (*) . Thus the crime is ever present before the eye of an incensed imagination as a probability which seems half a reality and which for that imagination often turns into a whole reality, even before rumours have been spread. When the rumour then emerges, it seems a thought spoken out loud; and it is not always easy to say where the fancies of imagination end and coldblooded invention begins.

7. *Degrees of Tension*

The difficult attempt to establish the cause of the difference of degrees of tension in group enmity cannot be totally avoided. Obviously, the degree of tension is determined by two factors: the *need* for expressing enmity and the *possibility* to do so. For the need exerts direct pressure upon the direction of possible expression; but the call of a chance for expression in its turn brings many hidden hostile feelings to the surface.

The influence of the second determining element is more easily estimated than that of the first. For it is infinitely difficult to establish the extent to which the sensitivity for suffering varies individually, in which way the mental transmutation into hostile feelings occurs from case to case, where the limit of accumulation lies, and how violent suffering must be to necessitate immediate expression of enmity. The fact that the individual disposition varies considerably in this respect is already

_____

(*) Whether as divine visitations brought down by the enemy's sin or (recent rationalisation) as by-products of atomic warfare. — 1949.

embodied in the experience which underlies the description of the traditional temperaments. In general we may readily observe how in vigorous individuals with a strong vitality the direct transmutation is more vivacious, and therefore the will to struggle more pronounced. It is further clear that particularly violent suffering cannot, or at any rate not for long, be retained, and requires an immediate outbreak; and it is, moreover, unmistakable that once the struggle has broken out, hate is for a while yet intensified by the uncommon suffering undergone as a result of the struggle. This additional suffering need, of course, not be accumulated, because the overt hostilities allow for its immediate expression; but it makes itself the more felt once the fighting has ceased, for then it is debarred from expression and must seek other ways: thence the remarkable degree of internal disturbance immediately after wars. But when the bitterness, the impotent will to express hatred, has abated, then physical and mental lassitude may lead to a distinct decrease of the need for hostile expression and so to a lessening of the tension.

Thus we find that strong dissatisfaction with existing conditions, especially when nourished by painful intervention of the opposite party, causes increasing pressure of the impulse to express hate, and therefore increased tension; in this case the increase appears to be due to material factors. But the dissatisfaction may also be of less material nature—i.e. not exactly a reaction to suppression or to the lack of first necessities—and appear as ambitious discontent and avidity for power of a group in still modest circumstances. Such groups develop an increasing impulse to expand, which engenders heavy tensions; and as long as a certain satiety and lassitude do not arise, *victory* in the struggle may still *increase* the tension: for it opens ways to the achievement of new and greater war aims. Strong vitality is always accompanied by strong dissatisfaction and a pronounced urge for struggle, so that in the surroundings of highly vital groups there usually is an increase in tension. This vitality is naturally often found in ethnical groups, for according to our present conceptions we cannot imagine it as due to other than physical causes; when a certain lassitude occurs in ethnical groups, then the vital individuals which remain seek by preference refuge in groups of another category, which offer conditions favourable for struggle in the shape of an ideology based on material discontent. Especially in the first stages of development, highly increased tension reigns also in the surroundings of groups of this type.

Far less basic, and therefore far more noticeable, is the influence of the *possibility* to express enmity on the degree of tension. Certain categories, in the first place the ethnical ones, are particularly suitable for the expression of the most dangerous instincts of hate, and so struggle between groups of such categories involves in itself a heightened degree of tension. Large ethnical-racial, ethnical-national and ethnical-language groups arouse by the very fact that they are felt to be the frame for ever recurring slaughter of men, an expectation of an opportunity of struggle which lends them a considerably higher tension than that found at the border of groups of lesser importance for mass struggle.

But in every group tension increases, often quite suddenly, as soon as a concrete chance to express hatred to a larger extent comes in sight. For the approach of a *possibility* of expression evokes precisely the repressed, i.e.

naturally the gravest, feelings of hate; *and so the technical possibility to express hate becomes a magnet which draws concealed hate to the fore, and thus increases tension to an extraordinary degree.*

In this way the most different circumstances may cause an increase of tension; it is, for instance, not infrequently due to a leader of genius that a group becomes unusually expansive and lets itself be led from struggle to struggle, from conquest to conquest. Such a group offers a great chance to express enmity, and often enough attracts even strangers; thus the appearance of a great leader (one remembers Alexander the Great and Napoleon) may cause enormous tensions in whole continents. The technical possibility to express enmity is, incidentally, always largely dependent on the policy of the group executive: a restless or clumsy policy causes frequent conflicts, and as soon as these announce themselves, concealed enmity desires break out throughout the masses, and cause such degree of tension that the executive is often unable to remain master of the situation. At the quietest of times an alarming message may be sufficient to evoke potentials of hatred which no one would have thought possible; and in past times, when thrones fallen empty were identical with approaching wars, the chance decease of a monarch was liable to unchain the most powerful excitement amongst nations.

Now the degree of tension existing decides the actual importance of a collision which has become a conflict. For while a clash which leads to conflict is by preference taken from a sphere which, like for instance the economic, is of great importance to man, this is by no means essential; the occasion need be of no actual importance; it may be of subordinate, and even of ridiculously slight, weight. For not the nature of enmity, but the existing degree of tension determines the violence of the outburst. Where tension between two groups is slight, or where they are allied against a third group, even the objectively most important contrasts are settled peacefully; if tension is high, then a word, a gesture, an inflexion of the voice may furnish the occasion for the most violent outbreak of enmity.

But as the tension present is increased by expectations of hostilities, it may be said *that the conflict derives its importance not only from the actual tension, but also' from that potentially available,,* i.e. from the hostile emotions called forth by the approaching opportunity for discharge. This attraction of the conflict for concealed hostile feelings favours the error that the conflict causes enmity. But in reality the nations care as little about unoccupied thrones as the mob about a stolen purse; and it is only the opportunity to let obscure enmity instincts work their will which excites nations at the approach of war, and the crowd in the street when a pickpocket is arrested: the conflict draws concealed hostile feelings to the light by promising them a chance of expression.

As a result of this attraction, the tension which occurs around groups with a materially attractive ideology is also fed by another source. According to the predominant philosophy of life release from poverty and distress is sought in different spheres; the force of discontent lends sometimes religious, sometimes social, and occasionally purely political groups a fighting strength which causes considerable tension; but this tension is yet increased by the fact that the group by its promise of conditions favourable for struggle releases much repressed hostile emotion and draws its carriers into the militant group. Thus we repeatedly observe in history the victorious progress of such movements, which in the end are carried far less by their original ideology than by the attraction of their success in the struggle. When such groups, as the result of a certain satiation, finally lose their impetus, and consequently their real attraction for individuals still in need of struggle—and some of these always remain—tension around them abates and passes, unless the state of weariness is general, to other categories which promise to relieve suffering which has become oppressive by yet other ways and means.

As the most violent emotions rule most exclusively, the maximum enmity tension passes always on to that category which at a given moment promises expression for the strongest enmity feelings. When in the election struggle political strife reaches its culmination, all other differences are for the time being relegated to the background; and as soon as organised murder by armed force, war, seems to approach, the tension between social, religious, political, and in brief, all categories which normally serve only the expression of minor enmities, disappears.

8. *Border Tension*

For every expression of enmity contact is necessary; and *close* contact is necessary where the expression of enmity consists of the intentional *avoidance* of contact; this avoidance, as we have seen, is the form which conditions of enmity tension assume when they are most durable and regular, i.e. in the long periods which lie between active outbreaks. In such times the large nucleus of the most extensive and important groups, such as those

of the national-ethnical category, has hardly any opportunity
for inimical reaction to the counter-group concerned. The
expression of enmity can only confine itself to unfavourable
criticism of the group character and the actions or, if necessary,
the presumed evil intentions of the foreign group executive;
but for the duration of official peace these activities exhaust
the range of possible forms of enmity expression for the main
body of the group. Only where a single member of the foreign
group penetrates into the group nucleus, does he automatically
become a target for the enmity directed against his group. And
even then, unless the differences in group characteristics are too
pronounced, does the absorptive power of the large group work
its way on the individual: the isolated foreigner is devoid of
means of self-defense, and may be absorbed without risk. Only
if a number of foreigners penetrate into the group at one and
the same time, and form a foreign colony within it, there arise
all those symptoms of tension which we usually observe only
at the normal place of contact, the border. Thus there manifests
itself what as a rule is designated as xenophobia. Apart from
these cases the main body of, for instance, the national-ethnical
groups is in a comparative state of rest; only on the group border
is the contact of the *more important* groups permanent, and only
there is the expression of hostile feelings within the frame of the
most important group possible; this possibility, as we have seen,
relegates the less important group categories to the background:
at the border of the group the antagonism of the most impor-
tant group categories takes effect. Thus there arises within the
group itself a *difference in the potential* of tension: a comparatively quiet nucleus is always surrounded by a border in a far

higher state of tension; where the members of opposed groups face each other in their advanced positions, there arises *border tension.* We find it on all state frontiers; it rules on the borders of ethnical-national and ethnical-language groups; other categories do not usually have so distinct a structure of a border surrounding a main body, but in the case of the large religious groups, for instance, border tension may often be clearly observed, though usually in the special and modified form from which we shall discuss in connection with the minority group.

At these group borders the members of officially perhaps friendly, but as neighbours in any case antagonistic, groups face each other in usually pronounced antipathy, which expresses itself in the avoidance, wherever possible, of such contacts which would seem to be demanded by the circumstances, and which cannot always be completely obviated. These unavoidable contacts lead to local clashes, and not infrequently to grave excesses.

It goes without saying that border tension is not completely dissociated from the general state of tension; where the latter is increased, border tension will also be stronger than, for instance, at times when the groups concerned are allied against a common enemy and therefore maintain pronouncedly friendly relations. But even in these cases border tension continues to some extent; a fact which may be exemplified by conditions in the world war, and its broad coalitions, where the intermingling of armies created far larger group borders between the allied nations on either side than those which exist in normal times, when each nation lives in its own country and has only restricted areas of contact with its neighbours.

As a result of this lack of contact, border tension under conditions of normal group distribution does not assume too much practical importance; the outbreaks of enmity which invariably accompany it are confined to comparatively very small areas. These areas are of special moment only inasmuch as they are prone to providing the occasions and consequently the subject matter for conflicts of which existing tension avails itself in order to induce outbreaks of enmity. Conflicts depend on friction, and therefore on contacts; consequently they will find their fuel most readily at the group border; and so it is hardly astonishing that in the struggle between nations, where enormous human masses must draw the matter for their conflicts from comparatively insignificant border areas, the conflict, the pretext for enmity, is so desperately disproportionate to the war itself, the real manifestation of that enmity; and that as desperate an unreason manifests itself in the attempt to motivate the war by the occasion which has triggered its eruption.

9. *The Minority Group*

Special, most particular and farreaching importance is attained by border tension when the major groups at whose borders it by preference appears do no longer form geographically circumscript closed bodies, but have in some way been broken up into isolated fragments which have become dispersed among large opposite groups of the same category. *Then the isolated group fragment contacts in all its members the opposite group: in sharp contrast to the latter it possesses no main body in a state of comparative rest; it is over its whole extent a group border, an army exclusively consisting of vanguards, and*

*therefore lives over its whole extent in a continuous state of
highly increased tension.*

This peculiar situation has peculiar consequences. The curiously unilateral distortion of the border relation is due to the fact
that the isolated group fragment in comparison to the opposite
group is in a striking numerical minority; we are, it appears,
dealing with the "minority group", of recent ill repute. The ill
repute derives from the circumstances that its presence is everywhere accompanied by particular conditions of uncommonly
high tension which become noticeable in this peculiar border
relation. When speaking of minority groups, one usually thinks
of ethnical or ethnical-national minorities; and these are indeed
of special moment because the ethnical category is as such a
highly important one, and because especially in the minority
relation its passive strength, the invariance of the principal group
characteristics, the physical and mental type, causes particularly
grave complications. There are, however, also numerous religious
minority groups which, on conscious purpose but therefore only
with the greater tenacity, preserve their group characteristics no
less successfully than the ethnical minority group. The social minority group exists everywhere: it has some traits in common with
the other categories of minority groups, but has strictly speaking
a different significance. In the minority group as everywhere do
groups of different categories coincide not infrequently; and this
tends to aggravate the situation still further.

The minority group is, notwithstanding its pronounced numerical disadvantage, by no means always weak and powerless; but it is
never on approximately equal terms with the majority group: it either
rules the latter or is ruled by it. Powerful minority groups are by

no means as rare as one might assume at first sight. The ruling social class is always a minority group; in the colonies it is at the same time a foreign minority within the national category; and it has often been so in history, when victorious nations used to abduct their vanquished enemies into slavery. The prevalence of ruling minorities may be based on powerful centres of which they are the advanced posts, but also on superiority in technical, particularly military and economic respects, a superiority which it takes the subjected groups often an astonishingly long time to attain. Even the powerful minority groups exist in a state of extraordinary tension; their position is always in danger and they protect themselves by special defense measures: they surround themselves by a protective armour of strict conventions setting their seal on every phase of a life which moves in strict and unchangeable tracks and so lends the individual the strength and security which he needs in his exposed position; thus an excess of group characteristics is created which makes desertion from the group, and, even more important, penetration of strangers into the group almost impossible. This is of so particular importance because the strength of the minority group lies not in quantitative but in qualitative elements; therefore it cannot expect anything but loss of strength from the absorption of foreign group material; and therefore it seeks its strength in absolute exclusivity.

The weak minority group also exists in a permanent state of increased tension; as long as its resistance and its will to exist have not been totally broken, it equally takes refuge in extraordinary defense measures; which are not at all dissimilar to those of the powerful minority group. For a persecuted group is even more in the necessity of seeking its strength and security in strict and unchangeable patterns of life, in a kind of impregnable base position where the individual, tired of the struggle, always again finds new sources of strength. And even more than the ruling is the persecuted group dependent on the unconditional solidarity of its members, and must therefore rely on its homogeneous closed structure; it will the more discourage the penetration of foreign elements as by virtue of its situation it is bare of attraction, and therefore regards the stranger who nevertheless demands admission with particular suspicion.

Both minority groups, though in themselves so different, have yet another trait in common: in respect of both there is a unilateral shift of collective responsibility. In the normal group struggle generalisation is mutual; in the minority relation it is almost wholly confined to the minority. The powerful ruling minority group feels of course a sort of collective contempt for the ruled majority, and even in the subjected minority there are traces of a collective unfavourable opinion with relation to the ruling majority: generalisation is too powerful a necessity in group life. But in general the minority regards the members of the majority group, nearly in the same degree as they themselves, as individuals; it tends to judge their actions *individually* according to some valid rule, and also to confine responsibility to the individual. For the majority group, whether ruling or ruled, always has that numerical overweight which favours the separate observation of individuals, and consequently a tendency to their individual judgment, even on the part of the minority. The latter, on the contrary, functions definitely as a closed unit; it lives under the unimpaired sway of the generalisation principle; each single one of its members is invariably regarded as representative; the action of the individual is reckoned against the whole group; the group and all of its attainable members are made responsible for every undesirable action of any other member, and revenge or punishment is, wherever possible, also exacted from every attainable member. With regard to the powerful majority group this possibility is slight; for it can avail itself of effective means of defense. But the weak and defenseless minority group is continuously exposed to such a generalising lust for revenge; and its situation is in every respect desolate.

While for normal group enmity a certain regularity in the mutual expression of enmity is characteristic, the antagonism between a powerful majority and a powerless minority is characterised by a onesidedness of hostile actions which is fatal for the minority. For the latter is exposed to continual attacks and must confine itself to laborious attempts to maintain its existence, without a chance to resist actively to any extent; even its passive means of defense are totally inadequate and its existence often has to rely on nothing but periodical flight from place to place. This onesided relation of permanent attack and failing defense is called *persecution.* Weak minority groups are usually persecuted more or less emphatically.

It goes without saying that permanent persecution does not only make heavy demands upon the power of resistance of the group, but may finally even undermine its will to exist. And for this mental collapse armistice is, as always, more dangerous than open war. At the very moment when relations have somewhat improved for the time being, terror of renewed persecution makes itself master of the persecuted minority group; only then is it overcome by the full misery of mental servitude; it loses the will to exist independently, and its members desire to be absorbed within the majority group. But the latter, now more than ever, emphatically rejects, out of the fulness of its natural superiority instinct, the contempted postulants who now also render themselves contemptible. The antagonism now appears as embittered, always aggressive enmity and unlimited contempt on the part of the majority, to which the minority responds with admiration and pronounced sympathy: *the antagonism assumes an unnatural, perverted character.*

The weak minority group lives in a state of increased hostile tension; but the degree of this tension, too, depends mainly on the state of the majority group; excitement of any kind, whether due to expansive activity or the result of crises, ill fate or disasters afflicting the majority group, are expressed to an increased extent against the minority. And as the latter is always a readily available and defenseless target for every need to discharge hatred, the excessive supply of suffering resulting from disasters can transform itself immediately into hostile acts against the minority group; which then becomes a scapegoat in an unmistakable and unadulterated form otherwise not often met with in group relations. As in all cases of immediate transference of hate it is attempted to impute at least part of the blame for the disaster to the scapegoat on whom it is revenged; and this is much easier in group relations, for so fantastic a suspicion as the poisoning of wells in epidemics or treason in case of a defeat is more easily imputed to that polycephalous

monster, the horrific minority group, than to any individual.

Horror, that most instinctive and most penetrating fear of the
unknown danger or the danger of the unknown, is usually most
pronounced where the minority group is determined ethnically.
The social and religious minority groups are also sources of
horror, but the most uncanny feelings are caused by the ethnical minority: for there the "otherness" springs from the depth
of a different nature and essence, from the "foreign" blood;
the ethnical minority has the emotional connotation of being a
foreign group, and remains so even if its members have been
living in the country of their residence longer than those of the
majority. *For the conception of the Foreigner is not determined
by geography, but a product of group phenomena.*

Man is not a foreigner because he *comes from* somewhere,
but because he *is* somewhere, to wit, amongst a group not his
own. The majority group as such regards the minority group
as a group fragment, a sort of splinter, which has penetrated
into its group body; and *for that reason* it regards the minority
group as foreign. As soon as man, even as a single individual,
penetrates into a group not his own, the unwilling host group
concentrates upon him all the hostile emotions usually directed
outward and upon neighbouring groups. We should not forget
that this merely happens because the neighbouring group
simply provides the most readily available opportunity for friction; the emanating enmity in itself has no preference for any
given object and is aimed at everything available. Therefore
it is of no account whether the foreigner's group of origin and
the host group were already on a footing of enmity or not; as

soon as he appears, he forms the border of a new neighbouring group, which has become such by reason of his proximity: he himself is the new group border; and he, fitly enough, becomes the object of the enmity tension which reigns there.

Consequently everything foreign is stamped with the trademark of inferiority which brands any enemy group. Most nations have, in addition to the special insulting nicknames used for their closest neighbours and special enemies, also a general term of contempt for anything foreign. In Jewish parlance the word "goy", which originally meant nothing but nation, and in the Scriptures is also used for the Jews, assumed the meaning of "foreign" nation and thus its present connotation of contempt. For the Greeks and the Romans the same connotation was borne by "barbarian"; to the Christian religions the invective is "pagan", to the Islam "giaour". In present-day Germany the word "Auslaender" has as unpleasant a flavour as in the English-speaking countries the term "foreigner" or "alien", and even the placid Dutchman thinks of nothing good when he uses his "vreemdeling". Contrary to most group phenomena this hatred of the foreigner must have drawn attention in comparatively early times. At any rate it has been honoured by the invention of a special term, and is called "xenophobia", strictly speaking: fear of stranger (*). After all we have said about the part played by fear in the enmity relation, the term will hardly need further explanation.

(*) I have searched all sources available to me for a term to indicate *hatred* rather than *fear* of the foreigner, but in vain; one might suggest "misoxeny" (on the lines of misanthropy) , but it does not seem that such a word actually exists.—Transl.

Originally, the foreigner is as such deprived of all rights, and even in the modern state his rights are restricted, be his activities ever so useful and his contribution to the demands and needs of the community ever so conscientious. As a temporary resident he is valued as an object of exploitation; when he settles permanently he is tolerated in modern countries out of considerations of reciprocity, but isolated like a focus of danger which cannot be rendered totally harmless. Of course there are always good people who take up his cause, for protecting the stranger is an outstanding virtue, regarded as such precisely because the stranger is in such great need of protection: he belongs to those outcasts whom the law and society fail to safeguard, and who are a charge upon the care of the virtuous. The isolated individual, though, will, unless he is a strong personality and comes from a group highly conscious of its own value, sooner or later lose the desire to continue belonging to his original group; as far as lies in his power he assumes all the variable characteristics of the receiving group, its languages, manners and customs, its morals and by preference also its religion. In the case of more pronounced ethnical differences the individual possibilities of assimilation are of course halted by the natural bar of the ethnical characteristics: he can do no more than produce, in collaboration with a member of the receiving group, a hybrid progeny which finally may merge into that group.

Assimilation is for its victims a bitter tragedy: it demands the sacrifice of essential elements of the individual personality; it places them in a position as unpleasant to themselves as to the outer world, with all the trademarks of the unharmonious and sham. The assimilant ratifies the inferiority and contemptibility of his own group, by preferring another; and thereby he also ratifies his own inferiority and contemptibility, for he is a product of this group. Moreover he must attempt to appear to the receiving group as something which he is not in reality: one of them; he would without warrant appropriate a privilege to which he is not entitled, namely the membership of the other group, which by its members is always regarded as a privilege; thus he must appear as an imposter. Like every imposter he fears the discovery of his deception: he trembles for the revelation of his real origin; he keeps himself under constant observation lest he betray himself by a word, a gesture, a look; his life has no more than the one aim and purpose: successful camouflage.

Naturally the isolated case has always only a closely limited effect within the small circle in which it happens to occur; single strangers are within larger groups so unimportant that they disappear without causing reactions worth mentioning. The minority group, however, is felt by the majority group as an accumulation of foreigners, which forms a permanent and, as a result of its, in the case of a group, yet increased natural resistance, yet far more complicated aliens problem. Each single individual of the minority group draws by its different characteristics the hate of the majority group upon himself; and by this difference he moreover draws an increased attention which causes the number of members of the minority group to appear much larger than it is in reality; and so the need for expression of hate has in respect of the minority group every imaginable chance.

But this very multitude of chances increases the difficulty of the problem presented by the minority group.

Firstly, hatred tends to the annihilation and expulsion of its object; but if it indulges in this tendency, it deprives itself of further favourable opportunities for expression, while the continued presence of a pariah flatters feelings of own importance and provides for permanent expression of hatred, at least in the less brutal degree. Thus different trends of the urge for hate expression come into conflict. Secondly, annihilation and expulsion of a minority group become easily a disadvantage for the majority group itself, because the annihilation affects economic forces of importance; not only the Pharaoh of the Bible wavered between the destructive desires of hate and the preservative tendency of the economic interest in respect of the Jews. And finally: it is true that in times of peace the urge to express enmity is largely repressed; but such a repression cannot but be advantageous to a prospering community life. The community suffers by living permanently in a state of extreme hostile excitement; and so the existence of minority groups is a curse to themselves, but far from a blessing for the majority group. To avoid mistakes it should once again be emphasized that the problem is never determined by the nature, character or activities of the minority group, but solely by its bare presence, by the *constellation*. For this renders permanent antagonism of not insignificant force inevitable.

Thus the majority group will often be unable to make up its mind as to the solution to be found for the minority problem; and this indecision is clearly expressed in the attempt at an answer which seems to offer the greatest advantages, and is often enough actually given a trial: *absorption*. The majority group as a whole regards absorption as desirable; and the minority is often willing. But the process must naturally take its effect at the individual level, and there the effect is opposed by the tendency towards repulsion. Thus it may happen that desertion from Judaism is made attractive by the socially desirable premium of a civil service position, but the deserting fugitive remains socially excommunicated even after his desertion. As a corrective to this process, the system of the entrance fee has become customary; the member of a minority group which enters the majority must compensate the stain of his origin by a special prestation. But though this fee is frequently tendered with the utmost willingness, the repellent force remains in general so strong that the greater part of the minority is, for all its good will, not admitted to absorption.

And so we have at least hinted at the essential issues of group enmity. An exhaustive description could not be given; we were forced to deny ourselves even the most cursory discussion of the phenomena of actual group struggle, the mechanism of alliances, the splitting and merging of groups, changes of group pattern, the effect of the group struggle on the group members, group executive and outsiders, and the various effects of the outcome of the struggle. For our task was only to outline the general frame within which the phenomena of antisemitism are contained; and the outline has possibly already become more detailed than the point of issue warrants.

A description of the principal forms in which anti-semitism appears will now have to establish to which extent they fit into the general frame of group phenomena.

Chapter VI

Manifestations of Antisemitism

After having been forced to pick our laborious way through a world of conceptions rarely visited by intellectual tourism, amidst a vegetation of partly unfamiliar terms, we can now with the greater confidence return to the familiar territory of antisemitic phenomena, keeping as far as possible to the well-known highways.

Antisemitic phenomena are usually qualified more particularly: we speak, for instance, of economic anti-semitism. The adjective seems to indicate a classification. In actual fact the commonly used classifying terms cannot be subsumed under a regular system, for sometimes they contain an attempt at an explanation, at other times again they describe the field in which the phenomenon occurs, or they may fulfill both tasks at the same time. Nevertheless it may be possible to use these common designations as a starting point for a discussion of the forms in which antisemitism appears.

Usually we speak of:
1.   Religious antisemitism,
2.   Economic antisemitism,
3.   Political antisemitism,
4.   Social antisemitism,
5.   Cultural antisemitism, and
6.   Racial antisemitism.

Finally we also know the seemingly most paradoxical but current expression: "Jewish antisemitism", meaning the hatred shown by Jews against other Jews. Though this form of antisemitism can of course not be treated on the same footing as the other forms, the language instinct with its usual intuition has not shot far from the mark in creating this expression. So-called Jewish antisemitism is also a group phenomenon, though a curiously perverted one; and we shall not fail to discuss it.

1. *Religious Antisemitism*

Religious antisemitism is the name for the enmity supposedly aimed at the Jews in their quality of followers of what is sometimes described as the Israelitic persuasion. The hatred apparent in this form of enmity is called religious hatred; and is thus characterised as of the same order as the enmity directed against the followers of many other religions.

And in fact, religious antisemitism is nowadays rather generally regarded as a religious group enmity, of which there are as many as there are religions. They are now rarely regarded as objectively justified, but rather considered as the result of a prejudice, which may be excused as backward, but is hardly ever defended in enlightened Europe. In other parts of the world it is different; and it has for a long time been different in Europe as well. There, too, a different religion used to be regarded as the most valid reason for enmity imaginable. And religious enmity, contrary to all other group enmities without exception, is the one form which might perhaps be regarded as to some extent normal; for while otherwise the picture of group enmity receives its most characteristic lines from a generalisation which is obviously contrary to all reason, religious group enmity may at least *seemingly* be interpreted as a sum total of (so-to-say) normal individual enmities.

Religious conviction pretends, possibly more than any other, to universal validity; thus it seems to gain in value, the more this validity is established. Whoever does not share the conviction, denies its validity, and diminishes its value. So it seems, at least; and one might say that the follower of a religious persuasion regards every dissenter as a personal enemy who by his unbelief depreciates a highly valued possession. Actually, this conception is completely false: the feelings of the true believer are different. The unbelief of others has never yet shaken anyone's belief in the truth and value of his own convictions, least of all in the heyday of religious persecution. In fact there also are numerous religious groups who pride themselves on the exclusive possession of their particular creed, segregate themselves anxiously from the surrounding world, and admit converts only when long and heavy trials have proved them worthy to be admitted to the chosen community. Actually this attitude would seem to make far better sense: the value of a possession is the greater, the less persons share in it; and the feeling of being chosen —the highest form of consciousness of value—must find most appropriate nourishment in the knowledge of the exclusivity of so precious a good.

But neither the one nor the other conception decides the attitude towards foreign religious groups. For this depends only on the relative strength of the groups and their position in the struggle. The colouring which the consciousness of value assumes is merely a result of this position. Religious groups do not differ in function from groups of other categories: they are on a footing of struggle with all neighbouring groups of their own category. Expansive religious groups regard the mere existence of dissenters as an insult, precisely as the powerful state regards the small neighbouring power and its will to be independent as a presumption. Non-expansive religious groups, like other groups in the same situation, prefer to find their strength in exclusivity. The *contents* of the creed are in this respect immaterial; and the differences in religious conception are in no relation to the degree of hostile tension. The most bitter and implacable enmity may be found between two sects who are concerned with nothing but the construction of a distinguishing formula for the indistinguishable difference of creed which is to be the criterium for their difference.

Thus Jewish religious conceptions and rites are never the real cause of enmity, though the need for justification has from time to time led to attempts to use them as such. A so-to-say normal ground for enmity might at the most be found in the circumstance that some Jews are supposed to have had a certain share in the crucifixion of the Founder of Christianity. But even if their guilt—which according to the then valid norms of justice, need not have been guilt at all—were established as a fact, the Jews in question have been dead for nearly two thousand years; and so this most absurd case of imposing collective responsibility known to history brands, clearer than anything else, an enmity attributed to such motives as a case of pure group enmity. But for us another question is more important. If today antisemitism is called religious hatred, it is in no way intended to cast any doubt on its nature of unreasonable and reprehensible group enmity. The intention is merely to deny it the character of an enmity determined by other factors, because thus it becomes possible first to minimise religious hatred as an almost overcome prejudice, and then to conclude that antisemitism, if it is nothing but that, is practically a thing of the past. The question is therefore: whether antisemitism really is nothing but religious hatred, whether it has at any time been no more than that, and why it has so long continued in that appearance. We have seen that often enough different categories may coincide within one group, and even that this unity is historically the original form. In that case there is, of course, also enmity between that group and its neighbour groups, but the principal enmity is directed against the *most important* category, and the characteristics of the thus overridden other categories descend to the level of auxiliary characteristics of the *chief* category. For the Jews, as for so many others, the ethnical and the religious category coincide; Jewish religion, with its (highly distinctive) rites and customs was a Jewish group characteristic which greatly impressed the non-Jewish population, but it was nevertheless no more than one of the characteristics—though the most definitely outlined one—of what was in the first place an ethnical foreign group.

And in fact we find on looking more closely that even in the time of the strongest religious persecution the anti-Jewish enmity was of another nature than contemporary enmities between religious groups of the same ethnical origin. The Jewish groups have always been treated as belonging to a foreign nation: they had to live in separate quarters of the towns, like even today the Chinese in America and Europe, and like the national minorities in various oriental towns. In this connection the famous controversy whether the Jews were from the beginning locked up in the ghetto or whether the segregation was at first voluntary, is of subordinate importance. For even if at first they lived together of their own free will, like today the Chinese in Rotterdam and New York, the freedom of this will is a very relative matter. Living together gives a certain feeling of security, and means escape from the hostile and expulsory tendencies of the ruling population. Moreover, the Jews in those times lived under the dearly bought and but rarely effective protection of foreigners' privilege. They were regarded and treated as nationally foreign groups, precisely like the non-Jewish foreign groups which in the Middle Ages were tolerated in a few trade centres—and which were also occasionally expelled.

If religious hatred had really been the determining element of the antisemitic attitude, then—and that always remains the formal proof in this matter—all enmity against the Jews should actually have disappeared as soon as differences of religion lost their decisive power as pretexts for enmity. We know to what extent anti-semitism has outlived the age of rationalism in which all metaphysical convictions were leveled down to the same value—or lack of value; we know that no change of religion could protect the Jew against antisemitism. Thus it follows that the ethnical category is the most important and determining one, the one against which antisemitism is directed. But there is good cause why it was Jewish *religion* which so long furnished the pretext for enmity; as long as religious feelings enjoyed overriding social validity, every persuasion which deviated from the Christian creed was sanctioned by the morals of the time as a cause for enmity, a cause invested by the forces which determine morals with validity of a far higher order than the mere hate of strangers. And in addition the religious group characteristics furnished the antagonism with even a better point of attack than the ethnical ones.

Jewish religion was and is a characteristic of the Jewish ethnical group, a characteristic like the Jewish nose, but a far more useful one. For it is to the group characteristics that enmity clings; to them it applies in the first place the method of degradation and devaluation which we have described in full detail; it is these which are branded as bad, ugly and disgusting by enmity, and thus become a justification for enmity. And for this purpose religious characteristics are more suitable than ethnical ones. For the ethnical characteristics are never so absolutely uniform and so firmly outlined as a creed and a rite which can be established beyond cavil and described in full particulars, while something like the national character can only be indicated by assumptions and interpretations. It is easy enough to say that the Jewish national character is evil, but we have seen to what pains modern antisemitism was put to establish Jewish inferiority even to its own approximate satisfaction. The Christian divines had not the least difficulty in proving to their flock that Jewish religion was false, and that the tenacity with which the Jews clung to it was evidence of incredible wickedness. It is of course also easy to say that the Jewish nose is ugly, and enmity in fact quite often uses derogatory esthetic judgments; but esthetic objections were even in the

Middle Ages no acceptable excuse for enmity, while everyone was satisfied when the Jewish ritual was denounced as wicked sorcery.

Whether the pretext for enmity is more or less easily found, is of course of little influence on the violence of the expression of enmity; reason always submits to the urge of instinct; but amongst a number of possible pretexts enmity always chooses the one most readily approved by reason and requiring the least elusive and tricky arguments for the creations of the necessary conceptions. Therefore difference of religion, with its exactly denned characteristics, is preferred as a pretext for enmity; and therefore Jewish religion was the preferred reason for the enmity against the ethnical group of the Jews, as long as religious notions had currency among the surrounding population; and where this is still the case, antisemitism often appears even today in the robe of religion.

2. *Economic Antisemitism*

While religious antisemitism is on the whole regarded as an affair of the past and its present remainders are depreciated as the shameful residue of the "dark ages", the actuality of economic antisemitism enjoys unconditional recognition.

The term may be intended to indicate the field in which the process occurs, and as such it is justified. Antisemitic occurrences are as frequent in the economic sphere as many other enmities, because the matter of conflict which unavoidably accumulates at this naturally sensitive point cannot but tempt every and any hostile feeling which seeks an apparently justified opportunity for expression. We should note, though, that the

expression of non-economic enmities in the economic field differs remarkably from relations of "normal" economic struggle,
a point which will soon be established.

In most cases by far the use of the expression does not confine itself to an indication of the field in which the phenomenon
occurs, but pretends to imply an explanation—and not always
the same explanation. Sometimes it is simply intended to claim
that normal economic friction produces normal enmities, and
that these are of course also directed against Jews, where they
participate in economic life; somewhat as follows: If an "Aryan"
shopkeeper has a competitor of the name Cohen (and particularly
if the competitor is successful) he will hate this competitor;
and as Cohen is a Jew, this hatred is called aiitisemitism. It is
clear that, if we understand the matter in this way, the so-called
antisemitism is in fact something different, namely competitive
jealousy which on account of its accidental object has been given
a wrong name. The antisemitic character of the incident is denied.
And that is the purpose of this interpretation: to state that the case
is in no way specifically antisemitic in nature and that the term
is merely used because the victim happens to be a Jew.

Now there are certain difficulties in maintaining this somewhat casual interpretation: the case Cohen differs too much
from the parallel case Smith or Brown. Our Gentile does not
confine himself to accusing Cohen of unfair competition, as
he does with Brown or Smith; in addition, and without rhyme
or reason, he publicly insults a Mr. Levy, a Jewish grain merchant with whom he has neither business nor social contacts: he
makes a habit of cursing the "b - - - - y Jews"; and he openly
declares that he is an antisemite. The explanation of this

so-called competitive jealousy must therefore take an additional step: Mr. Levy will be most willing to make it clear to us,
whether we ask him or not, that here we really have to do with
antisemitism, but that this is "only" a result of the professional
jealousy produced by Cohen's competition.

This, of course, does nothing to make us see why the competition of Smith does not cause our shopkeeper to foam at the mouth
with hatred of the Aryans, or why he blames all the Cohens and
Levys in the world for what he dislikes in the one insignificant
individual called Cohen. In fact it is the favoured theory of large,
mainly Jewish, circles that antisemitism is nothing but the hate
incurred by the Jews in the clashes of the economic struggle. A
certain transference of the hatred thus produced to other fields
is often assumed, though no further thought is given to the real
implications of this assumption. In its popular version the explanation says that antisemitism is "nothing more than" professional jealousy and envy of Jewish economic success, which is
regarded as remarkably great.

In dealing with this kind of superficiality, and in general with
the forms under which antisemitism appears, we must not forget
that the assumption of a fundamental enmity bare of all justified
motivation, which is vented only indirectly and under a variety of
pretexts, is, though not new, a highly radical conception, to which
even its theoretical adherents can almost never live up in the concrete
case. Again and again they succumb to the temptation of assuming as "normal" an enmity reaction as they can; how much more
readily will faulty and superficial explanations content those to
whom the notion of general and irrational hatred against the Jews

is *a priori* most unpalatable, and who resist that notion with all the power of their strongest instinctive conceptions.

This point should be clearly realised; for it is in itself none too easy to disregard in the expressions of economic antisemitism those characteristic differences which distinguish it so obviously from normal economic conflicts.

In the case of religious antisemitism we first had to show how, as a result of the coincidence of the religious and ethnical category in the Jewish group, an essentially anti-ethnical enmity could for so long a time find a particularly favourable point of attack and pretext for expression in the religious group characteristics. But there is no social-economic group with which the Jewish group coincides; on the contrary, the Jews are distributed over numerous social and economic groups of mixed ethnical composition. Consequently one would, assuming that antisemitism is of economic origin, expect them to experience, above and beyond individual competitive enmity, only the feelings directed against those hostile groups. If, for instance, the wholesalers look down on the retailers, then their contempt should not distinguish between the Jewish and the non-Jewish shopkeeper. But the characteristic point is that they do make a most noticeable difference; that in all economic conflicts the enmity effect with respect to Jewish objects is *not* the normal one; that an element *extraneous* to economic life interferes to *modify* the usual reaction. To express matters in terms of group theory: in the case of the Jews the antagonism of the ethnical groups overrides the antagonism of all other groups to which the Jews belong.

Let us first consider the simple and everyday case of competition. Normally, this bears a strictly personal character. What one objects to in one's inconvenient competitor is the fact that he exists; as this is not a "decent" reason for enmity, one likes to reproach him for the use of unfair methods; but this reproach is aimed at him personally alone, as is the envious enmity by which one responds to his success, if any. This changes as soon as a non-economic group antagonism intrudes itself into the relation. That may also happen in totally non-Jewish cases; enmities between all possible states, ethnical-national, purely ethnical, but, for instance, also religious groups readily intervene in the economic struggle. Where this is the case, the reaction against the competitor ceases to be purely personal: it seems as if it is "transferred" to all members of the group to which the man belongs and as if they are involved in the enmity "aroused" by him. We know that actually the reverse is the case: for enmity against, say, the Roman Catholics had already existed in our businessman for a long time; now a Catholic crosses his way in business, and that enmity is in a way confirmed in its justification; the Catholic competitor is no more than the live vindication of all the evil which has been imputed to his group long ago.

The same attitude is found in the Jewish object. It is by no means the case that Smith hates Cohen merely as a man and competitor, while Cohen, because he is a Jew, describes this hatred in the folly of his hypersensitivity as antisemitism. His inclinations rather take the opposite direction; he prefers to imagine that he affects his fellow-citizens only as man and individual. But he does not: the first thing which occurs to Smith as soon as he comes up against Cohen's competition, is the notion of the hated Jewish masses, of which Cohen seems to him to be merely the *typical, but in itself unimportant* individual case. What hinders him are *the Jews* in the incidental form of one of their number, a certain Cohen. And so Smith never says "this man", but "this Jew spoils my business". And he will go on to qualify the Jews as something unprintable which should be removed from the country by violent and equally unprintable means.

Thus we find that the in normal cases individual conflict derives its meaning from an existing group enmity which appropriates it for purposes of expression. In our case the group enmity is called antisemitism, and as it avails itself for its expression of an economic occasion, we may really call it economic antisemitism. Our opponent will admit this, but may claim that the whole enmity against the Jews is precisely a result of the Jews' success in business which, like success always does, evokes the hatred of the less successful. Now we would point out that firstly, Jewish success in business is often rather an imaginary affair and secondly, innumerable Jewish masses are notoriously as poor as church mice, so that their business successes cannot very well be the cause of an enmity which accompanies Jewish pauperisation as tenaciously as Jewish prosperity. The Jewish proletariat is exposed to no lesser enmity than the well-to-do Jews.

And moreover: competition in any case only arouses the annoyance of those whom it affects, success only the envy of those whom it leaves behind. Never yet has the president of a great power trust been disturbed by the thought that somewhere in the city a tobacconist makes his way, or that round the corner another goes bankrupt. Jewish competition, which is mainly middle class com-

petition (the "plague" of the Jewish middleman), is by preference denounced by the higher classes of society, who have no
personal contacts with the middle classes in question and are not
materially interested in their welfare. The successful business of
a Jewish shop cannot do them even imaginary damage, and the
expansion of a Jewish banking concern would probably rather
be to their advantage; for with Jewish finance and commerce
these circles often maintain not unprofitable business relations;
as we have seen, business interests can, if the advantages are
sufficient, override certain medium degrees of hostile tension;
though tension may reach a degree where profit is sacrificed
to hatred. In any case these circles are those which in the first
place voice complaints against Jewish intermediate trade and
Jewish capital; not because they suffer any real or imaginary
damage from it, but because they object to the occupation of
any place of importance in the economy of their nation, and in
fact any place at all, by Jews. And this opposition only makes
sense because they regard the Jews as a foreign, enemy group,
which for this reason should hold no economic power, and
strictly speaking should be completely expelled. This hatred is
purely hatred of the foreigner, of the ethnical minority group,
and wants to deprive the hated group of the economic means
of existence.

Incidentally, it goes without saying that any kind of success
and prosperity is begrudged to an unpopular group, and in this
sense the prosperous Jew may evoke the envious thought, how well
off "those people" are. But this prosperity is so offensive, and offensive in so different a way from that in the non-Jewish parallel case,
because one would prefer to inflict suffering on the detested group

or at least to see them suffer; and at any rate not to witness how they prosper increasingly. By the way: in Holland, where there is a Jewish proletariat, the poor Jewish hawker, who with endless trouble makes none too good a living, is regarded as the main source of antisemitic feelings. This assumption is wrong; the hawker incurs no worse enmity than the richest Jewish manufacturer; but it proves that Jewish wealth is no condition of antisemitism, and therefore not its cause. A further reason for the error that Jewish prosperity produces envy and consequently general enmity, is the sensitivity with which the people, the masses of the non-Jewish proletariat, react to Jewish wealth. It even is a frequent assumption that the most violent and most dangerous antisemitism arises where the people become aware of Jewish wealth. But this assumption also is not proof against investigation.

The worker hates of course all capitalists; but why are the Jewish enemies of his class singled out for special hatred? Why does the sight of a rich Jew cause him to feel something yet different from the general execration of the capitalist? Why does he perceive him as being of totally different nature? The Jewish capitalist is neither richer than his non-Jewish colleague, nor a harder master, nor a more rapacious exploiter; even if he wanted to be so, he could not, for the measure of exploitation is regulated collectively. The worker has therefore no reason to allot to the Jewish capitalist any priority of hatred. Nevertheless he bears the rule of his "own" capitalists with far greater resignation than that of a Jew; he regards the Jew as an interloper, his economic power as obtained unlawfully, by violence or deceit, his wealth as stolen goods and as a provocation. This additional element in his hate against the Jewish capitalist, this surplus which is not due to the economic relation, is anti-semitism; it is the enmity directed against the whole of the Jewish group, which reinforces his general hate of the capitalist; it is the same enmity which—a fact which often is, but should not be, overlooked—he also directs against his Jewish *class comrades. For antisemitism disrupts the pattern of the normal antagonism between the economic groups; and thus it also disrupts class solidarity.* This is, perhaps, a particularly painful chapter. Officially, the workers' parties pride themselves on protecting the Jews, fighting against anti-Jewish prejudice, and welcoming Jews within their ranks. Their position ought indeed to favour such a freedom of prejudice, for enslaved groups cannot and need not be particular in looking for help. And it is a fact that the workers' parties actually count a number of Jews amongst their leaders; but it is also a fact—which becomes more and more noticeable—that for quite some time these have no more been replaced by Jews, though there is no lack of Jewish candidates; the older Jewish leaders have lost much of their influence, though they are not exactly dismissed; replacements are recruited from non-Jews. In some countries, where there is no Jewish proletariat in the strict sense of the word, the expression of anti-Jewish tendencies amongst proletarian class comrades confines itself to this more and more popular method of shunting Jewish leaders to a side track; but where there is a Jewish proletariat, the non-Jewish workers face it with distrust, and often with undisguised enmity. This may be seen in England and America; it has become clear in a most painful way to the Jewish worker in Russia. With the Polish socialists also antisemitism has proved stronger than class solidarity. The people, the masses, have always strong antisemitic instincts; and no class solidarity, however sincere, is able to overcome them.

In the capitalist camp the development of antisemitic tendencies is not hampered by any ideology. The non-Jewish capitalist, though he belongs to what is always denounced as the Jewish class *par excellence,* and though in any case he has numerous Jewish fellow-capitalists, is in many countries an antisemite on principle, and proud of it. He organises antisemitic movements; and if he does so with an eye to the chance of distracting the attention of the masses from his own class, this only goes to prove that the antisemitic instincts of those masses give the stratagem a reasonable expectation of success. To his professional associations the non-Jewish capitalist does not, or only grudgingly, admit his Jewish colleagues, though his class interests demand friendly cooperation. But there, too, antisemitism hampers the normal economic necessities and disrupts class solidarity.

The non-Jewish capitalist may not love his "own" workers unduly; but still more than the Jewish worker, whom he completely debars from employment; as a rule, non-Jewish employers use Jewish labour only as a great exception. And so we come to the use of economic weapons in non-economic group warfare. For the employer is usually in a stronger position than the worker, and can use his position as a weapon.

In normal economic life the interested parties go by the rule of the greatest material advantage, and they use their power in this sense. But where group antagonism of another nature intervenes in strictly economic strife, there the economic means of power become subservient to this antagonism, even in express contradiction to the precepts of the rule of the greatest advantage.

Here it becomes most obvious how little such enmities are of economic origin; where necessary, the economic interest is *sacrificed* so that the enmity may be expressed.

In economic life, the most powerful factors are normally the buyer and the employer. In the purely economic struggle, both use their power in the interest of their material advantage. But when antisemitism, originating in a totally non-economic antagonism, steals into these relations, economic power turns away from its natural aims and places itself at the disposal of the hate, of the struggle against the hated Jews. Now the relation between employer and employed is a much closer one than that between seller and buyer. Thus, though at lesser degrees of tension the buyer disregards the Jewish source of an offer, or at least takes the Jewish offer into consideration if it is sufficiently attractive, the non-Jewish employer takes Jews into his service only as a great exception. The Jewish candidate must be able to offer quite unusual qualifications if he is to be employed at the same rate of pay as his average non-Jewish colleague. When tension is higher, the Jewish offer of goods is declined even if it is obviously more advantageous than that of the non-Jewish competition; and the Jewish candidate is as a matter of principle barred from any employment by non-Jews, even if he offers his qualifications far below their market value. *The antisemitism which, especially when it expresses itself in this way, is called economic antisemitism, proves to be a most uneconomical antisemitism.* It violates the golden rule of normal economic life, the rule of the greatest material advantage; the economic means of power are, against material interests, used to overcome the Jews.

As economic antisemitism one finally reckons the special form which has obtained currency as "business anti-semitism". The name indicates antisemitism blatantly displayed by businessmen for publicity purposes. It does not so much imply that this antisemitism occurs in business life, as that is *used* for business *purposes*. As such it is often presented as negligible; it is claimed that it is no real hate against the Jews, but only a calculated display. In the concrete case there may often be room for doubts as to the innermost feelings of the business antisemite, though the public display of a hostile feeling is not lightly to be interpreted as a sign of pronounced sympathies for the insulted group. But what seems to be the only essential point is that it is *possible* for antisemitism to be regarded as effective publicity; for this possibility can only exist when the tension of antisemitic hatred is so high that it does not only tend to the economic boycott of the Jews, but gives preference to suppliers who flatter its passions in the most obvious way. Neither the disruption of the economic enmity pattern by group enmities determined otherwise, nor the use of economic weapons in non-economic group strife are particular to antisemitism. We have already drawn attention to the influence of religious group antagonism. In districts with a mixed Catholic-Protestant population it is often customary to buy only from coreligionists; for employment, coreligionists are often preferred and personnel of other religions often rigorously excluded. The so-called foreign colonies live in a constellation of struggle in many respects similar to that of the Jews; their economic activities meet with the same reproaches as those of the Jews; at high levels of tension they are subjected to total boycott; the worker abroad finds employment almost only with compatriots. Also, the state often most consciously forces the economy to submit to the requirements of totally non-economic strife. This parallelism is hardly astonishing, for antisemitism is a group enmity like many others, and expresses itself in the same way; only there are but few minority groups which must forego the backing of a strong centre to the same extent as the Jews, and which therefore are exposed to the enmity of their opponents as defenselessly as the Jews.

3. *Political Antisemitism*

The expression "political antisemitism" has two meanings which may be distinguished rather clearly.

In the first place it is used to indicate antisemitism issuing from governments and authorities. In many countries the Government is engaged in more or less violent warfare against the Jews, and avails itself of legislative measures to deprive them officially of their rights, or to prejudice their interests indirectly. Where the Jews formally enjoy equal rights, they are hounded by vexatious administrative measures, or at least by the malevolent attitude of administrative bodies. And almost nowhere do they enjoy real, unrestricted equality, as the bureaucratic machinery can nearly always enforce a certain degree of discrimination against the Jews.

No serious attempt at explanation is forwarded for this type of political antisemitism, for on the Jewish side, the most fertile soil for attempts at explanation, the conviction is too deeply rooted that this "official" antisemitism, as it is also called, does the Jews extreme and inexcusable injury. It is either attributed to prejudices, which are regarded as particularly long-lived when they have settled in the official mind; or one attempts to persuade oneself that official antisemitism is something artificial, and merely the product of political opportunism; and this is the more readily believed as governments really often take anti-Jewish action in order to realise intentions of a totally different nature. Thus it is assumed that governments and politicians would as soon display a pro-Jewish attitude if it would seem more advantageous to the plans of the moment. The question why this is so remarkably seldom the case, is not further gone into. Because of its representative and in part formal nature, official antisemitism has in former times given much support to the erroneous assumption that for the Jews all should be well as soon as formal and, even more ideally, actual, equality of rights in relation to the state authorities would have been obtained by the Jews. The realisation that even formal or practical emancipation does not remove the hostile feelings from which official discrimination had arisen, could naturally only be gained in the later days of the era of emancipation, which now draws to its end.

As political we secondly describe the antisemitism which arises in connection with the political activities of Jews, and which of course is by preference regarded as the result of these activities: for the demand for "obvious" explanations and the dread of admitting a uniform general cause of antisemitic phenomena favour this interpretation.

In respect of official antisemitism the following may be remarked. The enmity of the population against a minority group regarded as foreign expresses itself most naturally and most vigorously in the measures of the group executive; in the countries where the Jews live, the governments of those countries. The struggle of the "native" population against the Jewish group can the more readily be entrusted to the government, as this holds the most effective weapons, and can use them without violation of the formal law. On the contrary, it can use the formal law itself as a weapon. A government which oppresses and persecutes the Jews, realises thereby its own wishes as well as those of the population. This fact is not changed by the circumstances that governments, in taking anti-Jewish action, occasionally pursue aims of their own.

It seemed, for instance, that the former Tsarist government in Russia was in the habit of taking particularly severe measures against the Jews or of provoking the outbreak of pogroms in order to divert the discontent of the population from the corrupt internal conditions of the Tsarist empire. This conscious application of a transference of enmity—which, incidentally, is highly characteristic—is by no means uncommon. The population may suffer through the inefficiency of the government, or sometimes through calamities against which the government is powerless; in either case there arises that form of suffering which we call discontent; somebody must be made responsible, and the first to be called to account for the cause of the discontent is the group executive, the government, which is expected to keep suffering out of the group's way. Also, in its character of ruling group, it is hated on account of the rule which it exercises within the whole group, and this hate is by preference expressed when discontent provides the pretext for expression; therefore discontent of the population endangers the position of the Government, which will be well advised to provide another victim for the erupting passions. A war might, for instance, be unchained; for therein feelings of hatred can be given the freest rein; but this stratagem can easily miscarry if the war is lost, and it is in any case safer to steer the emotions towards a defenseless group like the Jews. The government therefore takes measures against the Jews, in order to show the people that somebody is being punished for the suffering which has caused the discontent; or it encourages a direct outbreak of hate of the population against the Jews. But—and this is the point which is often overlooked—it can only do so because the population is in any case hostile to the Jews, regards them with suspicion, and is prepared to blame them for the existing abuses without more ado. It would be impossible for the government to select at random a few thousand citizens, and hand them over to the vengeance of the masses; for this purpose it needs a definite group which is already regarded with enmity: and no government could use the Jews for a scapegoat if it were not certain *that in gambling on the antisemitism of the population it always bets on a certainty.*

In general, though, the interest of governments in an antisemitic attitude is often strangely misjudged. Normally, a government must, in the interest of its own rule, conduct a policy of prosperity; it naturally aims at a minimum of internal friction. It wants the country to remain at rest. Thus it will often tend to master its antisemitic inclinations and protect the Jews: antisemitism which is not favoured by the government for some specific purpose is as a rule inopportune. Governments are thus often forced to declare themselves against antisemitic outrages; and at times they proceed against the Jews, contrary to their intentions and almost unwillingly, only in order to appease a strong antisemitic current amongst the population and to avert more serious disturbances.

As antisemitism lives within the population, it is also in principle of subordinate importance whether the Jews are, for any reason whatsoever, treated as equals before the law and in administrative practice. It facilitates their existence, often to a great extent, so that the Jewish efforts to achieve equality of rights are as justified as they are understandable. But equality of rights does not eliminate antisemitism, either on the part of the government or in the administration, for both are composed of members of the population, and the antisemitism of the population only varies with the degree of tension, and that depends on a number of conditions, but not on the legal position of the Jews. Rather is the latter a result of the degree of tension. Therefore, when tension increases, the legal status of the Jews may deteriorate again, as we have seen often enough in history; and advantages gained in this field are of no permanent importance. For the emotional background of anti-Jewish persecution undergoes no change even when the persecution is restrained or halted. The Jews who after the war expected miracles from solemn declarations, political emancipation, changes of government or special protective legislation, experienced bitter disappointments; the legal privileges were in part granted, but that did not mean the end of the enmity against the Jews.

The explanation of antisemitic trends as the result of Jewish activities in politics has of late been extraordinarily current. Jewish bolsheviki in Russia and Jewish republicans in Germany, in particular, are supposed to be responsible for the enormous growth of antisemitism after the world war. The superficiality of this assumption

is extreme, and illustrates not only the ease with which untenable justification for enmity are accepted, but also by its lack of
critical sense, the urgency of the need for explanation.

One might construct a situation in which Jewish groups as such
take part in the political life of their countries of inhabitation,
thereby become involved in unavoidable conflicts with other
parties, and thus incur their hatred. Even then it could easily
be shown that a primary hate of the Jews only avails itself of
the political conflict to find an adequate opportunity for expression. But it would at least have to be shown. In some of the new
states of Eastern Europe the Jews actually participate in national
politics as a Jewish group. Curiously enough, no particularly
antisemitic excesses have yet arisen from this participation.
There has, of course, been no lack of antisemitic insults in the
Polish Sejm; but it is in general regarded as self-evident that this
is no particular reaction to Jewish politics, but only a result of
a longstanding and well-known antisemitism, which is aired in
the Sejm as readily as on any other occasion.

In many other countries, however, the Jews participate in
the political life of their country of inhabitation neither within
the frame of a Jewish party, nor in the capacity of Jews at
all, but only within the general political parties, and only as
men, citizens, and party members. It is not astonishing that
in doing so they incur hatred or excite enmity (the common
form of expression is maintained for convenience's sake),
for political parties usually face each other with most vivid
enmity. But normally the Jews should incur no other enmity than their non-Jewish party comrades, and they should
incur this enmity only insofar as they personally take part in

politics. In fact they form an express exception from the hostility shown to their non-Jewish party comrades; the nature of their political activity is far less objected to than the fact that Jews are active in politics at all; all Jews are involved in the hate connected with the activities of only a few, and even non-Jews are made to answer for the political aid which they have allowed Jews to render them. And all this, though the Jews do not take part in politics in order to represent Jewish interests, and even avoid anything which may identify them as Jews. A statement as, for instance, that the monarchists in Germany hate the republicans, and that now a wave of antisemitism arises because amongst the republicans there are also Jews, or because the majority of German Jews support the republic, is unadmissible. In order to set the Jews apart among the mass of their non-Jewish party comrades, and to dedicate to them a special hatred, incomparably more violent than that directed against the others, one must regard them as a separate group to which as such one denies rights readily granted to others. And if one does so, there must be a pre-existent hostile attitude towards that group, which finds a welcome pretext for expression in the undesirable political activity of some or many of that group's members. By openly antisemitic sources this situation is in its essential points admitted. The nationalists' camp in Germany at present detests the republic, and consequently also the republican parties. But to the Jews it denies the right to influence politics at all, because they are regarded and hated as a foreign group. Offence is taken at the fact that Jews play a leading political part whatsoever; and they would not be tolerated in the nationalist parties either, even if the greatest ad-

vantage could be expected from their participation. And what
the declared antisemites admit openly without beating about the
bush, lives among the whole population as an unreasoned feeling.
For them also (and that applies even to peaceful Holland) the Jew
in politics is a stranger who meddles in matters which are none
of his business. Thus the officially pro-Jewish parties—which,
like incidentally all parties, readily accept the *anonymous* and
only for that reason not compromising aid of Jewish voices in
elections—must be most careful in employing Jews in leading
positions, as such use discredits the party among the masses. In
this case the priority of antisemitism is obvious to even the most
superficial observer.

The hatred supposed to be caused by the bolsheviki, that is
to say, the Jewish bolsheviki, hardly needs extensive discussion. For this "causation" is obviously far different from what
is regarded as a permissible and normal enmity reaction. In
Central and Western Europe the Jews are, if only because of
their economic position, in general pronounced anticommunists;
the Soviet state is a thought of terror to them, and among
the victims of the cancelled Russian public debt they rank
in an honourable place. In Russia itself the Jews are as such
persecuted by the Soviet authorities with something like
enthusiasm. If nevertheless the Jews are made responsible
for the unpopular activities of certain Jewish communists,
then this is an application of collective responsibility in the
grossest form. Doing so proves the existence of an anti-Jewish
group enmity strong enough to silence the objections of reason
even in the face of the most blatant unreason. For in this case
even the remotest possibility of apparent argument is shattered

by the simple facts: it is impossible even to pretend that Jewish communism is based on something like a general Jewish trait of character, and at the same time claim its complete opposite, capitalism, as a Jewish characteristic. And it seems somewhat pointless to blame all our good merchants, pillars of the community as they are, for the fact that comrade Sinoviev—or some other Soviet leader — originally called himself Apfelbaum. Nevertheless we may hear again and again that the Jewish Soviet politicians, assisted by international Jewish capital (which they fight to the last drop of blood) have planned a Jewish world empire (while they themselves have done their utmost to escape their Jewish antecedents and to russify the Jews of Russia) ; and that the first stage of that empire is the Balfour Declaration (the aim of which Jewish communists promote by zealously sending Zionists to Siberia) . Indeed, there are no limits to what suspicious hatred will imagine, and enmity-laden masses believe.

Political antisemitism in the sense of legal and administrative persecution has many non-Jewish parallels. Hated minority groups are deprived of their rights and persecuted throughout the world; in fact, the problem has a permanent actuality of its own. Cases corresponding to the antisemitism connected with the political activities of Jews are less frequent, because the Jewish dispersal is a unique phenomenon. There are, of course, other instances where members of ethnically foreign groups take a part in the national politics of another group abroad, of which they are regarded as the vanguards, and feared correspondingly; which, of course, lends the enmity directed against them a stronger appearance of justification.

Highly similar to the Jewish case is the distrust experienced at the outbreak of open hostilities by the members of a foreign nation which have become settled long ago. With the best of intentions it is impossible to believe in their fidelity to a cause which no one regards as theirs; their professions of solidarity and patriotism only strengthen the distrust, because "the gentlemen protest too much"; and the sacrifices brought by them are considered as a bribe, the payment of which seems to justify the suspicion which it is supposed to silence. The suffering of the Jews in this situation is the worse, the more sincere their devotion to the cause of their country of inhabitation is; but the enmity fostered against them cannot be convinced of this sincerity, and it is in vain that the Jews go to beg for confidence at the doors of their enemies, however bloody the casualty lists which they carry around on their pilgrimage.

Political antisemitism also recedes only when general conditions in the country of inhabitation have reached a certain stage of rest and stability. For antisemitism is not caused by any acts of commission or omission of the Jews, and these do not determine its degree of violence; it is a group enmity, and as such completely irrational; the level of tension depends on the situation of the majority group. Enmity against the Jews appears with such particular preference immediately after a war, and especially in the political field, because only at the end of the war the horrible suffering of' the struggle really attacks the masses, because it is only then fully realised, and because at that moment it cannot any more find an outlet in open battle. Therefore post-war periods are always periods of internal unrest. This particularly applies to the nations which have lost the war, and to those which have suffered most grievously in it. It is the tragedy of the Jewish minority groups that from the beginning of the Diaspora and until the present day they have been the always available and always defenseless victims of that increased urge for hate expression which has occurred after all disturbances in history; a tragedy only excelled by their own blindness, which prevents them from the full realisation of the true nature of their situation.

4. *Social Antisemitism*

We have already drawn attention to the importance of antipathy as the expression of even the slightest unfriendly feelings. Its bearers sometimes remain unconscious of it, and it is not always noticed by its victims. The smaller and smallest group formations are by their intimate nature fitted to serve as the frame for these slighter and slightest expressions of enmity; degrees of enmity which cannot make themselves felt within the larger groups, find a more favourable outlet in the minor formations. The social groups, with their often subtly shaded composition, are extremely sensitive instruments which register the presence of even the least feelings of antipathy with infallible precision.

Even where Jews have achieved full emancipation, not only in the eyes of the law but also, completely or almost completely, in political life—where, for instance, they have access to all, or nearly all, public offices—and where antisemitic feelings are rarely shown in public, the highly sensitive apparatus of society indicates with an astonishing precision the antipathy against the Jews which is present even at the lowest tension level of anti-Jewish enmity. The importance of this phe-nomenon is often minimised; and it is true enough that social antisemitism does not preclude the Jew from an otherwise toler-able life, though it wounds him precisely in the one point where he becomes most sensitive as soon as his life is free from mate-rial cares: in his social ambitions. But what is mainly misinter-preted is the nature of the antipathy; it is not realised that it is essentially equivalent to violent enmity and automatically grows more intense with any increase in tension. Not infrequently the very existence of social antisemitism is denied, in which case the social exclusion which is symptomatical for it is explained as normal social exclusivity.

Finally, we should not, after what we have already seen, be surprised to find social antisemitism, too, connected with an attempt at specific explanation: the social exclusion of Jews is attributed to their lack of qualities appreciated by society.

The equation of social antisemitism with normal forms of social tension and trends to social exclusivity rests on the same fallacy as the equation of economic antisemitism with normal instances of economic tension. *It is characteristic for the anti-semitic case that the normal relation of tension is disrupted in a way unfavourable for the Jew.*

There is no doubt that social groups keep themselves closed to each other, and particularly the higher against the lower ones. This seclusion finds its expression in various ways in the forms of social intercourse, and is the stricter, the more intimate the circle in question is. The most intimate circle is the family; and only those who rank as socially equal are regarded as worthy of admission to it. This is not changed by the fact that individuals in their matrimonial selection may sometimes disregard the wishes of the family, for marriage is based on a biological urge which seems to have some preference for crossing group barriers, and which does not even halt before the most pronounced racial differences. But the decisive social group, the family, resists such unions with all its power, and often punishes even minor non-conformities with excommunication.

The elements of similarity which determine a social group comprise profession, property, education, and in the higher classes also the constancy with which these elements have been present for many or at least a few generations. A person is, therefore, a social equal if he follows a calling of the same repute (the relative repute of callings varies with different nations) , owns approximately the same amount of property, has enjoyed approximately the same education, and if his forebears have already belonged to the same class for as many generations as possible. With the exception of the hereditary nobility the last desideratum is not insisted on too punctiliously, and it is usually sufficient if the antecedents of the grandparents are not compromising.

It might be regarded as normal that the nobility keeps its ranks closed to Jews, for even if a Jew achieves cabinet rank and landed property, he still lacks ancestors which have been patricians and landowners for centuries. But in his very contacts with the nobility the Jew is in a less favourable position than the Gentile who also has been the first of his family to become a landowner or minister. The admission of the Jew meets with greater difficulties; and is granted, if at all, only under more restrictive conditions. For the inferiority of the Jew in comparison to the non-Jew—and this is the point where antisemitism enters into the relation—must be *compensated*. It is this necessity which characterises social antisemitism in the various strata of society. The Jew is *not* regarded as equal, even if he has all the elements which would make a non-Jew equal; and in the middle classes these factors are often enough present on the Jewish side. The admission of the Jew into a non-Jewish circle must be bought with *special merits* to compensate the antipathy felt for his group. He must be able to produce a plus in property, professional standing, education, above that customary in the circle to which he seeks admission, or he must at least submit extraordinary talents, or preferably personal fame, as an entrance fee: as *a social being, he is only accepted at considerable discount.* He meets with greater difficulties in being admitted by non-Jews of his own social rank, than the non-Jew in approaching superior circles. This fact is not invalidated by the circumstance that occasionally marriages are contracted between Jews and non-Jews, in which the Jewish partner seems to be accepted at his full social value. For here it applies that marriages often disregard the social requirements of the family which in the best case reconciles itself, forced by circumstances, to the accomplished fact of the *mésalliance.*

Thus social antisemitism is not normal exclusivity; on the contrary, it distinctly differs from normal relations of tension between social levels; the social group structure becomes a means of expression for antisemitic feelings, and fulfills this function even at the lowest levels of antisemitism tension, consistently and without mercy.

It may be superfluous to add that social antisemitism

is not confined to the lesser degrees of tension. As every other form, it grows with increasing tension; then the exclusivity also affects the less intimate social formations and is applied more strictly; the entrance fee for the Jew is set higher and higher, until it finally ceases to be effective. Conditions at lower degrees of tension have been described in some detail because they are still present, and can still be clearly discerned, where antisemitic phenomena in other fields are nearly non-existent. This may also be explained by the fact that in social relations antisemitism may be expressed most easily and without any disadvantages: everyone is free to choose his social connections at will, and no one can be called to account for the social exclusion of the Jews. For that reason, social antisemitism is the preferred form of expression wherever other ways are, for some reason, not available. In the United States, for instance, antisemitic tension has at present reached a fairly high level; but it is inconceivable that the country of traditional freedom would see its way to re-strict the rights of its Jewish citizens, whether by law or only in administrative practice; the structure of Jewish economic life in the States makes it difficult for economic antisemitism to be ef-fective, though traces of it are already apparent. So antisemitism expresses itself with the more vigour in the social field, where the anti-Jewish boycott has assumed acute forms.

There should be no need at this stage to say much about the unpleasant Jewish qualities which are adduced in justification of such a boycott. Where it is by no means difficult for the imagination to provide the Jew with every and any moral inferiority desired, it should certainly be easy enough to ascribe to him those rather esthetic defects which make him socially impossible. Incidentally, the subjective nature of this sort of likes and dislikes is often admitted quite openly. We shall therefore only draw attention to a few special points.

The social talents are in the case of some Jews developed to a particularly high degree. They deploy an intellectual liveliness greatly appreciated in some non-Jewish circles. Such Jews are admitted, as long as one need fear no contact with their Jewish surroundings, and on occasions of a not too exclusive nature. The amusing and witty pet Jew is, for instance, invited to receptions which are open to a sufficiently mixed company, or alone, so that he cannot compromise his host.

These social advantages of the few are balanced by an objective disadvantage in the many who in strange and hostile surroundings feel themselves obliged to keep an anxious watch over their own attitude and actions, and are, as far as possible, at pains to conceal their descent; and who therefore are unable to attain the restful lack of self-consciousness of the remainder of the company. It is clear that this no doubt awkward self-consciousness is a result of existing enmity rather than its cause. A specific excuse often forwarded for social antisemitism is the importunity ascribed to the Jews. This importunity forms a rather peculiar chapter of its own: —

In Central and Western Europe the Jews have been granted equality before the law; practically, this is not always and not everywhere implemented, but the Jews are—apart from their religious persuasion, and that also differs amongst the remainder of the population—expected to behave as if they were in all respects normal citizens. Napoleon expressly required them to cease regarding themselves as a nation which permits itself the luxury of its own national aspirations. This requirement became the express or implied condition for emancipation; and it is no more than natural that the Jews failed to see why their status of normal citizens should fail to apply in respect of society; admission to non-Jewish society could not but appear to them natural consequence of emancipation, and their attempts to draw this consequence become importune only because in reality their emancipation is purely fictitious, and the antipathies against them continue unchanged. At this point we become aware of the quandary in which the non-Jewish population found itself when faced with the attempt to emancipate the Jews. The emancipation was an attempt to liquidate the Jewish problem. According to its trend, the aim should have been the absorption of the separate Jewish groups. The Jews themselves did, and for the main part do even today, strive to achieve this aim. But the non-Jewish population cannot force itself to swallow the bitter pill, even when in the particular individual case it is gilded by a large entrance fee. And thus the Jew remains suspended between yea and nay: supposed to be a goodly citizen of equal rights, he is yet repelled everywhere; expected to submerge within the nation of the country of his inhabitation, he is ever again denied.

But when he recalls his dignity and attempts to secure an independent future for his own nation, then those who have most crudely refused his advances accuse him of lacking love for the nation in whose midst he lives. For the attitude of the majority is, also with regard to the Jewish minority, ambiguous: in theory it demands absorption, but in practice it takes fright at the implementation; in theory it demands expulsion, but when it comes to the point, it clings with a perverted affection to the pariah whom it has become accustomed to despise and to abuse. Small wonder that the Jew, drawn forcibly from his ghetto, could neither anticipate nor understand this paradoxical attitude: as long as he believes in the liquidation of the Jews as such, he attempts to achieve it, and his principal way of escape from the Jewish group is his personal social betterment. Admission to non-Jewish circles flatters his vanity, because it seems to confirm the exceptional nature of his individual qualities; fame, riches, and respect, on the other hand, provide him with the means to purchase admission to the non-Jewish circle; and thus the idea of Jewish liquidation, once instilled in the Jewish masses, has produced that feverish urge to improvement of their social status which in its expression is rejected as importune, because in reality the hated or at least despised group is not regarded as equal.

In this connection *we* cannot omit some remarks on the term "the new rich". At times it seemed as if the new rich and their so noticeably unpleasant characteristics were regarded as something specifically Jewish. This was principally due to the particular conditions of observation under which a minority group such as the Jews lives. Even before the war there were non-Jewish upstarts enough, but the Jews were more readily noticed, because they belonged to a minority group under constant and hostile observation, under which, moreover, the individual always evokes the conception of the whole group. The post-war period has produced non-Jewish new rich in such an overwhelmingly multitude and so suddenly, that even the cartoonists finally began to draw the Newlirich family with non-Jewish faces. It should not be necessary to say much about the way in which the type of the Jewish upstart is generalised, and the whole Jewish community is made collectively responsible for its new rich and the unpleasant way in which they make themselves noticed. This effect is in striking contrast to that of the gentile new rich, who are only noticed as individuals and whom no one regards as representative for their nation. The painful special situation of the Jewish minority group is again demonstrated in this case. And it should not be forgotten that there is no question of deliberate ill will of the majority, such as one always assumes in acts of over-hostility, but of the unavoidable effects of group psychology, which even with the best intention cannot be continually corrected in the mind of those concerned.

Though the conception of the "new rich" as a Jewish monopoly cannot be maintained any longer, it is still often enough presented as the real cause of social antisemitism. This explanation is rarely forwarded from the Jewish, but so much the oftener from the non-Jewish camp. According to it, social antisemitism would be nothing more than a reaction against the type of the new rich, which happens to be represented by Jews, but there would be no specifically anti-Jewish flavour to it.

That the impression of the new rich is repulsive, is a fact. Newly gained riches are displayed with more ostentation than good taste permits. The new rich are as a rule unable to regard their fortune as the natural, essential, but in itself contemptible attribute of a class in which such fortune is normal. They want to find out what they can get for their money, and in how far it can replace qualities not contributed by a lowlier past. The opulent of old standing, who dictate the rules of good taste, dislike the thought that the visible characteristics of the upper class rest for a good deal not on inner qualities, but on possessions which may equally well fall into horny hands. Therefore they reject the ostentatious display of worldly goods as repulsive, and lay the heavier a stress on those hallmarks of their class which are inaccessible to the newcomer.

The Jewish new rich cannot expect any better treatment than their Gentile fellow-sufferer; and in general, though perhaps not from case to case, it would be difficult to show that when the Jewish upstart is put in his place, the process applies to the Jew as much as to the upstart. But it is easy enough to show that the Jew is repelled even if he is no upstart. For many Jews were already well-to-do when they left the ghetto; neither riches inherited for generations, nor discretion in their use are rare amongst Jews. On the contrary, the Jews were here as ever motivated by the desire to invalidate antisemitic reproaches; as soon as they could at all afford to do so, they excommunicated the acquisition of money with a certain fanaticism, and turned to learning; in the display of their possessions they often exercised the most rigorous restraint; they acquired such knowledge as was there to be acquired and cultivated their taste in strict conformity to the accepted standards; they trained themselves in the skills of the body fashionable in Europe, and learned how to conduct themselves in society. But all this did not help them to overcome the dislike against their being Jews, which remained and still remains; a dislike to which the Jew is exposed, be he ever so well educated, ever so sensitive, ever so civilised; at the most one could say that in that case he prefers not to expose himself, but that proves nothing against the fact as such. Actually, many Jews have in the course of time come to the conclusion that intercourse with non-Jewish society should be confined to the unavoidable. There is much to be said for such a conclusion; only, it does, of course, not mean the—no longer intended—elimination of social antisemitism, but the acknowledgment of its existence.

5. *Cultural Antisemitism*

Contrary to the forms of antisemitism described so far, cultural antisemitism is not rooted in the mind of the general population, but a plant cultivated in the glasshouses of so-called scientific antisemitism; with more pains and care than the result warrants, for it has remained a poor growth. No general and popular antisemitism is expressed in the cultural field; for the people care little about cultural matters in any specialised sense, and as far as they take any practical interest in them, they are incapable of perceiving any possible Jewish influence in the products of culture. One might say, as has been said, that one of the most popular German folk songs was written by the Jew Heine, and that it is therefore a product of culture infected by the Jewish or Semitic plague; but the essay in which the disease is clinically described reaches only a restricted circle of readers—and even there it finds more faith than understanding. To the people it matters little what is written in their songs, as long as it satisfies certain primitive emotions. The more complicated products of culture almost completely escape the awareness of the masses.

In its cultural colouring, antisemitic feeling manifests

itself only amongst a restricted range of persons, who are mainly themselves engaged in the arts and sciences, and who naturally seek to express their antisemitism in the first place in their own domain, particularly as they usually find many Jews there. In general w^{r}e may say that in the field of culture Jewish contributions, if they are not accepted with either grace or gratitude, are at any rate thoroughly exploited. In a few cases, of course, the hatred of the Jew has proved so strong in this sphere as well, that the advantage which a Jewish scientist could bring to the public cause has been sacrificed to it. Thus there have been instances of famous Jewish scholars being expelled from their chairs, because antisemitic sentiment revolted against their Jewishness. It may, of course, be said that this does not do honour to antisemitic sense, but where hatred exceeds certain limits it disregards all considerations, even those of its own advantage.

The theory of cultural antisemitism is in principle that the national culture must be cleansed of the foreign cultural influence of the Jewish mind; at times the stress is laid on the mere foreign nature of this influence, and then the hatred of the foreigner is apparent in its distinct special aspect of fear, of xenophobia. But usually the Jewish influence is in addition condemned as inferior. This inferiority can of course not be established by objective rules; but the devaluation process in the antisemitic conception has been discussed at length, and it is obvious that it affects Jewish contributions in the field of culture as much as Jewish characteristics.

Just as it is attempted to explain economic antisemitism as competitive envy, cultural antisemitism is occasionally attributed on the Jewish side to envy of non-Jewish colleagues caused by Jewish achievement. Doubtless jealousy and envy also occur in the cultural field; and they may even assume acuter forms, because the importance of the achievement is not so readily measured as in the economic sphere, and because the artist and the scholar feel a far stronger need than the merchant to be convinced not only of the value, but of the special value of their achievement. The merchant reads the value of his achievement on his balance sheet, and is satisfied if he sees yearly improving results. The scholar or artist must first obtain the confirmation of the value of his achievement from others, convinced as he may be in his own mind; and he will always suffer from the feeling of having achieved no more than mediocrity, for in science, and even more in art, only the outstanding is fully recognised. No wonder that the natural jealousy among scholars and artists is notorious. But this jealousy can hardly assume an antisemitic character except when the individual offensive Jewish case can be projected upon a whole hated community; when there is at least a latent hatred against a group whose feared influence becomes manifest in the successful artistic or scientific achievement of one of its members.

A professor is, of course, only human, and we can readily understand how painful these indefatigable, conscientious and painstaking people are affected when somebody who has learned nothing more than they, who has passed no other examinations and can avail himself of no other means of research, produces out of the fortuitous blessing of a gifted mind, as in play, all those new and enriching ideas which years of assiduity could not squeeze out of their own thinking equipment. If such a genius is one of theirs, they will admire him enviously and secure a share in his fame by proclaiming him as the flower of national science which, so to say, they produce collectively. The flower is then the beautiful and plainly visible, but strictly speaking secondary product of their silent toil. But how different is the reaction if the unfortunate hero is called, say, Sigmund Freud. We are here not concerned with the question whether Freud is more or less important than is generally assumed; it suffices that he is admired and regarded as a genius. Then the Jewish name immediately evokes the impression of the groveling crowd of the hated foreign nation; it seems *a priori* impossible that anything really great, noble, pure, beautiful, etc., can issue from those inferior minds; thus what appeared to be a discovery of genius cannot really be founded on anything but a vainglorious parade, publicised by shrewd propaganda; everything new and surprising in our man's argument becomes proof of a hunt for cheap effects, a speculation on the public's hunger for sensations, painfully contrasting with the tedious soundness of the conventional scholarly disquisition; the stress on sexual aspects found in the thesis of the Jew is regarded as the best proof for the moral perversion of his corrupt race. By such considerations and interpretations antisemitism disparages the achievement, brands it with the taint of the inferior, the *corruptive,* and with something like a silent roar of triumph enmity springs from its ambush to grasp this new proof of its everlasting justification, this exceptional opportunity of coming to the light.

The mechanism of this process differs in no way from other forms of antisemitic expression; it is only characterised as an instance of cultural antisemitism because it occurs in the cultural field, i.e. uses pretexts drawn up in terms of culture. And it matters little whether the pretext is furnished by a Jewish scholar or a Jewish artist.

The "numerus clausus", the exclusion of Jewish students from universities, had better be regarded as a form of political anti-semitism, for this measure is intended to prevent the Jews from enjoying the benefits of higher education, and so to render their existence more difficult. If, however, we consider this restriction in the light of the desire to keep the participation of the Jews in the cultural life of the country of inhabitation, and thus their cultural influence, within the narrowest possible limits, then we may also speak of cultural antisemitism. Insofar as the "numerus clausus" movement is implemented by the non-Jewish students, it also bears some of the traits of social antisemitism.

Such difficulties of classification often arise when it is attempted to assign any given antisemitic phenomenon to a form of appearance; and no wonder, for what is essentially one and the same group enmity seeks and finds its expression in all fields which come into consideration; any more precise qualification of antisemitism has merely the one justification of describing the field in which it happens to become manifest.

Resistance against foreign cultural influences is of course a frequent occurrence, and by no means restricted to the antise-mitic relation; for the national culture provides numerous and important group characteristics, and any attempt to transfer these, even to the most limited extents, is felt by the foreign group as an attempt at penetration, and resisted as such. But in normal conditions this resistance is directed against foreign nations whose cultural influence is feared as a pre-liminary of political penetration. In this respect, too, the dispersal has created an abnormal situation for the Jewish groups: their cultural activity, which in the diaspora cannot even be specifically Jewish, is not backed by any imperialist threat, but insofar as it is perceived as Jewish, it is invested with a disintegrating nature by a hatred which requires a conception of fear if it is to be able to regard its hostile expression as a defense, and thus as justified.

6. *Racial Antisemitism*

Another expression sometimes met in discussions is the term "racial antisemitism". The difficulties offered by the concept "race" have been sufficiently exposed at an earlier stage. The Jews are an ethnical-historical national community, and there would be no objection to the additional interpretation of the enmity directed against this group as race hatred; but that term is often, and especially in America, understood to refer only to contrasts between major ethnical-racial groups distinguished by essential differences in pigmentation—in other words, between the black, white and yellow races. Thus it becomes possible to state that there is no antisemitism in America, as antisemitism is racial hatred, and racial hatred in America refers only to the coloured races.

The word derives its particular importance as a definition of antisemitism from its use in the technical anti-semitic literature which attempts to establish the inferiority of the Jewish or Semitic race, and thus the justification of antisemitism. Though much has already been said on this subject, a few additional remarks may be permitted.

In every group antagonism the opposite group is branded with the conception of a certain inferiority; but the antisemites have, perhaps for the first time, elaborated the stratagem into an actual system. Nor is this surprising: for notwithstanding all the natural clashes which unavoidably result from the close contact between Jews and non-Jews it is not too easy to find sufficient pretexts for enmity against the Jews. The reason is, of course, not any outstanding excellence on their part—they are no better than others—but the fact that, being everywhere weak and defenseless minorities, they are of necessity everywhere harmless. Their always precarious position, their dependence on so uncertain sentiments as the tolerance of majority groups, *forces* them to extreme caution and to an attitude as blamelessly conform to local standards as possible. Their situation obliges them to avoid offense. Of course this does not lessen the hatred directed against the group. Exemplary behaviour only prevents hatred from using convenient channels of expression and forces it into less easy ways. Hatred can only become more acute if its chosen victim fails so signally to provide a handle for legitimate expression. This, obviously, is why the suspicions which serve instead of actual transgressions are so remarkably wild, confused and improbable, why they so clearly bear the imprint of a desperate and tortured imagination; the supposed Jewish conspiracy for the conquest of world dominion is a case in point. This, also, is the reason why the proclamation of Jewish racial inferiority, argued with a pathological ingenuity only paralleled in some forms of lunacy, had to become the pivotal element of the whole antisemitic ideology. This, we may finally add, is why the antipathy of antisemitism can hardly direct itself against any Jewish actions, and even not easily against faults of the Jewish character, which can never be more than an assumption; it must find its real object in the *outward appearance* of the Jew: in his facial type, his gestures, his diction, in short all those things which are obviously and specifically Jewish, but totally unsuitable for ethical valuation. Here again the esthetic supplements the ethical condemnation. For the majority group also dictates the esthetic standard; it sets the canon of human beauty, and brands whatever is divergent, different, hated, as ugly, disgusting, *hateful.* This shift from esthetic to ethical deprecation—we have already mentioned it in passing—is quite a regular feature of the enmity relation: the type of the foreigner is regarded as ugly, and only appreciated insofar as it approaches that of his own group; in the conception of those who hate, the exterior of those who are hated is distorted to hatefulness. Thus the hated enemy is also painted as the prototype of ugliness: in the war, each nation used to draw its enemies with all the marks of hideous bestiality. As a further stage, ugliness is then again taken as the outward expression of mental turpitude, which is supposed to leave its mark on the outer appearance; for *mere* esthetic objections as reasons for the expression of enmity do not receive the necessary sanction of the sense of justice. In this way the Jewish nose becomes the symbol and even the physical symptom of Jewish importunity; the Jewish eye the sign of Jewish faithlessness; the Jewish smile proof of cunning, deceit and treachery. What is felt as Jewish inferiority, what pains the eye, what gives offense, what always and everywhere activates latent enmity, is in the first place the Jewish exterior: for that can really be identified as characteristically Jewish. Not for nothing have so many Jews attempted to suppress and conceal their Jewish characteristics as far as possible; not without good grounds have they imitated at least the variable characteristics of their majority groups with painstaking exactitude. It has, of course, not helped to eliminate or alleviate antisemitism; *the attempt was no more than an evasion of its effects by means of camouflage.*

Everything characteristically or representatively Jewish falls prey to contempt, and is branded as bad, ugly, disgusting and vulgar (*) ; and thus debased it draws the particular manifestation of antisemitic hatred which cannot bear to see anything Jewish left intact, even if it is only a Jewish graveyard.

The usually undeniable unreason of these manifestations of hatred, always offensive to an impartial sense of justice, should cause no wonder: it is characteristic for every mass enmity; and in the same measure as the tension present is higher, the forms it assumes are coarser and more violent.

There are as many racial enmities in the world as there are different races, different ethnical groups. The enmity between such groups need in itself be no more violent than that between groups of other categories. But the permanence of physical and mental characteristics hampers fusion and absorption, or, where the difference between the characteristics is great, as good as makes them impossible. Therefore the ethnical group is a particularly suitable formation for struggle; its characteristics are flags and standards which cannot be concealed; the enemy is easy to recognise, and desertion difficult or impossible. Racial or ethnical group distribution therefore always maintains a dominant function as the line which in mass enmities divides the human masses into hostile camps. The difficulty of fusion and absorption moreover sets a more

---

(*) Not on purpose and consciously, of course, but purely by instinct.

extreme target for the struggle, which can only aim at annihilation or subjection of the opposite group. Subjection is a bad second choice, but the whole of humanity is in these days so closely knit together by common interests that annihilation cannot too easily be accomplished; if the attempt is made, a third group will find only too welcome an opportunity to take a hand in the fight, for there is no better and more creditable pretext for the expression of enmity than the rendering of aid to the persecuted.

These conditions determine the tenacity of antisemitism, the fundamental impossibility to reconcile the contrast which it expresses, and the apparently senseless concurrence of the gravest and the most frivolous expressions of enmity which all seem to lack true adequacy. The total extermination of Jewish groups is rare; the large-scale slaughter of part of them only too frequent; from time to time Jewish groups are expelled from their countries of inhabitation and thus given the opportunity of escaping slow or sudden annihilation by flight; and where they stay, they live in conditions which, even in case of benevolent or at least condescending tolerance of their "hosts", bear the marks of a more or less pronounced subjection, a more or less profound slavery. And this slavery has led to the development in many Jews of the perverted hatred against their own group which is to form the last point in our discussions.

7. *"Jewish Antisemitism"*

Like all perversions, so-called Jewish antisemitism is a morbid condition, traces of which may on close observation be found in normal situations.

We must always bear it in mind that collective self-respect derives from and is built on the individual; and so is collective self-overestimation. Man values the groups to which he belongs so highly, because they are *his* groups, because they have the invaluable advantage to count *him* among their members. This does not necessarily mean that the other members always prove themselves worthy of this advantage. On the contrary, they often fall short of the exalted example as which the person concerned fondly regards himself; in which case he will exert himself with loving care to raise his group comrades to what he believes to be his own level; he thinks that they should behave as he thinks fit and proper. As the others from their side probably see matters in the same light, there will often be differences of opinion, and the attempted education will only lead to disappointments; then our man says bitterly: "Well, that is what we are like." But by "we" he means not himself, but only the others. In this way it comes about that collective self-overestimation, the group feeling of superiority, does not exclude a self-contempt which seems to be its irreconcilable contradiction. The apparent contradiction dissolves if we consider that the collective self-contempt (often no more than mild disapproval) refers to one's fellow group members, but never to oneself; whom one always regards as exemplary.

Moreover, what relates to oneself is, for all esteem, common and familiar; it lends life its indispensable rest and security, but in attraction it is exceeded by the unfamiliar. Thus, even in the case of normal nations, all things foreign seem attractive when the individual uses them to make himself remarkable; and for all his uncanniness the foreigner may well possess the fascination of being different, which within the "domestic" group means being unique. But even in the normal case the foreigner and what belongs to him are only taken as a model, when the receiving nation has a feeling of subservience in respect of the giving nation; which need not imply any politically defined relation of dependence.

In the enslaved group all consciousness of own value has been lost. Even the most inferior specimens of the ruling group are regarded as beings of a higher nature; they are the standard for all notions of the good, the true, the beautiful. If only within his own imagination, the member of the enslaved group compares himself to the ruling group, and regards himself as an exceedingly favourable exception from the inferiority of his group comrades, on whom he looks down with the identical contempt in which they are held by the ruling group.

Notwithstanding all persecutions, the Jews had until the beginning of the era of emancipation lost *comparatively* little of their self-respect, and none of their will to exist as a nation. They had met all tribulations with the strong conviction of their superiority as the chosen people, and allowed nothing to rob them of the hope for their return from exile to their own land. But heroism supports nothing as badly as a certain alleviation of conditions. The emancipation, though only the deceptive sunrise of a dark and stormy day, had broken the Jews' belief in themselves and their mission, and therewith also their real will to exist as Jews; the results of this collapse have even today been overcome but to an infinitely small degree. No one who is not intimately acquainted with Jewish conditions can conceive the extent and violence of a mass disease which in this extent is probably unparalleled. Originally it had attacked only the occidental Jews; meanwhile, a considerable part, if not the majority of the Jews of Eastern Europe have also been infected. Even where the Jews have recovered their national consciousness, the after effects are usually still felt. The clinical picture of the disease is more or less as follows: —

The non-Jewish surroundings, as they appear from time to time, have for the Jew become the standard and model in every aspect of life. Ideas and conceptions, customs and habits, standards of beauty and canons of ethics, morals and conventions, capacities and achievements, in short, everything characteristic for any given non-Jewish majority, are *enthusiastically exalted* by the Jewish group which lives in its midst. Attempts are made to shape the whole of Jewish life in the image of the adored ideal. Even what has formally been retained as a Jewish characteristic, namely the Jewish religion, is adapted to the surrounding world, at least in its conceptions and notions, and often also in its external form. Even where there has been no reform movement, Jewish religion becomes a rite, the Jewish code of life a set of tenets, the synagogue an Israelite church, and the organization of the national group a church council. This process is called assimilation, though it far exceeds any involuntary adaptation. Some regard this assimilation as desirable, others as wholly, still others as partly unavoidable; its existence is everywhere admitted.

But this glorification of everything Gentile must of necessity find its complement in the *rejection* of everything Jewish; which, in extent, intensity and real character, is usually misjudged. It has its roots in the collective consciousness of inferiority, which has here been characterised as perverted. Strictly speaking, the term "collective" must here again be understood as exclusive of the individual, who assumes the inferiority of all or nearly all Jews, except himself. For the individual always lives under the illusion, so senseless to any impartial observer, that he himself has reached the heights of the non-Jewish ideal, that he has freed himself from the inferior Jewish qualities; he may even make an exception for some persons from his nearest surroundings, whom he is accustomed to see as individuals and so has detached from the collective impression; but the remainder of the Jews, and everything that is Jewish, he regards as inferior, sometimes by way of a considered opinion, but always emotionally, even where he is not aware of this emotion, and would indignantly deny it if charged with it. In reality he has taken over a good share of the anti-semitic attitude, of the antipathy against everything characteristically Jewish; *and his reaction to his own group is the attitude familiar in group psychology in relation to a hostile foreign group.* To his consciousness the Jews appear as something collective; in the individual he mainly recognises the group being, the group average; he drags Jewish characteristics down into the sphere of devaluation and aims his antipathy at them; he believes in specifically Jewish evil qualities; and he interprets, precisely as the enemy, Jewish actions in an unfavourable sense, in order to regard them as confirmation of his justified dislike. Also he applies collective responsibility to the Jews: when a Jew arouses his displeasure, he is inclined to say: "That is what *they* are like" and "one must keep out of *their* way"; at the same time he judges the members of the majority group, as if he were one of them, by strictly individual standards.

In one respect only the perversion fails to have effect;

even Jews who have gone far astray are still sensitive to Jewish achievements which are admittedly superior to the accepted rules; then they find a shameful joy in the memory of their own Jewishness, and readily include themselves in the appreciation occasioned by the Jewish performance. For, after all, Jewish self-respect is only buried and covered up; the Jew must remain a Jew as long as he lives, and under the ashes of his admiration of the foreigner there still glows a spark of Jewish group feeling, ready to be fanned into flame by an auspicious wind. Only, the enmity of the surrounding world has so heavily born down on the conception of the Jewish character, and has exposed Jewish achievement to so strong a devaluating tendency, that Jewish spiritual heroes of the highest rank must appear on the scene, if in their Jewishness they are to receive the unwilling applause of the world; *and only this applause recalls the Jewish self-respect to consciousness: its rare manifestations are totally dependent on non-Jewish opinion.*

We would make it overly clear that these manifestations of perversity are in no way due to the conscious and considered acquisition of antisemitic opinions: those are rejected by most Jews as malicious insanity; and if a few Jews finally accept them in conscious reason, they do so only by way of an *ex post facto* theoretical superstructure for what primarily were unreasoned emotions. Only in a few isolated cases are Jews so lacking in good taste as to profess their antisemitic convictions in public; and only this attitude is usually called Jewish antisemitism. But its emotional basis, the perversion of the group feeling, has attacked and poisoned the half- and unconscious emotions like an epidemic of insanity. That is why Jews are horrified when in the presence of non-Jews some "coreligionist" talks with his hands or in other ways proves himself a Jew, or even if he only pronounces the dreaded group name; that is why they anxiously and over-critically watch every Jewish action; that is why they discover inferior Jewish qualities in the conduct of a Jewish adversary; and that is also why towards other Jews, even if they are no personal acquaintances, they so readily assume a familiarity which does not so much breed, as it is bred by, contempt.

So deeply has the consciousness of inferiority corroded the Jewish soul, that it can only with great difficulty be uprooted even in those Jews who have awoken to a new Jewish will to live. The very notion of a Jewish renascence, be it ever so fair, still carries a flavour from an ill fated past: a connotation of liberating the Jews from an imaginary inferiority; and thereby it has done untold harm to the whole of Zionist ideology. It is clear that only a new generation of Jews, grown up in full freedom and outside the atmosphere of antisemitism, will be able to see itself as a normal nation, which derives the conceptions of its worth or unworth, whatever they may be, from no foreign and hostile world, but only from itself.

Conclusion

With the consideration of the forms in which antisemitism manifests itself we have reached the end of our discussion. It had to show that antisemitism must be regarded as a special case of a general phenomenon. Antisemitism was established as a group enmity, which in its turn ranks amongst group phenomena in general. The group was described as the instrument for the distribution and expression of love and hate; and it followed from the description that neighbouring groups of the same category cannot but live in mutual contrast. The tension which exists between the groups and the enmity which becomes manifest is in no way a product of the qualities or actions of the opposed group; the tension results from suffering of most heterogeneous origin, which is transformed into enmity ready for expression, and in the creation of which the objects of the enmity have in general no part. What seems to have aroused the enmity, what is adduced by outsiders as its explanation and by those concerned as its excuse, is merely the occasion which makes the expression of enmity possible by furnishing it with a concept of justification.

Antisemitism appears as a special form of that group enmity which directs itself against ethnical minority groups of inferior strength. Their weakness and defenselessness lend to the antagonism between them and the majority group that onesidedness in which the majority group acts exclusively in the offensive, while the minority barely defends itself. The minority is often exposed to downright persecution, cannot always escape partial annihilation by flight, and is not infrequently exposed to the destructive influence of slavery.

A discussion of antisemitic manifestations had to establish that the various forms in which antisemitism appears admit of no separate explanations, but that there also the apparent causes are only occasions, mere pretexts for the expression of one and the same enmity, with causes which lie deeper, and which in all its manifestations and consequences takes its place amongst group phenomena in general. It might at the most be said that the peculiarity of the Jewish dispersal adds some special, but by no means essential, traits to antisemitism; apart from the Jewish case there could hardly be any instance of ethnical groups, completely isolated and defenceless, which lack a central core, but are nevertheless conceived of as connected; but this circumstance does not affect the cause, violence or manifestations of antisemitism. Against this, the enmity which is everywhere and always again directed against the Jewish groups makes by its extent and continuity a strong impression on the human imagination and causes the notion of a phenomenon which is unparalleled in its essential nature as well. This impression is erroneous; for all the characteristic criteria of antisemitism can be observed in other group enmities, so that only the particular nature of the object lends a different colour to the enmity directed against it.

For clarity's sake we shall yet point out some of the conclusions which follow from what we have established.

As the expression of enmity within the group relation is an absolutely *primary* necessity, which *freely creates* a distorted and debased impression of the hostile group character out of the fulness of its emotionality, *exploits* always available friction and its opportunities for conflict in order to gain a pretext for its manifestation, and if necessary *provokes* it or *motivates* it by the assumed dangerousness of the other party; as all these matters are as they are, neither the behaviour nor the qualities of the opposite group exert any influence on the degree of enmity or the violence of its expression. Particular harmlessness or exemplary behaviour of the opponent only calls for less plausible and more fantastic pretexts for enmity.

Therefore it is immaterial what or how the Jews are or act. Therefore it is useless if they attempt to eliminate antisemitism by their behaviour. For if they attempt to take the objections of their enemies into consideration, then any other attitude will be objected to in the same way, simply because it is a Jewish attitude; and it will in addition be mocked, because it is an unnatural and assumed attitude. Under favourable conditions the Jew may for a time be able to conceal himself from the expressions of antisemitism; but he can never please his enemies, and his will to conform will only bring him the reproach of characterlessness.

And as antisemitism is not provoked by real faults or offenses, it is an error to believe that the Jew may overcome this enmity by his personal qualities or achievements. Outstanding success may at times provide him with the entrance fee to the portals of non-Jewish society, but antisemitism itself is eliminated by no success, no virtue and no achievement; like a burning sun it shines upon the just and the unjust Jew alike.

It is even hopeless to argue against antisemitic reproaches and accusations, and to establish their lack of good grounds; for they are not the causes of antisemitism, but only its pretexts. When the reproaches are actually so invalidated that they lose their usefulness for the antisemite—and their fictitious nature renders this improbable—he only finds himself in the necessity of producing others; and he will assuredly produce them. Naturally we shall nevertheless continue to refute accusations, to denounce lies and to uncover forgeries; but we should not do so without being aware of the ultimate pointlessness of such a defensive.

We shall again be shocked, we shall again cry out in despair, when tomorrow again Jews are, somewhere in the world, murdered, tortured, outlawed; we shall appeal to the conscience of the nations and call our persecutors to account for their deeds, even as we are prepared to account and be responsible for our every action. But we should not blind ourselves to the realisation that no penitential sermons can change human nature, that no indignation can prevent enmity from transforming itself into hostile desires, that the phenomenon of group enmity cannot be banished from the earth by exhortations, and that whatever has been done to bring the world to a more peaceful condition has so been done by measures calculated to affect human nature as it is and not as it should be.

We are not entitled to expect that the psychological conditions from which group enmity springs will be changed by the protestations of our moral indignation; it is not clear how our protests could possibly achieve what not even the own interests of the majority group have been able to bring about: a change in the disastrous and hapless instincts which, rooted in the abysses of the human mind, have but too often been repressed by inhuman exertions, and have as often erupted again with the violence of the forces of nature.

This is not to say that the particular form of group enmity which we call antisemitism is ineradicable. *For its results,* with all their particular and for us Jews so fateful consequences, *only derive from a disastrous constellation.* We cannot change human nature. We can, with or without good cause, hope that after another three thousand years it will conform better to our longings and dreams of moral perfection than it has done during the last three thousand years of Jewish history. In any case, there is no sense in expecting that this change should now suddenly come about within the next few centuries.

It is, however, by no means impossible to change the group conformation of human masses. This can be accomplished within a limited period. Only because the Jews live everywhere as dispersed, weak and defenseless minority groups, does that enmity which exists between groups everywhere, assume in respect of the Jews such a particularly dangerous, deleterious, destructive character. If this constellation can be brought to an end, then antisemitism, with all the characteristic manifestations which have made the history of the Jewish dispersal an uninterrupted *via dolorosa,* will also once and for all be liquidated.

A Jewish nation which lives in close settlement within its own country will probably be exposed to the hostility of the surrounding nations, and live in alternating states of war and peace, as has ever been the way of the world. But the enmity between the Jews and their neighbours will then be no more than a normal enmity between one nation and the other, and not that onesided and accursed hatred which has haunted the fragments of a tortured people through twenty centuries and over the whole of the inhabited world.

This has nothing to do with the question whether the Zionist aspirations are capable of technical realisation. They might conceivably fail through practical obstacles of various nature. At present the expectations of the movement seem favourable; time must tell whether they will turn into reality. But that there is *no other possible way* to make an end of antisemitism, that, we believe, has been established in this book beyond all possible doubt.

THE END

Index

For Product Safety Concerns and Information please contact our EU
representative GPSR@taylorandfrancis.com
Taylor & Francis Verlag GmbH, Kaufingerstraße 24, 80331 München, Germany

www.ingramcontent.com/pod-product-compliance
Ingram Content Group UK Ltd.
Pitfield, Milton Keynes, MK11 3LW, UK
UKHW010813080625
459435UK00006B/60